# The Red Brigades and left-wing terrorism in Italy

In their basic relation to themselves most people are narrators ... What they like is the orderly sequence of facts, because it has the look of a necessity, and by means of the impression that their life has a 'course' they manage to feel somehow sheltered in the midst of chaos.

R. Musil (1979) *The Man Without Qualities*, London, Pan Books, Vol. 2, p. 436.

# The Red Brigades and left-wing terrorism in Italy

Edited by
## Raimondo Catanzaro

**Pinter Publishers**
London

© Raimondo Catanzaro and contributors 1991

First published in Great Britain in 1991 by
Pinter Publishers Limited
25 Floral Street, London WC2E 9DS

**British Library Cataloguing in Publication Data**

A CIP catalogue record for this book is available from the British Library
ISBN 0–86187–893–0

Typeset by Communitype Communications Ltd, Kettering, Northamptonshire
Printed and bound in Great Britain by Biddles Ltd of Guildford and Kings Lynn

# Contents

# List of contributors

**Gian Carlo Caselli** is a judge at the Court of Turin.

**Raimondo Catanzaro** is Professor of Sociology at the University of Catania.

**Donatella della Porta** is Guggenheim research fellow at the Wissenschaftszentrum in Berlin.

**Max Kaase** is Professor of Political Science at the University of Mannheim.

**Luigi Manconi** is lecturer in Sociology at the University of Palermo.

**Claudio Novaro** is a lawyer at the Court of Turin.

**Sidney Tarrow** is Professor of Government at Cornell University.

# Preface

This volume deals with the analysis of the Red Brigades and left-wing terrorism in Italy. It contains the main results of a research programme that dates back to June 1982 when the Istituto Cattaneo was commissioned by the regional government of Emilia-Romagna to carry out a study on political violence and right-wing and left-wing terrorism. Thus, at the basis of the programme lies a civil commitment to dealing with a phenomena that for more than a decade has painfully and seriously afflicted Italian society.

The research on which this volume is based took place in three phases. In the first phase (1982–3) the existing information on Italian terrorism was assessed and systematically classified, both at the level of empirical description and that of conceptual definition. The research theme was developed in close collaboration with the leading scholars working in the field and focused on the analysis of the specific characteristics of terrorism in the Italian context in comparison with the terrorist experience in other countries. On the basis of this preliminary work, the second phase of research (starting in 1984) was aimed at generating original and systematic research in two directions. The first was the creation of a documentary archive for the collection and analysis of material on terrorism. This consisted of judicial sources (preliminary and final sentences, the transcripts of judicial cross-examinations, etc.), and documentation produced by the terrorist groups themselves (leaflets avenging kidnappings and other actions, programmatic documents, the texts of 'strategic decisions', and documents on dissociation, etc.). The second direction of research was an investigation of the life histories of terrorists. To this end, a total of fifty-three in-depth interviews were carried out, of which twenty-three were with right-wing terrorists and thirty with left-wing terrorists. The interviews were carried in such a way as to guarantee the inclusion of as broad as possible a range of orientations and positions that emerged within the Italian experience throughout the duration of the terroristic phenomena. The third phase consisted of the long, difficult and complex work of analysing the documentary material and the screened and transcribed interviews.

No research activity, particularly when it extends over such a long period of time and has such a large research group, can develop without the support of a multitude of institutions and individuals. Among these I wish to express my gratitude to the Scientific Committee headed by Luigi Pedrazzi, and to its members, Augusto Balloni, Luciano Bergonzini, Francesco Berti Arnoaldi, Massimo Brutti, Gian Carlo Caselli, Leopoldo Elia, Vittorio Grevi, Ferdinando Imposimato, Federico Mancini, Nicola Matteucci, Arturo Parisi, Gianfranco Pasquino, Stefano Rodotà, Giovanni Tamburino, Angelo Ventura, Piero Luigi Vigna and Luciano Violante. Their constant and painstaking coordination and their experience as judges, lawyers, parliamentarians and academics proved invaluable throughout the course of research.

Special thanks are also due to the then Minister for Justice, the On. Mino Martinazzoli, without whose understanding the programme would never have been possible, and to Dr. Nicolò Amato, the director general of the *Istituti di prevenzione e pena*, whose cooperation enabled us to carry out the interviews with imprisoned terrorists. The interviews of left-wing terrorists were carried out by Donatella della Porta, Giuseppe De Lutiis, Patrizia Guerra, Luigi Manconi, Domenico Nigro, Claudio Novaro, and Luisa Passerini. My thanks go to them and to all those interviewed, who willingly allowed us together to reconstruct the – often painful and traumatic – episodes in their lives. Taking this into consideration and in order to respect the confidential nature of the interviews, their names have not been cited in full in this volume. The transcription of the interviews were carried out by Claudia Sofritti and Lucia Trippa. The latter was also responsible for coordinating and archiving the documentary material.

Throughout the entire course of the programme I have had the constant and active support of both the president of the Istituto Cattaneo, Luigi Pedrazzi, and of its administration, first in the shape of Arturo Parisi and, during the last year of research, of Piergiorgio Corbetta, together with the collaboration of Piero Bongiovanni, Giovanni Cocchi and Mirella Marani. This book would have stayed in the drawer had the translation of the manuscripts (with the exception of the chapters by Max Kaase and Sidney Tarrow) and the overall production editing not been entrusted to Clare Tame (Research Associate, European University Institute, Florence). Her careful and scrupulous work merits more than the ritual thanks normally made on these occasions.

Finally, my very particular thanks go to Arturo Parisi, not so much for having proposed my candidature as the director of the research programme, so much as for having testified – as part of the Scientific Committee and with the help given in times of difficulty – to the inestimable value of friendship.

Raimondo Catanzaro
Bologna, July 1991

# Introduction

## *Raimondo Catanzaro*

A theoretical-methodological preface

Today, at the beginning of the 1990s, the season of Italian terrorism seems to be something firmly set in the long-distant past. However, eight years ago, when the research on which this book is based began, we were still in the thick of the terroristic offensive; knowledge about the phenomenon was very limited. At the beginning of the research, the first element that had to be taken into consideration was constituted by the specific characteristics of Italian terrorism. First, it is characterized by its duration in time, by far superior to that of similar phenomena (that is, terrorism of a non–ethnic and non–nationalistic character) in other European countries, such as France and West Germany. Secondly, the Italian experience has witnessed the coexistence of various sorts of right- and left-wing terrorisms and of different groups within these two alignments. These groups use different strategies. They are characterized on the right by indiscriminate massacres for which – in the majority of cases – no responsibility is claimed; on the left by attacks carried out against well-chosen human targets for which responsibility is inevitably claimed; and with some attempts by the right to mix with clandestine groups and to imitate their strategies and slogans. Thirdly, it is characterized by the existence of a succession of different generational waves of militants in the armed struggle.

The literature on Italian terrorism has tended to consist of an excess of interpretations of a general and sometimes purely speculative nature, with a lack of serious research. To some extent this is still true today. There was not even any basic documentation sufficient to undertake an empirical survey; the interpretations of terrorism in Italy were mostly based on macro-variables relating to the political system, ideology and to factors of economic and social crisis. There is then a two-pronged challenge facing any academic wishing to undertake empirical research:

the need to construct a broad, reliable system of documentation and to avoid resorting to a broad outline of the overall situation.

At the same time, we did not wish to reject such outlines in the analysis of the origins of Italian terrorism out of hand, but rather to stress the possible negative consequences arising from these interpretations. In fact, we may give a totally black-and-white picture of the situation, in which the contradictions of the protagonists are simply eliminated. So, for example, we have descriptions in which the powerful armed strength of the terrorists confronts the stable, compact state which is fighting against the poisonous growth on its healthy body. We should instead ask whether or not important elements of disorganization and improvisation are not present in a significant number of terroristic actions, and whether there was not a worrying underestimation on the part of the government, of the terroristic phenomenon and a marked inability to understand its roots and motivations. We may also fall into a form of overdeterminism, so that the protagonists in the conflict – in particular, the terrorists – are envisaged as mere puppets manoeuvered from above, either by *cattivi maestri* (literally 'bad teachers'; Marxist intellectuals who supported a proletarian revolution), or by the secret services. In either case, these phenomena have clearly existed, and to a not insignificant extent, but they must be accorded the weight they merit. Terrorism with the range and breadth of Italian terrorism cannot have been exclusively the fruit either of subversive internal or international plots, or of political preaching or incitement to violence.

In the research programme we wished to avoid resorting solely to this sort of interpretative approach. It appeared to us to be more interesting and fruitful to organize and carry out an empirical survey that could provide answers to some of the following questions: along which life-course must an individual travel in order to choose to join the armed struggle? What are the transitions and turning points? Can we single out the types of life-course? Is the choice to join the armed struggle the fruit of an individual or a collective decision? What differences exist – if any – between various generations of terrorists? Are variables such as social background, position within the group and the existence of solidaristic or social networks relevant? Why among subjects belonging to the same political group have some followed a path that led them to the armed struggle while others have stopped half-way or have not even begun the journey? And finally, what life-courses and motivations produce the phenomena of *dissociazione* and *pentitismo*?[1]

To answer these questions means to investigate the historical-social conditions that translate into the determinants of individual behaviour. It seemed therefore important to take the individuals themselves, their life experiences and the conscious or obscure reasons underlying their choices as the starting point, rather than the armed groups and their organization and ideology. Thus, the best way to answer the questions appeared to be to reconstruct the life histories of the subjects who were protagonists of the armed struggle.

Such a reconstruction poses complex problems of method and content. Since the aim was to single out an 'anthropological' base for the behaviour of terrorists, we chose to use the unstructured interview (with only an outline interview) as the primary instrument for obtaining information on the variables that we considered essential for the reconstruction of the life-courses and turning points, and the claimed continuity and hidden interruptions.[2]

In the selection of the subjects to interview we took into consideration the following variables: the name of the group within the vast and heterogeneous universe of left-wing terrorism to which the protagonists belonged; the generational waves of the phenomenon; the territorial bases of activity; the sex of the protagonist; and the functions carried out within the group (leadership or simple militancy).

Clearly then, the information gathered using the interviews is not relative to *facts* (for which other sources exist, in our case essentially the documentation on judicial sentences and judgements, statements of cross-examinations and material produced by the terroristic groups themselves), so much as on the experience of the subjects, and the emotions, sensations, traumas and internal conflicts derived from this experience and the way this is reconstructed and perceived; the construction of the image *per se* of others and of the world around them; the degree of complexity of these images; the representation of the social reality in which they lived, the membership group, other organizations, the state and the perception of the sense and the meaning of violence; and the way in which these images vary according to the changing experience of the armed struggle and clandestine life. In other words, with the creation of this source we wished to reconstruct the subjective environment of the protagonists of the armed struggle and terrorism, and to investigate how this experience was lived daily within the terroristic groups.

The aim of the interviews was also to combine two elements of the same importance in the understanding of the terroristic phenomenon: factuality and subjectivity. Such coupling was possible through the analysis of both the content of the biographical reconstruction carried out by the subject, and of how much of his account is borne out by the documentary sources. It is not accidental that we talk of *coupling* and not of *synthesis* between the two types of information, because the reconstruction of the events made by the judiciary and that of the life-courses of the interviewees are located on different levels.

We must nevertheless not totally overlook the fact that the reconstruction of the internal – individual and collective – dynamics of the clandestine groupings, to which we had access through the mirror of the memory presented by the interview, are important for the overall picture of research on terrorism carried out up until now. A particularly interesting hypothesis would be to link the mechanisms of reproduction and the repertoire of terrorist actions to the progressive narrowing down of their political, cultural and social horizons following entry into clandestinity, and as a result, the emergence of the logic of competition and conflict between the various groups: logics that have often been the principal, if not sole, determinants of the strategic or tactical choices operated by terroristic groups.

## Terrorism and the movements

If we look at the date of the events, the first neo-fascist-type massacre that marked the beginning of the cycle of terrorism took place on 12 December 1969 at the *Banca dell'agricoltura di Milano*, in Piazza Fontana, that is, in the middle of the 'hot autumn' of worker and trade-union unrest that followed in the wake of the 1968 movement. If again we look at the phase in which the terrorist presence was strongest and most dangerous in terms of the number and quality of attacks, we are forced to admit that it began in 1976–7, simultaneously with another process of broad-based collective mobilization. At first sight terrorism seems therefore to emerge and develop in connection with the high waves in the cycles of protest, collective mobilization and the formation of the movements. It is on this consideration that the first series of research questions is based.

Since nothing is more fascinating than undertaking research of the obvious, we posed ourselves what is normally considered as a self-evident truth in the form of a question: is terrorism the child of the movements, from the protest cycle and collective mobilization? or is it not rather the consequence of the end of the movements, and of the beginning of their crisis, of the non-integration of radical and extremist groups into legal politics, and of their organizational collapse? Whatever the reply to this question, one of the elements to investigate concerns the choice of individuals and groups to make the transition or the leap to the militancy of the armed struggle. This in turn poses a second question. It is well-known that not all those who took part in the extremist organizations involved in the movements travelled along a path leading them to terrorism. Why then did only certain individuals and not others take up the option of the armed struggle and who are they? And why did this occur at certain times rather than others?

A reply to these questions can be found by investigating the points where the individual life-course intersects with political experience. In particular, the investigation of individual life-courses allows us to check in what historical-social circumstances this meeting between the subjects and politics took place, when and through which political groups, and in what way it was characterized. Other apparently important elements in understanding the relationship between movements, groups and individuals are constituted by the age of entry into active politics and the ways in which political socialization has occurred. In this respect, the circumstances in which protagonists have had substantial experience of legal political activity before their contact with arms and organized violence are very important. On the basis of the life-course data and from the observations of the interviewees, it would appear that the absence of such experience was an important factor in the elimination of objections to the use of arms. Finally, as far as the genesis of terrorism is concerned, a significant element appears to be constituted by the bonds of solidarity and by the networks of social and affective relations that induce individual and collective choice.

To these questions, posed in the context of the research on the individual life-courses, we must add the need to analyse the characteristics of the movements and the cycle of protest of the 1970s. It was at this point that the need to broaden the area of research – even if this basically followed the lines of the biographical data – and to establish contact with scholars who had carried out studies on aspects of the Italian situation relevant to the understanding of terrorism, became obvious.

The analysis of the features of the cycle of protest and of the collective mobilization that swept over Italy from the end of the 1960s, and its relationship with terrorism, is a thematic nucleus around which revolve some particularly interesting questions. Is it true, as Sidney Tarrow asks, that the characteristics of the cycle of protest were such as to enable us to forecast its outcome and hence the emergence of terrorist groups? Can we claim that the violence only led to outcomes such as the products of terrorism, or inversely can we single out the processes of the institutionalization of political participation that follow from the cycle of mobilization? Tarrow's response is that the terroristic experience emerges not from the movement itself, but from its collapse.

This does not mean that there were no links between the movements and terrorism. Some aspects of the movements, which were internalized by the subjects during or even before the process of collective mobilization, turn out to be qualifying elements of the associational characteristics of the armed groups, in particular left-wing groups. Among these we find affective and ideological solidarity. In this respect we can ask, together with Claudio Novaro, whether solidarity in some way determines the choice of the armed struggle on the part of groups of young militants that passed from the experience of the *servizi d'ordine* of *Lotta Continua*[3] to the area of *Senza Tregua*, and subsequently to clandestine militancy in *Prima Linea*. If we accept the answer implicit in the reconstruction of Novaro, that is, that these elements of expressive and ideological solidarity underpin the social construction of an identity that extends – even today – beyond the experience of the armed struggle, then these can be considered, in the perspective of the analysis of the individuals involved in terrorism, as motivational elements in the choice of clandestinity.

If we analyse the situation from an organizational rather than a protagonist-individual perspective, then another question emerges: whether these elements constitute incentives for militancy in clandestine organizations which, given the high cost of their maintenance, are particularly difficult to maintain. In this perspective we can ask what role is played by ideology and solidarity in the functioning of clandestine organizations? Do they constitute symbolic resources that allow the cohesion, maintenance and reproduction of armed groups? Alongside these symbolic resources, what role is played by material rewards?

Hence solidarity, material rewards and ideologies must be interpreted as resources and as instruments of the cohesion, maintenance and reproduction of armed groups, which, in as far as the modality of their reproduction is concerned, follow dynamics that are partly similar and partly different to those that characterize groups carrying out legal political activity.

One of the problems that emerges here relates to the different weight exercised by ideological and solidaristic incentives in the different individual histories and in the choice of adhesion to the armed struggle or of the continuation and confirmation of such a choice. It would be interesting to conduct an analysis – as yet lacking – of the reasons for the predominance of one or other type of incentive according to the territorial and generational context in which they operate, and according to the different ideological characterization of the groups.

## Ideologies and images of the political system

Thus we come to another commonplace about Italian terrorism: the problem of the ideological origins and the spiritual fathers of these generations of terrorists. In particular, the problem has a double profile: the reference to political ideologies and to the images of the system of power and politics; and the conflicting value systems of terrorists and society, in particular with reference to the problem of violence as a weapon of political competition.

The question normally posed about the relationship between terrorism and ideology is whether terrorism is the child of a particular ideology, and if so, which. Thus posed, the question implies that certain ideologies are generators of terrorism, in particular those ideologies that contain an invitation to the use of violence or its justification. In this way, however, we cannot give discriminant replies to the question about the influence of ideologies in determining the choice of violence. Historically it is a given fact that the ideological catchwords to justify the use of violence have the most varied roots. What we wish to put forward is that ideologies should be more appropriately considered as resources available to the actors to legitimate political action or to justify the use of violence and the armed struggle, rather than as the original cause of violence and terrorism.

In the light of this premise we can read the questions contained in the chapter by Luigi Manconi about the ideological formulation of the Red Brigades during the constituent and initial phase of their existence. Is it true that at the base of such a formulation – which certainly conditioned that formation of other left-wing terrorist groups with different strategies – we find the reference to the bible of Marxist-Leninism, backed up by the *operaista* tradition?[4] Or is a more important reference linked to another tradition – that of anti-fascism and the Resistance?

Manconi opts for the second direction: that the ideology of the Red Brigades (BR) is better understood in terms of the traditions of the partisan struggle rather than those of Marxism. This thesis is confirmed by the experience of other terrorist groups, for example *Prima Linea* in the Val di Susa which is dealt with in the chapter by Claudio Novaro. The *brigatista* formulation of the image of the absolute enemy, the state, anti-state action and the plan to build an armed counterpower, correspond better to this line of interpretation than to interpretations that trace BR ideology to Marxist-Leninism.

Within the spectrum of Italian left-wing terrorism, the BR are the longest-lasting terrorist group with the most coherent strategy. Their strategies of action and their organizational structures, broadly documented in the chapter by Gian Carlo Caselli and Donatella della Porta, have nevertheless passed through various phases. The persistence of the BR logo undoubtedly constituted an element of continuity, but was nevertheless unable to paper over the fractures between the imprisoned leaders and those acting outside. Nor was it able to guarantee an effective strategic continuity in the succession of the various leaderships, in particular after the kidnaping and killing in May 1978 of Aldo Moro, the President of the Christian Democratic Party.

The problem of the consistency between the terroristic strategies used by the BR – above all, the kidnappings and popular trials – and the ideologies and images of the world recalls the possible influence of justicing experience derived from the impact of Latin-American terrorism. It also recalls, however, the theme of the reciprocal image of the adversary. Faced with the image that the Red Brigades had of the state, what image did the state have of the Red Brigades? Was it a sharp, clear-cut image or indistinct and cloudy? Did the state appreciate the danger that terrorism constituted for its institutions, to understand its roots and manifestations?

If we read the declarations made by the Presidents of the Council of Ministers during the *anni di piombo* ('years of lead'; the period when terrorism posed the greatest threat to Italian democracy), their references to the problem of terrorism reveal how, over and above the rhetoric about the dangers for the democratic state and the state of emergency, government behaviour was characterized by the total absence of a clear image of the terroristic phenomena, its components and the effective threat it posed for the democratic institutions. Even when the attack on the state reached a peak with the abduction and killing of Aldo Moro, we are confronted by the limited nature of the declarations about terrorism periodically made by the heads of government to parliament. Not only was there a clear underestimation of the entire phenomenon, but 'red' terrorism was undervalued as much, if not more, than 'black' terrorism. We can put forward the hypothesis that this relates to the political climate of the mid-1970s, with an attitude that – stressing the recurrent danger of a rightist *coup d'état* – is connected to the tradition of the foundations of legitimacy in the creation of the Republic of Italy from the ashes of the fascist regime.

In this respect we need to ask whether the recall to the anti-fascist tradition and to the tradition of the Resistance as a foundation of the democratic state did not at that time tend to legitimize the existence and actions of both legal politics and violent action. In other words, we could put forward the hypothesis of Manconi on the recall to the tradition of the Resistance by the BR and how much the argument about the attitude of government can be integrated in a more comprehensive overall picture. The dispute between opposing political forces, that is, between the legal political actors on the one side and illegal political actors on the other, but also among the former, was also a dispute over symbolic values and who had more right to claim continuity with the constituent foundations of the democratic state. The strong symbolic influence of such foundations may have undermined the terrorist group's ability to understand which were the effective transformations taking place in society and within the state. Nevertheless, this symbolic influence undoubtedly determined the inability of the political parties, government and institutional political actors, to understand the dynamics of terrorism.

Another equally weighty observation can be linked to this: that is, the relationship between the initial inability of the repressive apparatus of the state to beat terrorism effectively and the deviations of the secret services, and the analysis of terrorism made by the political forces and the parties. Perhaps it is no coincidence that the deviations of the secret services, the conniving between P-2 (a secret Masonic lodge, *Propaganda Due*, suspected of having organized a *coup d'état* in the 1970s), the subversive right and members of the intelligence agencies and state officials, and their infiltration of right- and left-wing terrorist groups came about in a situation of a marked inability on the part of the government and political forces to understand, forestall and fight the different terrorisms.

However, we do not wish to link the dialectics of violence exclusively to the relationship between the state and the terroristic armed counterpowers. Another line of investigation that should be followed up is that of the relationship between theory and praxis, between preaching and practising violence.

## Terrorists and violence

In the fiery climate of the early 1970s, the fear of a *coup d'état* undoubtedly influenced individual and collective decisions to resort to violence as a weapon of political competition; this theme of violence is dealt with in the final chapter of the book. It is in the brutal practice of political murder, kneecapping, inflicting injuries, massacres, and in the violation of the physical and moral integrity of individuals that the continuity and interruption in the life histories of the protagonists are revealed. Here we also find indications of the structural reasons, the environmental and social processes, and the individual crises that subsequently led to the phemonena of *dissociazione* and *pentitismo*.

The problems of interruption and continuity in the life histories of terrorists are particularly important for the exponents of red terrorism, above all in relation to the phenomena of *dissociazione* and *pentitismo* (both phenomena occur little and are qualitatively ambiguous in the experience of the subversive right). To what extent did individual reflection and the political and organizational crises of the groups influence the decision to dissociate? What weight did the legislation that granted the reduction of sentences to the *pentiti* have on the internal dynamics of the groups and individuals?

It is certain that individual crises of militants together with the organizational disintegration of clandestine terrorist groups influenced the decision to abandon the armed struggle. The dissociation of most left-wing terrorists is characterized by a renunciation of terrorism without collaborating with justice; it coexisted alongside the repentence and collaboration with the authorities on the part of others. Such behaviour relates back to the problematic, intricate relationship of left-wing terrorists with violence and in general to the question of what is understood as political violence.

Starting by answering this question, Max Kaase asks himself whether there are any *a priori* reasons why subjects should abstain from the use of violence as an instrument of political competition. According to the answer given to this question we can then ask whether the reasons for the episodes of violence are not often to be found in the interaction between demonstrators and the forces of law and order.

While these questions deal with the practice of violence, other questions examine attitudes: that is, the cultural system of values. We can in fact ask whether the extension of the violent repertoire is not to some extent connected to the fact that the cultural sense of the violent action, subjectively understood for the protagonists, is not univocal. In particular, developing the analysis of Max Kaase, we can ask what is the relationship between the instrumental aspects and the hedonistic-expressive aspects of violence?

In this respect, we can ask how the impact with arms took place and how it was interrupted. For left-wing terrorists there seems to be an intricate link between the use of violence in street demonstrations and in clashes with the police during marches, and the cold-blooded, ends-oriented determination to strike defenceless people typical of terrorist acts directed against single individuals. It is this relationship that enters a crisis, as we shall see in the last chapter, transforming what was an element of strength in the membership of the group into an element of weakness of the reproducibility of violence.

## Continuity and interruptions in the biographical life histories

Given the shape we wished to give the research, the choice of one empirical method of investigation is derived from a criticism of the reductionist definition of the phenomenon: that is, with those that trace terrorism to the preaching of violence, those that only examine variables of a socio-psychological nature, or those that limit themselves to emphasizing the dynamics of the political or party system. Hence we chose the method of the biographical reconstruction of individual experience. The interviews on the life histories are a course in the memory on the part of the subject interviewed. This induces the protagonist to rethink the sense of his or her life-course, to reinterpret its continuity and interruptions, and to relive its junctures, transitions and turning points. It is also an understanding of how and in what way the breaks in the biographical life history are acknowledged, or, conversely, that continuity is strongly sought.

The biographical courses presented to us by the protagonists of the armed struggle fall essentially into four categories: two are centred on the breaks or interruptions and two focus on the continuity of the life-course, that distinguish old and new generations, i.e. the historical leaders and new 'conscripts'.

The first type of image is that of the continuity of the life history: a continuity relived with strong emphasis on the personal aspects of the succession of events in terms of individual choice, where the emphasis on the political is less important. In this first type of reconstruction of the biographical life history, continuity is seen as a return: a return to the environment and in the environment of the community that had been abandoned for the sake of terrorism. This abandonment is reinterpreted as a mistake committed in a fundamentally just course of action, a course of action that the community itself, with its tradition of anti-fascism and the Resistance, indicated. It is an error of course that it is possible to undo in so far as there is a primary community, with its network of social relationships, that is willing to forgive a prodigal child. This version of the personal continuity is centred on the community of membership and is found in first- and second-generation left-wing terrorists belonging to the Red Brigades or *Prima Linea*. It has particular social background characteristics: working-class or labouring origins, in some cases from families who had migrated from the South, integration in an industrialized context with strong labour traditions and characterized by the presence of a strong Communist-oriented community subculture.

The second type of image is once again characterized by the continuity of life-course events but with the emphasis on political aspects. Here we are mainly dealing with subjects from the post-1977 period of left-wing terrorism who do not interpret the political plan they had sought to develop as being a complete failure. We could say that, while in the first case (that of personal continuity as a return) the protagonist lives the crisis of dissociation as the failure of his or her political experience, and this in turn generates the need to reconstruct a personal identity through narrative continuity, in this second case political identity is maintained even after dissociation and the subject centres the reconstruction narrative of his identity on the maintenance of the relationship with fellow militants or, at least, with people who had made choices of political militancy similar to his own in the second half of the 1970s. Here the protagonist tends not to see events of continuity rather than interruption. In this sense, while in the first case it seems to be a return to the private sphere and a rejection of political militancy, in the second case dissociation is aimed at the recovery of spaces of political expression. Such attitudes seem to be the outcome of one of the aspects most firmly internalized by the protagonists: the emphasis on collective solidarity of a strongly expressive nature as an end in itself. From this point of view we can perhaps understand the reason for the emphasis on the political aspects of the life history. For these generations, the transition to the armed struggle appeared to respond to the need to defend their primary solidarity networks. Such networks were the melting pot in which personal needs and political motivations were moulded. This gave rise to the emphasis on political continuity and the gathering together of the greater part of the most strictly personal aspects of the protagonist's life experiences under this heading.

In the third type of narrative identity constructed by the interviewees, the life-course is reinterpreted in terms of interruptions or breaks at the level of personal experience. It deals with cases where we get a glimpse of a sort of conversion process, sometimes expressed in clearly religious terms. In these cases the life-course is reconstructed as an experience broken into two parts by an interruption. This interruption is the transition from the previous definition and is totally centred on the values and the practice of violence, whereas present experience is characterized by the discovery of human values. In some cases this discovery is experienced as a conversion to Catholicism. Here the past is seen as characterized by fundamental errors; the political plan the protagonist had for a long time believed in, and for which he may have taken up arms or justified the sacrifice of human life, is now considered to be non-existent and judged as bogus.

Finally, the fourth and last type of narrative identity reconstructed by the interviewees is defined in terms of discontinuity with the emphasis on political factors. It is a mirror case of the second type of reconstruction and here too typically deals with subjects who have lived through the experience of the 1977 movement and who have successively belonged to *Prima Linea*. Unlike the second type of reconstruction, however, the protagonist here has taken part in the 1977 movement without a solid background of previous political experience. Here the strongest aspect was, using the words of one of the interviewees, what we could define as a 'pack identity': something that is simultaneously deep and superficial – a question of 'feeling', a moving together in which the personal is submerged in the collective and the political is reduced to the personal. The strongest, but probably also the most naive, consequence of this type of involvement is the subjectively rooted belief in a communion of needs and the image of a communitarian universe constituted by a homogeneous unity of aspirations and intentions. This sort of image of political and personal identity breaks down following the impact with the reality of prison. In prison the terrorists discovered that the political prisoners did not at all share those homogeneous characteristics, aspirations and objectives that seemed common to the movement of 1977 and to its armed developments.

> We are all people without an identity ... people with a heavy past ... and a vacuum in the future ... I internalized a sort of nausea for politics.[5]

This total break with past experience, this definitive collapse of the hopes of a dreamt-of world, this discovery of the absolute futility of the plan pursued, leaves no room for ascribing a sense to the recovery of personal relationships that can even happen following a prison experience. Unlike the first three cases, where personal identity is salvaged at the level of primary – affective or political – relationships, here dissociation has led to an – as yet – unresolved crisis of personal identity, and to a future without hope. It is this inability to hope for a future that is perhaps the most extreme and marked demonstration of what we have lost with the experience of terrorism. Certainly, it has been primarily the terrorists themselves who have lost part of their lives in this experience, but perhaps we have all lost something on account of terrorism. In reconstructing the life histories of the protagonists during those years the aim has been to reveal the experiences and contradictions typical of the daily life of terrorists, a life it would be a mistake to interpret as either exceptional or extraordinary. Indeed, their lives, even if the protagonists sometimes describe them in terms of 'heroism', appear in a light of normality that makes them, precisely for this reason, emblematic of the history of the generations that fought – and lost – in the attempt to reconcile the demands of solidarity, the myths of the violent transformation of society and ideological constructions.

Thinking back to those years, reconstructing those dynamics, reflecting on the errors made and reconsidering the turning points through the medium of memory are ways to make a critical reappropriation of what we have all lost. If it is true that, in the words of Musil, 'one is never so near to oneself as when all has been lost',[6] the reflection on the way in which we have become lost and the experience of this loss can contribute to an understanding of the recent history of a country like Italy which, perhaps more than any other European country, has suffered from terrorism.

## Notes

1 On *dissociazione* and *pentitismo* see the final page of Chapter 3.
2 The outline of the open-ended interview is reproduced in the Appendix.
3 On the *servizi d'ordine* see note 15 in Chapter 6.
4 On the *operaista* tradition in Italy see note 2 in Chapter 4.
5 Interview with 'Francesco', p. 7. Interview carried out by Domenico Nigro.
6 Taken from R. Musil (1982) *Die Schwärmer*, Cologne, Rowohlt TB.

# 1
# Political participation, political values and political violence

## Max Kaase

### 1.1 Introduction

This chapter deals with political violence, its diffusion, its determinants and its relationship to other forms of political participation. Violence is one constitutive element of the human condition; it exists everywhere and at all times although it is not equally frequent at all times and in all societies. The control of violence has been a major concern wherever people have interacted to form societies and, particularly, polities. Violence has a particularly destabilizing quality because it cuts across all rules, is independent of all specific forms of social and political organization and therefore threatens the precise existence of society. Can we reasonably argue along those lines without attaching a specific meaning to the concept of violence? We think not. Take, for example, Galtung's famous definition of violence as being present:

> when human beings are being influenced so that their actual somatic and mental realizations are below their potential realizations ... Violence is here defined as the cause of the difference between the potential and the actual.[1]

This definition has served as the basis for the concept of 'structural violence' which, as can easily be seen, is so broadly applicable that it describes all social relationships of superordinance and subordinance and is therefore, in the end, devoid of any substantive, distinctive and analytical meaning. By contrast, in this chapter violence is regarded as all forms of direct or indirect physical damage by individuals intended to be inflicted on other individuals or things. Political violence thus refers to all acts of wilful physical impairment.[2] At this point we should distinguish between political violence in general and political terrorism; the latter uses political violence as a means in a means-ends calculating process in conscious avoidance of direct confrontation with police forces; it aims at a breakdown of societal interaction. Thus, political terrorism is regarded here as a specific sub-category of political violence. Since the studies and data on which this chapter is based do not contain information on political terrorism, and for other reasons briefly elaborated upon later in this section, political terrorism is not further discussed in the paper.

Obviously, political violence up to this point has been regarded as an activity produced by individual members or groups of individuals in a given society outside the state, as societally-based violence. Political violence can, however, also be and frequently is carried out by the state. Here we usually speak of repression. In fact, if we systematically distinguish between the *source* of violence and the *addressee* of violence, we get the following fourfold typology:

Table 1.1 Typology of violence

| Addressee of violence | Source of violence | |
| --- | --- | --- |
| | State | Societal groups |
| State | *Coup d'etat* | Revolution, protest, terrorism |
| Societal groups | Repression | Civil war, unrest, anomie, turmoil |

Which types of violence are, or have been, most frequent is a matter of historical perspective. Certainly, one important qualifying variable is the kind of political order that exists and is regarded as legitimate at a given point in time. For instance, *coup d'états* usually take place at the transition from a democratic to a non-democratic political order, or within the latter. Furthermore, state repression under a democratic regime is extremely limited and usually bound by the proper operation of law. The violent fights between societal groups are normatively – but not factually – excluded as an acceptable mechanism for conflict solution in democratic societies; their innate logic and *raison d'être* should have made the exercise of physical violence superfluous. If this perspective is adopted, then it follows automatically that the state monopoly on violence is convincingly *established and must be accepted as legitimate*. Needless to say, the exercise of that monopoly in order to become and remain legitimate has to follow the rule of law. *The rule of law, a competitive political process, and the state monopoly on physical violence constitute the core of the modern democratic constitutional state.*

Of the various types of political violence cited in the above table, two are particularly relevant for democratic polities in reasonably 'normal' operations: the 'repression' cell and the 'revolution-protest-terrorism' cell. On the above *a priori* grounds the 'revolution' element will be excluded from further consideration – revolutions in democratic societies only arise under 'non-normal' operating conditions. The 'terrorism' element is left out because it does not involve any sizeable part of the public and does not possess broad legitimacy. This leaves us with the 'repression' cell and the 'protest' element which have two major considerations in common: they both confront the state and societal actor(s) and they both involve, at least potentially, the mass public. This latter factor is important because democratic polities derive their legitimacy precisely from the people; major changes in orientations of violence lead to broad repercussions for the polity. We should point out that the emphasis on democratic legitimation chosen in this chapter does not reflect any claim that a legitimacy crisis is the only conceivable, and certainly not necessarily the gravest, threat to the overall stability of democratic polities.

## 1.2 Political participation and political violence: theoretical foundations

When the waves of political unrest hit Western democracies in the 1960s, a wealth of explanations was offered by ingenious social scientists and others. Few of those explanations, though, were based on reliable empirical evidence. Thus, the *Political Action* study (Barnes, Kaase, et al., 1979) had a natural focus. What were the *conditions, structure and meaning* in particular of those kinds of political involvement that were then termed protest behaviour? While in the beginning, the protest perspective dominated public perceptions and scholarly debate alike, a new view of uninstitutionalized political participation slowly emerged. This view was based on a particular variety of democratic theory that emphasized a broader role for the individual citizen in political involvement. The participatory revolution, as it is sometimes called, challenged the limited perspective of democracy as a unique set of rules for the regular, institutionalized exchange of political authorities. It characterized the existing system of political institutions as outdated and identified the quest for more political and social participatory rights as the core problem of political order in Western democracies. It was unclear, however, what place the use of political violence should occupy in terms of democratic theory.

We already maintained almost a decade ago that a micro-theory *alone* could not account for the emergence of direct, uninstitutionalized forms of political participation in the late 1960s and early 1970s. Factors like the spectacular increase in the level of economic well-being and educational attainment, the growing physical and cognitive distance to the Second World War and the spread of electronic mass communications – particularly television – (Kaase, 1986), are all important macro-societal conditions for the changes in political involvement by many citizens in the Western democracies.[3] These changes could not be *systematically* empirically related to the micro-data collected by the *Political Action* group. Nevertheless, the analyses in *Political Action* followed a theoretical model outlined in the 1979 volume as follows:

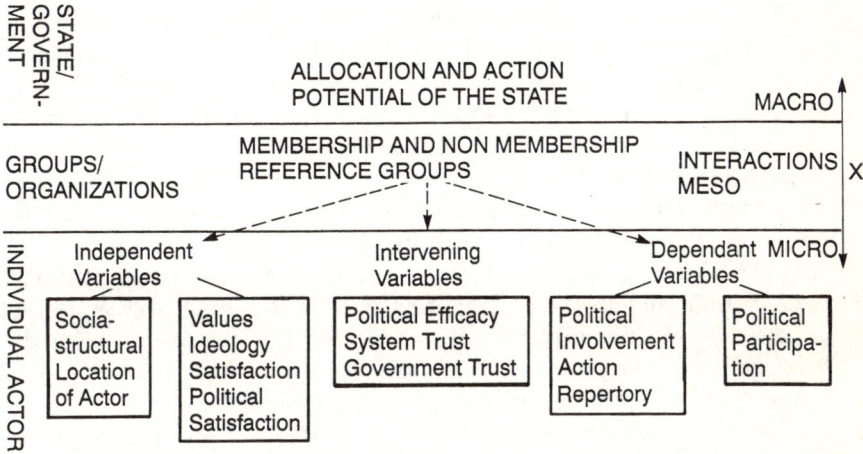

Figure 1.1   A model of political action and mass participation

This model clearly entails the dynamic multilevel properties needed to understand rationally all forms of political participation as a result of individual inclinations and beliefs, involvement in personal networks and organizational memberships and a set of institutional conditions ranging from electoral laws to the availability of plebiscitary political channels. Obviously, the model is weak in specifying the developmental perspective and the concrete interactions between the macro-, meso- and micro-levels of the system bringing about individual action.

Although a full test of the complete model was not achieved in *Political Action* – thus making the model more of an heuristic device for guiding analyses and interpretations – it is worthwhile mentioning some of the most pertinent findings for the 1974 data-point of the study. Our main finding was that conventional participation in the late 1960s and early 1970s had been supplemented by a second direct-action-related dimension of unconventional participation. We demonstrated that while the concrete incidents of such behaviour were still relatively scarce, there was a substantial willingness among the population of the eight countries studied to engage in acts of unconventional political participation *under specific circumstances*. This willingness was heavily concentrated on the cluster of issue-specific, legal and unconventional participation, whereas affinity with the sub-dimensions of civil disobedience and violence was limited to a small part of the population. Furthermore, we argued that the interaction of stable economic growth and the extension of higher education created – as Inglehart maintained – a potential for new, post-materialist values, including the desire for more political participation in determining our own lives. This value change also led – particularly in special sub-groups of the population – to the emergence of new issue priorities and the 'new politics' as they were called by Hildenbrandt and Dalton (1978). On these grounds it seemed plausible *and* could be empirically validated that young, well-educated persons were the main carriers not only of preferences for post-materialist issues but also of positive *attitudes* towards unconventional political participation. The finding that the strong statistical relationship to young age considerably weakened the closer one moved to *actual* unconventional participation hinted at the importance of intervening factors in the process of *mobilization* to action,[4] but also at the special impact of the existing pro-participatory *Zeitgeist* on the educated young.[5] But once again, it was unclear where political violence fitted in.

One of the topics which received a lot of attention was the question of the relationship between conventional and unconventional participation. Not knowing then what we know now, we might have expected – especially under the protest perspective – a negative correlation between the two, indicating that the formal and informal sectors of political participation were drifting apart. What we found instead was a positive though modest correlation between the two dimensions. This led us to conclude that we were witnessing an expansion of the political repertoire of the general public in Western democracies in the postwar period; the dimension of unconventional participation was being added to the conventional, electorally-oriented dimension that itself had only been *fully* established in those countries in the 1920s and 1930s. As a consequence, we combined the two dimensions resulting in the typology of a political-action repertoire. The findings with respect to this typology gave rise to the warning note in the concluding chapter of *Political Action* where we argued that the dimension of unconventional political participation contained a problematic mix of instrumental and expressive political orientations. This led us to reinforce Huntington's (1974) sceptical reflections on the future of democratic politics.

At this point we must point out that very little of our thinking was concerned with political violence *per se*. While events of political violence command a tremendous amount of attention on television, and in this sense alone can create a completely false public perception of the importance and frequency of political violence, we were struck by the consensus among mass publics in eight democracies regarding the disapproval of and the rejection of political violence.

There is no point in discussing the validity of these data at great length

Table 1.2   Approval of and participation in violent actions

| Countries | Approval of Violence | | Participation in Violence | |
|---|---|---|---|---|
| | Against Persons % | Against Things % | Against Persons % | Against Things % |
| Great Britain | 1.1 | 1.4 | 0.6 | 0.2 |
| Federal Republic | 1.2 | 2.5 | 0.3 | 0.3 |
| The Netherlands | 0.9 | 1.5 | 0.8 | 0.4 |
| Austria | 2.4 | 2.7 | 0.4 | 0.2 |
| USA | 0.9 | 1.7 | 0.7 | 1.1 |
| Italy | 1.1 | 1.4 | 0.5 | 0.3 |
| Switzerland | 1.7 | 1.7 | 0.3 | 0.2 |
| Finland | 0.4 | 0.8 | 0.8 | 0.5 |

since no other comparative information on the subject is available. Thus while there will always be some doubt as to whether violence-prone individuals were systemically excluded from the respective national samples, one conclusion is warranted: political violence in democratic polities is a taboo phenomenon.

The important question as to whether there is nevertheless a link between non-violent legal direct participation, non-violent illegal direct participation (civil disobedience) and violent participation, in the sense that displaying the first type of behaviour increases the probability of exercising the second, and so on, will be taken up later in the chapter. What needs to be spelt out here is that the widely shared rejection of violence does not automatically warrant the conclusion that there is a firm societal basis against political violence. A couple of points should be addressed in this context.

First of all, an early study by Blumenthal (1972) revealed that one way in which an individual can overcome that societal taboo on violence is to redefine certain actions so that they are no longer regarded as violent. The Blumenthal study of American males showed that there are indeed group-specific differences in the way certain actions are defined as violent or not. Obviously, the more encompassing and vague the societal definition of violence – as in Galtung's concept of structural violence – the easier it is to define violence subjectively such that actions used by individuals and their sympathisers that are violent or on the brink of violence are redefined such as to be conceived as non-violent. Vice versa, actions by opponents and their sympathisers may be labelled violent and thereby socially castigated although they are not physically violent. The less precise the societal definition of violence, the higher the probability of such group-specific interpretations of violence, and the lower the likelihood of the general acceptance of *one* concept of violence. If such ambiguities are reinforced – as in the case of the former Federal Republic of Germany – through the legal process, then this further reinforces the actual use of violence.

Such considerations sharpen our view of the problem of justifying violence, be it moral or rational. If certain types of behaviour are heavily negatively sanctioned – as is the case with physical political violence – then it requires a particular effort to *justify* such non–acceptable acts. We have little quantitative information about the types of justification that have gained currency *vis-à-vis* political violence. However, one such type of justification is the rational calculation of violence and its ensuing success in achieving the desired goal; the more effective violence is considered to be, the more likely it is to generate support. According to the *Political Action* study, in seven of the eight countries examined, between 3 per cent and 12 per cent of the mass public regard personal violence and/or violence against property as effective. In parenthesis, we should mention that in Finland this figure rises to around 40 per cent. These data clearly show that the number of people who regard violence as effective is substantially higher than those who approve of it. The obvious countermeasure against the application of physical violence in a means–ends calculation is that authorities do not give in to demands supported by violent actions.

The second type of justification is moral. In such cases, the goals pursued by an individual or a group of individuals are held so dearly that even the most extreme action is considered acceptable. There is evidence that such justifications are not only employed in complicated situations such as that of Northern Ireland and the Palestinians, but also in Western democracies. The West German discussion on the validity of the majority principle in democratic decision-making is a good case in point (Guggenberger and Offe, 1984). Since there are no *a priori* criteria that rank one set of issue priorities over another, a generalization of this type of justification invalidates the basic principles of democratic decision-making, bringing the peaceful political process to a halt.

In countries where the democratic tradition has suffered an interruption we often find another justifying principle for political violence: violence in order to prevent an attack or a *coup d'état* against the democratic state. Whereas philosophers of democratic thought accorded a role to this type of justification – the right, even the duty, of the citizen to kill the tyrant – the West German example shows there is an ideological bias in its application:[6] individuals on the left of the political spectrum are more predisposed to tolerate this type of violence. While this ideological bias can easily be explained in historical terms – the left part of the ideological spectrum is most clearly opposed to national Socialism, having suffered particularly from it – it is nevertheless important to see to what extent this extreme situation (the tyrant's murder) is generalized on the one hand and 'eased–up' on the other, thus creating an argument that can be used – once again – to justify almost any kind of political violence.

We have touched on the justification issue because normative justification by society at large constitutes, in our view, one of the major facilitating factors for the application of physical violence in political matters. There may be controversy on the question as to whether direct or indirect democracy is the most appropriate way to organize citizen participation within the polity. Such a controversy may be resolved, however, without endangering the democratic process. The same is not true with regard to political violence, not even with regard to illegal non-violent forms of political participation. These modes of political participation have one thing in common: *if applied on the large scale* they bring the institutionalized and lawful solution of controversial political matters to an end. Why is it then that among political activists in democracies, despite the ban on violence, there is still an openness, at least intellectually, towards the use of physical force in political strife?

We have already given one of the answers: it pays. It pays in terms of results and because state repression as an obvious successful countermeasure to political violence is alien to democratic ideology. It is no accident that collective participation in violent political acts is rarely sanctioned by the courts. Violence is also sometimes regarded as legitimate because it is easy to recall that many existing societies are so unjust and undemocratic that almost any measure to improve the political situation appears justified. The problem here is that it is easy to extend this sort of reasoning to any kind of political order, to forget the conditions and consequences of political violence in a legal perspective. It is one thing to ponder, as an intellectual, on the virtues and necessities of political violence to obtain a better world, and quite another to think through what political violence means for the entire population of a given society.

One element of modern societies deserves special mention here: the mass media, particularly television. It is well-known that in a rational calculation of the pros and cons of political violence for a given group, the positive effect on goal achievement through mass-media reporting of political violence plays an important, even a strategic, role. Much demonstrative violence – and this is particularly true for political terrorism – would never take place were it not for media reporting. Activists know, as do journalists, that the mass media are inextricably caught up in the logic of their own operating rules. The problem is aggravated because mass-media reporting creates a public image of omnipresent and widespread political and other forms of violence, thereby reducing the individual threshold for its use.

Modern democracies seem to become increasingly politicized (Dalton, 1988), though on a less-informed level (Kaase, 1986). Politicization means more concern with issues, more- and not less-ideological stance and also the likelihood of a higher degree of participation. Are there then innate boundaries between legal and illegal uninstitutionalized forms of political participation? Once we adopt a *legal* perspective to politics, the answer is likely to be 'no'. If this is true and if we accept the premise that political violence is a problem, then it is even more important to establish empirically the status of political violence in liberal democracies. We shall examine this in the following section.

## 1.3 Political participation and political violence: the facts

The analysis of developments in participatory behaviour and attitudes, including political violence, requires good data: that is, data that reflect the underlying theoretical approaches properly, which are as factual as possible and which are longitudinal. There is no point in discussing these important but cumbersome matters in any detail. Let it suffice to say that the data situation on political violence in general is very poor and that there are basically two types of data relevant for its study: data describing concrete events or event sequences of political protest and violence, and survey data that reflect in one way or another the behaviour and/or attitudes of individuals in this area. The complex research designs necessary for the study of political violence must combine such data types and even additional information, e.g. process-produced data from police or court registers. The more longitudinal a study perspective becomes, the more difficult it will be to produce such complex data structures; usually the empirical researcher is more than happy if he has access at least to some reliable longitudinal data. For reasons of cost and accessibility, the researcher is more likely to obtain longitudinal-event data than survey data. Here the data put together by the Yale Political Data Project and its successors are particularly relevant (see Taylor and Jodice, 1983). The two following Tables contain information on events in the area of political turmoil (see note 1 to Table 1.3) and politically motivated deaths; both indicators are standardized according to population size.

Unfortunately these data do not cover the post-1978 period. If we look at the *development* of the two indicators over time (at five-year intervals), then three observations emerge. First, it is obvious that within a given type of event, countries can occupy different positions at different times. Thus, there seem to be country-specific events and processes that influence the level of turmoil or political deaths over and above general trends. Secondly, countries clearly do not switch ranks at random. Country specificities of a structural and more permanent nature can account for a consistently low, medium or high level of turmoil and/or violence. Thirdly, there is overwhelming evidence of a substantial increase in turmoil and violence since 1967. This trend emerges if we sum the standardized scores across countries within time periods (Greece, Portugal and Turkey which have had changes in their political order in the period under review have been excluded from these calculations).

These data support the popular notion that the politically quiet 1950s and 1960s were indeed followed by an acceleration of turmoil and political deaths in the 1970s. The lack of more recent figures makes it

Table 1.3 Turmoil in democracies 1948–1977: events per capita

| Countries | 1948–1952 per capita | rank[3] | 1953–1957 per capita | rank | 1958–1962 per capita | rank | 1963–1967 per capita | rank | 1968–1972 per capita | rank | 1973–1977 per capita | rank | Total number of events[4] |
|---|---|---|---|---|---|---|---|---|---|---|---|---|---|
| USA | 2.43 | (16) | 3.32 | (10) | 27.34 | ( 6) | 67.89 | ( 2) | 47.68 | ( 3) | 14.82 | ( 8) | 3199 |
| Canada | 4.37 | (14) | 1.91 | (12) | 7.26 | (12) | 17.81 | ( 5) | 22.89 | ( 9) | 4.83 | (17) | 117 |
| Ireland | 26.95 | ( 7) | — | (14) | 3.53 | (17) | 48.68 | ( 3) | 223.43 | ( 1) | 86.23 | ( 4) | 116 |
| United Kingdom | 7.11 | (13) | 0.79 | (13) | 23.59 | ( 7) | 10.82 | ( 8) | 81.48 | ( 2) | 93.93 | ( 3) | 1205 |
| France | 28.51 | ( 5) | 31.31 | ( 1) | 32.84 | ( 3) | 7.80 | (11) | 23.88 | ( 8) | 33.07 | ( 5) | 739 |
| Belgium | 89.14 | ( 2) | 15.78 | ( 5) | 73.19 | ( 1) | 16.90 | ( 6) | 7.27 | (16) | 6.09 | (16) | 187 |
| Netherlands | 3.96 | (15) | 2.79 | (11) | — | (18) | 4.88 | (14) | 1.53 | (20) | 10.30 | (11) | 29 |
| Luxembourg | — | (19) | — | (14) | — | (18) | — | (19) | 29.50 | ( 7) | — | (20) | 1 |
| West Germany | 26.40 | ( 8) | 10.69 | ( 6) | 4.33 | (15) | 16.43 | ( 7) | 18.45 | (11) | 7.13 | (15) | 465 |
| Switzerland | 2.13 | (17) | — | (14) | 5.59 | (13) | 1.71 | (18) | 17.56 | (12) | 15.30 | ( 7) | 26 |
| Austria | 64.89 | ( 3) | 5.76 | ( 8) | 28.38 | ( 5) | 2.76 | (16) | 4.03 | (17) | 10.61 | (10) | 82 |
| Italy | 62.65 | ( 4) | 18.06 | ( 4) | 19.70 | ( 8) | 10.01 | ( 9) | 32.48 | ( 6) | 25.81 | ( 6) | 847 |
| Portugal | 1.19 | (18) | — | (14) | 58.92 | ( 2) | 7.58 | (12) | 35.92 | ( 5) | 430.27 | ( 1) | 468 |
| Greece | 10.58 | (11) | 27.63 | ( 2) | 3.60 | (16) | 73.68 | ( 1) | 46.63 | ( 4) | 189.25 | ( 2) | 306 |
| Turkey | — | (19) | 7.97 | ( 7) | 18.54 | ( 9) | 7.06 | (13) | 10.23 | (13) | 9.03 | (12) | 164 |
| Denmark | 28.18 | ( 6) | 22.52 | ( 3) | 32.74 | ( 4) | 2.10 | (17) | 8.12 | (14) | 13.93 | ( 9) | 49 |
| Sweden | 7.13 | (12) | — | (14) | — | (18) | 9.04 | (10) | 18.64 | (10) | 7.24 | (14) | 33 |
| Norway | 18.38 | ( 9) | — | (14) | 5.59 | (13) | 32.23 | ( 4) | 2.58 | (18) | 7.49 | (13) | 24 |
| Finland | 129.71 | ( 1) | — | (14) | 11.29 | (11) | — | (19) | 2.17 | (19) | 4.30 | (18) | 60 |
| Japan | 14.94 | (10) | 5.57 | ( 9) | 16.26 | (10) | 2.93 | (15) | 7.86 | (15) | 1.62 | (19) | 457 |

1 According to a suggestion made by Charles L. Taylor, protest demonstrations, political strikes and riots were treated as constituting one single dimension of *turmoil*, i.e. of small threats to the system with (mostly) the intent to change some kind of government policy. Therefore, the event-counts for the three activities were summed up within countries to create that single indicator of turmoil.

2 The absolute number of events is misleading if not standardized according to the population size of the given country. While this standardization may well give rise to other objections, for the descriptive purposes of this chapter it seems perfectly adequate. Standardization was achieved by dividing the absolute number of events by population size and multiplying it by a factor of 10,000 to arrive at a number reasonable for comparisons between countries. The population size used for standardization was always taken from the middle year of the given time period, i.e. 1950, 1955, and so on. All data were taken from the file documented in Taylor/Jodice 1983: 22–36. The data were supplied by the Zentralarchiv für Empirische Sozialforschung der Universität zu Köln. My thanks go to Dieter Fuchs and his colleagues from the Central Archive who provided me with the computations.

3 If countries had identical values, identical ranks were assigned to them.

4 Some observers may wonder whether the number of events is not too low. Taylor/Jodice (1983: 10–15) explicitly state that they decided to use but two sources for the information retrieval about events. Then they state (15): 'The application of additional sources will add cases and will increase the attribute information that is available on both the existing and additional records.'

Table 1.4  Deaths from political violence in democracies 1948–77: events per capita

| Countries | 1948–1952 per capita | rank | 1953–1957 per capita | rank | 1958–1962 per capita | rank | 1963–1967 per capita | rank | 1968–1972 per capita | rank | 1973–1977 per capita | rank | Total number of events |
|---|---|---|---|---|---|---|---|---|---|---|---|---|---|
| Greece | 12295.80 | ( 1) | 0.0 | ( 8) | 0.0 | (11) | 5.85 | ( 3) | 3.41 | ( 8) | 33.59 | ( 4) | 9341 |
| United Kingdom | 1.19 | ( 9) | 0.0 | ( 8) | 0.57 | ( 9) | 0.0 | (10) | 99.86 | ( 1) | 159.50 | ( 1) | 1463 |
| USA | 1.44 | ( 7) | 0.54 | ( 7) | 2.38 | ( 7) | 12.66 | ( 2) | 4.69 | ( 7) | 0.84 | (15) | 434 |
| Turkey | 0.0 | (11) | 1.26 | ( 6) | 16.72 | ( 3) | 15.73 | ( 1) | 14.48 | ( 3) | 29.59 | ( 5) | 267 |
| Italy | 13.90 | ( 3) | 3.53 | ( 1) | 4.58 | ( 6) | 0.77 | ( 7) | 6.91 | ( 4) | 20.54 | ( 6) | 259 |
| France | 0.72 | (10) | 1.84 | ( 3) | 21.67 | ( 2) | 0.41 | ( 9) | 1.97 | (13) | 7.94 | ( 8) | 164 |
| Belgium | 4.63 | ( 5) | 0.0 | ( 8) | 6.56 | ( 5) | 0.0 | (10) | 71.59 | ( 2) | 2.03 | (13) | 81 |
| Portugal | 0.0 | (11) | 0.0 | ( 8) | 27.19 | ( 1) | 2.17 | ( 5) | 2.32 | (11) | 43.37 | ( 3) | 66 |
| West Germany | 1.20 | ( 8) | 0.0 | ( 8) | 0.0 | (11) | 0.68 | ( 8) | 5.44 | ( 6) | 2.92 | (10) | 61 |
| Japan | 1.20 | ( 8) | 1.78 | ( 4) | 0.21 | (10) | 0.0 | (10) | 2.01 | (12) | 0.99 | (14) | 60 |
| Ireland | 0.0 | (11) | 3.42 | ( 2) | 0.0 | (11) | 0.0 | (10) | 6.77 | ( 5) | 150.11 | ( 2) | 50 |
| Denmark | 32.78 | ( 2) | 0.0 | ( 8) | 0.0 | (11) | 0.0 | (10) | 0.0 | (15) | 0.0 | (17) | 14 |
| The Netherlands | 0.0 | (11) | 0.0 | ( 8) | 0.0 | (11) | 0.0 | (10) | 0.0 | (15) | 9.56 | ( 7) | 13 |
| Canada | 0.0 | (11) | 0.0 | ( 8) | 1.12 | ( 8) | 3.05 | ( 4) | 1.40 | (14) | 0.44 | (16) | 12 |
| Austria | 5.77 | ( 4) | 1.44 | ( 5) | 0.0 | (11) | 1.38 | ( 6) | 2.69 | ( 9) | 2.65 | (11) | 10 |
| Sweden | 0.0 | (11) | 0.0 | ( 8) | 0.0 | (11) | 0.0 | (10) | 2.49 | (10) | 4.82 | ( 9) | 6 |
| Finland | 2.49 | ( 6) | 0.0 | ( 8) | 6.77 | ( 4) | 0.0 | (10) | 0.0 | (15) | 0.0 | (17) | 4 |
| Norway | 0.0 | (11) | 0.0 | ( 8) | 0.0 | (11) | 0.0 | (10) | 0.0 | (15) | 2.50 | (12) | 1 |
| Luxemburg | 0.0 | (11) | 0.0 | ( 8) | 0.0 | (11) | 0.0 | (10) | 0.0 | (15) | 0.0 | (17) | 0 |
| Switzerland | 0.0 | (11) | 0.0 | ( 8) | 0.0 | (11) | 0.0 | (10) | 0.0 | (15) | 0.0 | (17) | 0 |

Source: Taylor and Jodice (1983) pp. 48–51.

Table 1.5   Sum of political violence scores across countries

|          | 1948–52 | 1953–7 | 1958–62 | 1963–7 | 1968–72 | 1973–7 |
|----------|---------|--------|---------|--------|---------|--------|
| Turmoil  | 516,88  | 118,50 | 291,63  | 251,99 | 549,55  | 342,70 |
| Deaths   | 65,32   | 12,55  | 43,86   | 18,95  | 205,82  | 364,84 |

difficult to assess developments in the 1980s. A limited empirical assessment can be made for at least the three countries in the *Political Action II* study (Germany, The Netherlands and the USA) up to 1979 for the turmoil dimension. These data confirm that individual countries perform rather idiosyncratically over time. They also show that the three countries, taken together, do not display a lower level of turmoil in 1978–82 than in the previous period, although we must bear in mind that this summary finding for the three countries is produced almost exclusively by the USA.

Table 1.6   Average number of incidents of turmoil (demonstrations, political strikes and riots) in The Netherlands, West Germany and the United States 1968–82[1]

|           | Time Intervals | | | | | | |
|-----------|---------|--------|---------|---------|---------|-------------------------------------|-------------------------------------|
| Countries | 1968–72 | 1973–7 | 1978–82 | 1965–74 | 1975–9[2] | Year of First Study 1974 | Year of Second Study 1979[3] |
| The Netherlands | 1.53 | 10.30 | 13.24 | 9.98 | 11.77 | 2.94 | 2.94 |
| West Germany | 18.45 | 7.13 | 10.68 | 37.07 | 13.62 | 1.95 | 0.49 |
| United States | 47.68 | 14.82 | 59.55 | 96.06 | 80.12 | 3.51 | 21.27 |

1 Data for 1968–72 and 1973–7 are taken from Barnes, Kaase et al. (1979). All other data were kindly supplied by Dieter Fuchs from the Zentralarchiv für Empirische Sozialforschung der Universität zu Köln. The data are standardized according to population size and multiplied by a factor of 10.000. Results were cut off after the second decimal.
2 Time intervals reflect the time frame set in the individual country studies. The five-year time frame applies only to The Netherlands. The data for West Germany represent the 1971–80 time period, for the United States the 1972–81 time period. These periods differ according to the year the second wave of interviews was conducted.
3 For West Germany the year is 1980; for the United States the year is 1981.

For the West German case we are in the lucky position of being able to build on a time series on the number of political demonstrations, including the percentage of violent political demonstrations. These data are collected annually by the state and federal ministries of the interior and are derived from police accounts (see Table 1.7)

The data again support the claim that there was more uninstitutionalized political activity in the 1980s in West Germany than in the second half of the 1970s. It is remarkable that in *relative* terms the number of demonstrations where violence occurred diminished and now appears to be wavering at around the 4 per cent mark. In *absolute* terms this is not true, so it is a matter of evaluation how these data are interpreted. If we accept the premise that demonstrations usually confront protesters and police and thereby create a distinctive chance of violent encounters then the shrinking percentage of violent demonstrations does *not* warrant a conclusion of growing violence in West Germany. In order to generalize this finding we would need data from many other countries. As long as such data are not available, the West German case is an interesting example, no more. It may be worthwhile to make a comparison between these data and the number of violent incidents documented by the authorities, and with the number of cases where people were found guilty of violent actions.

Table 1.7   Number of violent demonstrations in West Germany, 1975–86

| Year | Number | % violent | Year | Number | % violent |
|------|--------|-----------|------|--------|-----------|
| 1975 | 2,551 | 8.2 | 1981 | 5,772 | 6.2 |
| 1976 | 2,956 | 6.5 | 1982 | 5,313 | 4.3 |
| 1977 | 2,887 | 8.7 | 1983 | 9,237 | 3.0 |
| 1978 | 2,980 | 7.0 | 1984 | 7,453 | 3.1 |
| 1979 | 3,327 | 2.9 | 1985 | 5,691 | 3.6 |
| 1980 | 4,471 | 3.2 | 1986 | 7,143 | 3.7 |

Table 1.8   Number of violent incidents and court convictions for violent action, 1985–6

| Number | Left | | Right | |
|--------|------|------|-------|------|
| | 1985 | 1986 | 1985 | 1986 |
| Violent incidents | 1,604 | 1,904 | 77 | 71 |
| Court convictions | 597 | 410 | 140 | 135 |

*Source: Innenministerium,* 1987: pp. 140–2; 195–9.

Next to the clear preponderance of 'left' versus 'right' violence, which we will return to later in the chapter, there appears to be a rather high number of violent incidents, whereas successful repression by the state does not appear to be extraordinarily high. Comparative data would be necessary to evaluate the above accounts properly.

We have already pointed out and supported by empirical findings, that in 1974–6 attitudes towards political violence as well as reports of past violent behaviour are extremely scarce for the general public (operationalized as those aged sixteen years and over). For 1980 the respective figures for the three countries remaining in the second wave of the *Political Action* project have not changed (detailed figures are given later on in this section).

In evaluative terms, this is reassuring. For social science research, however, this encompassing rejection of participation in acts of political violence by the public at large, as represented in national sample surveys, creates a statistical problem because there are simply not enough cases for a thorough analysis. This is an important reason for the fact that in the following analyses other forms of uninstitutionalized political participation – legal or illegal – will be put to the fore. We shall begin by examining findings from a study on political participation and political violence conducted in West Germany in 1980 and 1985 (Uehlinger, 1988). In this study representative samples of the population aged sixteen to thirty-five (1980) and sixteen and over (1985) were asked their opinions on twenty-two activities, including violence against persons and property. The question was threefold: which activity would people choose in order to influence political outcomes? (normal); which activity would people choose if the authorities were slow to respond to requests? (escalation); and which activities had been used in the past? After a variety of dimensional and cluster analyses had been performed, Uehlinger came up with the following results:

Table 1.9   Distribution of various types of political participation in 1980 and 1985

| Types of Participation | Participation | | | | | | | | |
|---|---|---|---|---|---|---|---|---|---|
| | Normally | | | Normally plus Escalation | | | Already Done | | |
| | −35 years | 36 years+ | | −35 years | 36 years+ | | −35 years | 36 years+ | |
| | 1980 % | 1985 % | 1985 % | 1980 % | 1985 % | 1985 % | 1980 % | 1985 % | 1985 % |
| Citizen role | 95 | 95 | 97 | 95 | 95 | 97 | 75 | 84 | 82 |
| Issue–specific Participation | 80 | 78 | 59 | 88 | 88 | 72 | 48 | 43 | 34 |
| Party–oriented Participation | 50 | 37 | 27 | 63 | 54 | 38 | 12 | 10 | 13 |
| Civil disobedience | 17 | 21 | 8 | 35 | 34 | 16 | 5 | 6 | 2 |
| Political violence | 5 | 7 | 4 | 13 | 15 | 8 | 1 | 1 | 1 |

*Source:* Uehlinger (1988) p. 142.

As in the *Political Action* study, reports on *past violent participation* are extremely rare. It is a different story altogether, however, if we look at the *inclination* to pursue political goals violently or through acts of civil disobedience. Depending on the circumstances, between two million (normal) and six million (escalation) West German citizens can at least imagine the use of political violence to further their cause; for civil disobedience the respective figures vary between seven and fifteen million. These seem to be quite remarkable numbers that do not fit the notions of law-abiding Germans at all well. There are apparent boundaries that usually prevent our *thinking* about our own violent or disobedient actions turning into true actions. Nevertheless, these data signal a degree of acceptance of illegal forms of political participation that does not square with the logic of democracy as being the kind of political order where political controversy is enacted on the basis of the rule of law and constitutional rules of the game. For reasons of incompatibility, we are unable to make direct comparisons between the Uehlinger and *Political Action* data-bases. We can, however, show the 1974 and 1979–81 findings for the question whether we might participate in violent actions if the situation appeared to require it.

Table 1.10   Willingness to participate in violent actions, by country

| | GB % | D % | NL % | AU % | USA % | I % | CH % | FIN % |
|---|---|---|---|---|---|---|---|---|
| **Personal violence** | | | | | | | | |
| Would do if important | 1.0 | 0.7 (0.7)★ | 2.1 (0.8) | 0.9 | 0.7 (0.5) | 0.3 | 0.5 | 0.3 |
| Might do in a particular situation | 3.7 | 4.6 (3.4) | 3.7 (4.6) | 3.7 | 4.8 (5.4) | 2.8 | 4.7 | 2.5 |
| | 4.7 | 5.3 (4.1) | 5.8 (5.4) | 4.6 | 5.5 (5.9) | 3.1 | 5.2 | 2.8 |
| **Violence against things** | | | | | | | | |
| Would do if important | 0.5 | 0.7 (0.5) | 1.3 (0.3) | 1.1 | 0.2 (0.4) | 0.4 | 0.5 | 0.2 |
| Might do in a particular situation | 1.9 | 2.6 (2.6) | 2.6 (1.5) | 2.0 | 2.7 (3.3) | 2.9 | 2.9 | 3.4 |
| | 2.4 | 3.3 (3.1) | 3.9 (1.8) | 3.1 | 2.9 (3.7) | 3.3 | 3.4 | 3.6 |

★Figures in parentheses refer to 1979 (NL), 1980 (D) and 1981 (USA).

The *Political Action* data are more difficult to interpret than the Uehlinger data because the wording of the question invites affirmative responses from quite different justification backgrounds. But these results certainly indicate that the Uehlinger findings for West Germany in the 1980s are not completely out of line with those for the 1970s and that West Germany is in no way atypical in comparison to other Western democracies. Thus violence, at least in the minds of a small but significant section of the population, is regarded as a viable political choice if the circumstances are right; this is even more the case for the activity dimension of civil disobedience (where the figure for West Germany in 1980 is 30 per cent). It remains to be seen whether this potential for violence is a resource that can be systematically exploited as a recruiting ground for political terrorism. We shall turn to this question in the concluding section.

Uninstitutionalized political participation has long been regarded as a way for underprivileged people to make elites take notice of their grievances. The following section of this chapter will therefore briefly discuss the socio-structural bases of political participation before turning to the relationship between political values and political participation.

## 1.4 The socio-structural correlates of political participation

When it comes to the analysis of those socio-structural factors most strongly associated with political participation, the socio-economic standard model comes immediately to the fore (Verba and Nie, 1972; Verba, Nie and Kim, 1978). This model claims universal currency and indicates that it is the socio-economic resource level of the individual that has the most impact on the individual level of political involvement. Barnes, Kaase et al., (1979) could demonstrate that the general model is also valid for unconventional, uninstitutionalized modes of political participation. Table 1.11 gives a quick assessment of the 1974 and 1979-81 socio-structural correlates of political participation and changes in them for The Netherlands, West Germany and the United States. The data for other countries would not systematically differ from those displayed here.

These analyses produce two major results. First, in a static perspective both types of political participation remain positively and almost equally related to education as an important indicator of the individual socio-economic resource level, reinforcing the validity of the 'standard model'. Furthermore, unconventional involvement is clearly related to age. Sex differences in political participation are much more pronounced in the conventional than in the unconventional realm where women in all educational groups have considerably lessened the gap between themselves and men. The minor impact of age on conventional participation partly reflects the curvilinear nature of that relationship and partly the important compositional effect of age cohorts with respect to education in so far as there is a positive correlation between young age and higher levels of educational achievement in all three countries. Obviously, this correlation reflects the enormous extension of the system of higher education.

Secondly, with regard to changes in the structure of relationships over time, we are impressed by the high degree of stability reflected in these data. This stability goes beyond that observed in the marginal distribution of the respective variables. It gives an idea of the extent that conventional as well as unconventional forms of political participation are embedded in a framework of institutions, organizations and networks that elicit the behaviour in question in a collectively predictable fashion.

Let us pursue this a little further. On the one hand, the analyses in *Political Action* and elsewhere (e.g. Uehlinger, 1988) have shown that young age is an integral part of orientations towards unconventional political participation. On the other hand, precisely its uninstitutionalized character indicates that favourable attitudes have to be transformed into action through a process of mobilization; a process that should to some extent function independent of age in that it pulls into action people who are accessible to a mobilizing corporate or individual actor at a given point in time. Mobilization into action should therefore be less dependent on individual resources, best measured as education in the sense of a generalizable resource. We are

Table 1.11   Socio-demographic correlates of conventional political participation scale and protest potential scale 1974 and 1979–81: multiple regressions[1]

| Participation Scale Year and Type of Study | Sociodemographic Correlates | | | | | | R[3] | R[2,4] |
|---|---|---|---|---|---|---|---|---|
| | Age | | Sex | | Education[2] | | | |
| | beta | b | beta | b | beta | b | | |
| 1. THE NETHERLANDS | | | | | | | | |
| **1.1 Conventional Political Participation Scale** | | | | | | | | |
| 1974 Cross Section | .11 | .01 | −.17 | −.55 | .32 | .46 | .36 | .13 |
| 1979 Cross Section | .07★ | .006★ | −.14 | −.41 | .29 | .36 | .32 | .11 |
| **1.2 Protest Potential Scale** | | | | | | | | |
| 1974 Cross Section | −.24 | −.03 | −.11 | −.42 | .14 | .23 | .34 | .12 |
| 1979 Cross Section | −.30 | −.03 | −.08 | −.28 | .08 | .12 | .34 | .12 |
| 2. WEST GERMANY | | | | | | | | |
| **2.1 Conventional Political Participation Scale** | | | | | | | | |
| 1974 Cross Section | −.06 | −.007 | −.29 | −1.19 | .23 | .39 | .41 | .17 |
| 1980 Cross Section | −.01★★ | −.001★★ | −.30 | −1.09 | .23 | .33 | .41 | .17 |
| **2.2 Protest Potential Scale** | | | | | | | | |
| 1974 Cross Section | −.28 | −.03 | −.13 | −.42 | .19 | .25 | .41 | .17 |
| 1980 Cross Section | −.28 | −.03 | −.06 | −.19 | .15 | .20 | .36 | .13 |
| 3. UNITED STATES | | | | | | | | |
| **3.1 Conventional Political Participation Scale** | | | | | | | | |
| 1974 Cross Section | .14 | .02 | −.15 | −.62 | .32 | .56 | .34 | .11 |
| 1981 Cross Section | .13 | .01 | −.09 | −.38 | .31 | .58 | .32 | .10 |
| **3.2 Protest Potential Scale** | | | | | | | | |
| 1974 Cross Section | −.35 | −.03 | −.07 | −.24 | .21 | .30 | .47 | .22 |
| 1981 Cross Section | −.41 | −.04 | −.03★★ | −.10★★ | .22 | .31 | .52 | .27 |

1 Entries are standardized (first column) and unstandardized (second column) regression coefficients. Regression coefficients displaying a ★★ are not statistically significant at least at the .90 level of confidence, those with a ★ are significant between the .90 and the .95 level. All unmarked coefficients are statistically significant above the .95 level of confidence.
2 Education is coded in five-category ranking from 1 (elementary school) to 5 (university).
3 Multiple Correlation Coefficient.
4 Multiple Regression Coefficient.

aware of the fact that the data available – representative cross-sections of the population aged sixteen and over – are not well-suited to analyses dealing with mobilization processes. Nevertheless, we shall try to approach the mobilization phenomenon by speculating that mobilization should show up: generally in a lesser predictive power of those socio-demographic indicators already found to be associated with positive direct-action orientations; and specifically in a lessened impact of the age variable the closer we draw to action. Let us recall once again that there is evidence to support such speculations in *Political Action* although at that time we were not interested in pursuing the matter any further.

Table 1.12 gives the results of a multiple regression analysis with age, sex and education as independent variables and three types of scales of unconventional political participation, each varying in its degree of closeness to direct action, as dependent variables.

The first question to be answered by this analysis is to what extent the variance explained jointly by the three structural independent variables decreases the closer we come to actual unconventional participation. In all three countries the findings are clear to slightly varying degrees: the amount of explained variance in actual participation is about half compared to the direct action orientation farthest away from participation. This reinforces the notion that actual participation in unconventional politics greatly depends on situational factors and is less dependent on individual characteristics.

The second question refers to the extent to which the explanatory power of each of the independent variables is influenced in the multiple regression depending on which scale is treated as the dependent variable. The most noticeable thing here is that in all countries and at all points in time the impact of age is reduced by far the most the closer we draw to action.

The findings for the gender variable are more ambiguous. While its explanatory impact in general is relatively low, which is unconventional compared to conventional political participation, there is only a slight tendency for this gap to be reduced the closer we come to true unconventional action. This is, however, the tendency we would have expected from the theoretical reasoning underlying this analysis.

Finally, with respect to education as a resource, it does not come as a surprise that this resource becomes more important the more action is called for. Nevertheless, education is an important antecedent for unconventional political participation as well as for positive attitudes towards unconventional political participation.

We must bear in mind that these analyses did *not* include the dimension of political violence because of the small size of the sample. Uehlinger's (1988) data for West Germany corroborate the above findings from *Political Action* in all major aspects. In particular, the inclination of the young and highly educated to take part in acts of civil disobedience reinforces the notion that uninstitutionalized forms of political participation as a *contemporary phenomenon* is systematically related to causes other than economic deprivation. We should also mention that the Uehlinger data on political violence do *not* show a

Table 1.12   Socio-demographic correlates of unconventional political participation scales I, II and III 1974, 1979–81 and 1985–6[1]: multiple regressions[2]

| Unconventional Political Participation Scales | Socio-demographic Correlates | | | $R^4$ | $R^{2,5}$ |
|---|---|---|---|---|---|
| | Age | Sex | Education | | |
| 1. THE NETHERLANDS | | | | | |
| **1.1 Unconventional Political Participation Scale I** | | | | | |
| 1974 | −.04 (−.00)★★ | −.09 (−.14) | .19 (.13) | .24 | .06 |
| 1979 | −.14 (−.01) | .01 ( .02)★★ | .14 (.08) | .22 | .05 |
| **1.2 Unconventional Political Participation Scale II** | | | | | |
| 1974 | −.21 (−.03) | −.12 (−.49) | .12 (.22) | .31 | .09 |
| 1979 | −.27 (−.03) | −.08 (−.25) | .02 (.03)★★ | .28 | .08 |
| **1.3 Unconventional Political Participation Scale III[6]** | | | | | |
| 1974 | −.34 (−.05) | −.13 (−.58) | .11 (.23) | .41 | .17 |
| 1979 | −.32 (−.04) | −.11 (−.46) | .08 (.15) | .37 | .14 |
| 2. WEST GERMANY | | | | | |
| **2.1 Unconventional Political Participation Scale I** | | | | | |
| 1974 | −.12 (−.01) | −.09 (−.14) | .28 (.19) | .36 | .13 |
| 1980 | −.13 (−.00) | −.06 (−.07) | .27 (.13) | .34 | .12 |
| 1985/86 | −.17 (−.01) | −.05 (−.10) | .29 (.40) | .39 | .15 |
| **2.2 Unconventional Political Participation Scale II** | | | | | |
| 1974 | −.25 (−.02) | −.13 (−.43) | .22 (.29) | .41 | .17 |
| 1980 | −.27 (−.02) | −.08 (−.22) | .21 (.24) | .39 | .15 |
| 1985/86 | −.34 (−.03) | −.11 (−.31) | .23 (.46) | .48 | .23 |
| **2.3 Unconventional Political Participation Scale III** | | | | | |
| 1974 | −.32 (−.04) | −.13 (−.57) | .17 (.32) | .43 | .19 |
| 1979 | −.32 (−.04) | −.08 (−.36) | .17 (.30) | .42 | .17 |
| 1985/86 | −.36 (−.03) | −.16 (−.50) | .21 (.44) | .51 | .26 |

*continued*

3. UNITED STATES

**3.1 Unconventional**
  **Political**
  **Participation**
  **Scale I**

| | | | | | |
|---|---|---|---|---|---|
| 1974 | −.12 (−.01) | −.13 (−.26) | .27 (.24) | .35 | .12 |
| 1981 | −.16 (−.01) | −.05 (−.10)★ | .29 (.26) | .38 | .15 |

**3.2 Unconventional**
  **Political**
  **Participation**
  **Scale II**

| | | | | | |
|---|---|---|---|---|---|
| 1974 | −.24 (−.02) | −.13 (−.41) | .24 (.32) | .41 | .17 |
| 1981 | −.29 (−.02) | −.11 (−.35) | .23 (.31) | .45 | .20 |

**3.3 Unconventional**
  **Political**
  **Participation**
  **Scale III**

| | | | | | |
|---|---|---|---|---|---|
| 1974 | −.37 (−.04) | −.11 (−.48) | .20 (.34) | .48 | .23 |
| 1981 | −.38 (−.04) | −.11 (−.45) | .21 (.39) | .51 | .26 |

1  1985/86: West Germany only.
2  Entries are standardized (first column) and unstandardized (second column) regression coefficients. Regression coefficients displaying a ★★ are not statistically significant at least at the .90 level of confidence, those with a ★ are significant between the .90 and the .95 level. All unmarked coefficients are statistically significant above the .95 level of confidence.
3  Education as type of school; see Barnes, Kaase et al. (1979) p. 585 for details; for West Germany in 1985–6 a three-category variable – low, medium, high – was used.
4  Multiple Correlation Coefficient.
5  Explained Variance.
6  The categories of 'have done', 'would do' and 'might do' were combined to construct the 3rd scale.

clear preponderance of highly educated individuals. It must remain an open question as to whether this means that political violence is clearly separated from *all* other forms of uninstitutionalized participation, including the non-violent illegal ones, where Uehlinger had observed heavy emphasis of better-educated individuals, or that it is the particular quality of the mobilization into action together with the characteristics of the given situation that are the decisive intervening variables to determine who participates violently and who does not.

In summary, the findings reinforce the point that actual participation in direct-action politics must be explained by studying the concrete process of mobilization and the interaction between individual properties and predispositions on the one hand and between situational factors and intermediary organizations on the other.

## 1.5 The ideological and value bases of political participation and political violence

Values are collective conceptions of what is regarded desirable in a given society at a given time. In this sense, values possess an integrative function on the macro-level for the society at large and on the micro-level for individual attitudes and for the construction of coherent belief systems; thereby they may also have a steering potential for individual behaviour. This is, abstractly speaking, why values may become important antecedents of political participation.

Surprisingly enough, values as a central category of functionalist sociology hardly played any role in empirical research in the 1950s and 1960s. Only an article by Ingelhart (1971) started the stampede of value studies of which there are now so many. The course taken by the discussions on the role of ideology in politics was quite similar although here the decisive stimulus came almost ten years earlier in a study by Converse (1964). The scholarly debate on the Converse study places much emphasis on the *formal* structure of ideologies as encompassing belief systems. In the context of the *Political Action* study, Klingemann (1979) extended the approach and findings beyond the American case initially analysed by Converse. In terms of *content*, for Converse the only logical choice available for the study of ideological belief systems *in mass publics* was the liberal-conservative dimension. Inglehart and Klingemann (1976) could show that – based on the analyses of the Eurobarometer data – in Europe the only ideological yardstick of general currency is the left–right schema. Here left means opposition to hierarchical socio-political organization and favourable orientations towards changes to achieve greater social and political equality; right refers to the opposing principles.

For the purposes of this study, there is no point in dwelling on the details of the debate that has accompanied the empirical study of both ideology and values since their heyday. Suffice to say that despite all the criticism levelled at the two concepts and their empirical use, both have sustained a surprisingly high amount of explanatory power. One of the positive side-effects of these raging controversies has been that hardly any survey study in empirical political sociology has been able to omit these concepts from its questionnaire. Hence, quite a lot of evidence on these concepts and their relationship to other variables has been accumulated over the years. We shall build on this evidence in the following discussion. This evidence also permits us, with one *pars pro toto* exception, to forgo the presentation of detailed empirical analyses.

Ideology and values as operationalized through Inglehart's materialism–post-materialism index and through the left–right self-anchoring scale have been, at least over the last twenty years or so, systematically interrelated in the sense that leftism and post-materialism are positively correlated. The most important qualification of this relationship that has emerged from recent research (Inglehart, 1988; Fuchs, 1989) is that a distinction between the old and new left needs to be made in the sense that the 'old' left (the working class) is predominantly materialist and the 'new' left (young postbourgeois *Bildungsbürgertum*) is predominantly post-materialist. In terms of Western party systems, this situation has created a tremendous strain on the integrative capabilities of the traditional social-democratic parties such as the Labour Party in Britain and the SPD in Germany. In terms of political participation *in general*, this distinction between the old and the new left has become relevant because, starting with *Political Action*, analyses have continuously and consistently shown that it is particularly the left post-materialists who are inclined to turn to uninstitutionalized modes of political participation.

When dealing with the moral justification of political violence in section 1.2 we referred to the fact that these justifications often build on issues that are regarded as highly important and in need of immediate repair, such as the environment, so much so that violent actions are deemed necessary to get fast results. It is not surprising that it is precisely the left post-materialists who stand for these issues.

Table 1.13 presents the corresponding findings for the West German part of the 1980 *Political Action II* study together with not-directly comparable results of a 1985–6 study of a cross-section of 1943 voters in West Germany. The part of the table that refers to 1980 contains the *mean* values of three measures of affinity to civil disobedience (scale I pertains to those who have done or would do the activity; scale II pertains to those who have carried out or would carry out the activity; and scale III to those who have done, would or might do the activity – see also Table 1.12). If a respondent answered affirmatively *to any one of the four possible items* of civil disobedience (participate in rent strike/ participate in wild-cat strike/occupy a building/participate in violent street demonstration), he or she was coded '1', so that the scale value for a respondent can only be either '1' or '0' and for groups of respondents varied between '0' and '1'. The 1985–6 part of the table was constructed following the same basic logic with two differences: the data refer to *legal* uninstitutionalized activities (signing petitions, participation in peaceful demonstrations, boycotts, citizens's initiatives); and the scores are summed *across the four items* giving us an index with values between '0' (no activity chosen) and '4' (all activities chosen). As a consequence, *group means* can also vary between '0' and '4'.

The same pattern emerges for all three types of scales (I, II and III) and for both points in time. Post-materialists are, in every position on the ideological spectrum, by far the most direct action-prone group, both as regards civil disobedience and legal uninstitutionalized participation. Respondents to the left are also much more likely to be active than those to the right; this finding shows up most sharply when comparing the left post-materialists with the right materialists. These data also indicate that, at least in Germany, values are more influential on affinities towards direct political action than on ideology.

In summary then, when considering the above data and the discussions in the literature, we can speak of a special and clearly contoured

Table 1.13   Civil disobedience (1980), unconventional political
participation (1985–6), values and ideology in West Germany: mean
values

| Values | 1980 Ideology | | | |
|---|---|---|---|---|
| | Left (1–4] | Middle (5–6) | Right (7–10) | All Respondents |
| *Particip. Scale I* | | | | .00 |
| PP | .03 | .00 | .00 | |
| PM | .00 | .01 | .00 | |
| MP | .00 | .00 | .00 | |
| MM | .00 | .00 | .01 | |
| *Particip. Scale II* | | | | .08 |
| PP | .36 | .16 | .09 | |
| PM | .19 | .03 | .02 | |
| MP | .14 | .04 | .03 | |
| MM | .05 | .02 | .02 | |
| *Particip. Scale III* | | | | .31 |
| PP | .80 | .52 | .54 | |
| PM | .49 | .32 | .26 | |
| MP | .41 | .23 | .21 | |
| MM | .28 | .16 | .15 | |
| **1985–6** | | | | |
| *Particip. Scale I* | | | | .62 |
| PP | 1.81 | .96 | .76 | |
| PM | .63 | .65 | .46 | |
| MP | .70 | .31 | .35 | |
| MM | .37 | .19 | .21 | |
| *Particip. Scale II* | | | | 1.58 |
| PP | 3.07 | 2.28 | 1.94 | |
| PM | 2.06 | 1.94 | 1.47 | |
| MP | 1.71 | 1.14 | 1.19 | |
| MM | 1.35 | .68 | .75 | |
| *Particip. Scale III* | | | | 2.65 |
| PP | 3.82 | 3.51 | 3.15 | |
| PM | 3.43 | 3.06 | 2.64 | |
| MP | 2.60 | 2.22 | 2.27 | |
| MM | 2.56 | 1.82 | 1.68 | |

syndrome of political orientations that combines young age, economic
and cognitive resources, left ideology, post-materialism, specific political
issues and an affinity to uninstitutionalized modes of political participation. Whereas these orientations are held by individuals and groups of
individuals, the mobilization for action can build on new social networks
found in large metropolitan areas and increasingly identified as the

carriers of the new social movements (see for instance Melucci, 1980 and 1984; Donati, 1984; Kaase, 1990). This additional element of networks can, almost *ad libidum*, create the situational constellation where activists and police are confronted and political violence so frequently occurs. Here we find one of the bridges between political protest and political terrorism: many personal accounts by terrorists testify that it was the experience of such violent confrontations with the police that finally paved the way for the decision to join or to create a terrorist group.

At the end of this section a qualifying remark needs to be made. Detailed accounts of terrorism, as the five volumes on terrorism produced by a group of West German researchers in the early 1980s testify, and of violent political confrontation at demonstrations, sharpen the sense for the *specifics* of a given situation in explaining political violence and political terrorism. Hence the analytical perspective of the *survey researcher* that we have adopted in this study may systematically – because of the internal logic of survey research with national samples – blend out relevant information on the varieties of political violence, terrorism and their social and political antecedents. The picture drawn here, therefore, is a summary that of necessity lacks detail and differentiation.


## Conclusions

The empirical-longitudinal study of uninstitutionalized political partici-pation in general and of political violence in particular suffers a great deal from the lack of appropriate data. Nevertheless, the descriptive information presented in section 1.3 documents with sufficient reliability that illegal political participation and political violence are scarce but fairly regular elements of political life in Western democracies. We have seen that on the one hand political violence is almost uniformly rejected as an acceptable means of participation. On the other hand, we have discovered mechanisms that relieve some of the taboo pressure originating from the concept of violence. Furthermore, it could be shown that there is no firm mental block that would definitely exclude the use of violence from citizens' action repertoire. This phenomenon is most evident in the relative ease with which, under certain circum-stances, people consider the use of illegal non-violent actions.

This information is highly pertinent because path analyses between various modes of participation detected by Uehlinger (1988, pp. 204–17) clearly indicate that there is a strong, positive path between civil dis-obedience and political violence. Since these analyses are cross-sectional, nothing can be said about the causal relationship between the two modes.

It is plausible, though, to assume that once a citizen has crossed the border from legal to illegal uninstitutionalized participation, the threshold of political violence has been lowered to such an extent that it is only a question of situational factors as to whether or not violent actions are performed. From here, it is only a small step to terrorism, to the individual inclination to systematically plan violent actions from the underground.

These considerations point to the need to deal more effectively with non-violent illegal political participation. This is easier said than done, given that in democratic polities repressive measures impinge on the basic rights of citizens too quickly to be generally available as a cure. Research has shown that repression in totalitarian systems is extremely efficient in containing political violence. In democratic systems, however, repression is likely to be counterproductive. This, incidentally, is part of the rationale for terrorist attacks because terrorist groups, such as the German *Rote Armee Fraktion* (RAF), have always argued that terrorism forces the state to become more repressive and thereby undermines its own legitimacy.

It appears that in the age of the omnipresent and ever-responsible welfare-state political violence among social groups has receded or disappeared altogether, whereas violent confrontation between social groups and the state seems to be a fairly common feature. This situation is particularly critical for a democratic system because, as has been pointed out, the state here is caught in the unfortunate role of being either too repressive or not repressive enough to guarantee the orderly conduct of social and political life. Therefore it is absolutely mandatory for the state to train police forces such that the probability of violent encounters between demonstrators and police forces is substantially reduced. In the West German case, this has led to the development of complex training programmes for the police and has been relatively successful in reducing violence at demonstrations. The coexistence of instrumental, goal-oriented and hedonistic political action and violence (see Barnes, Kaase et al., 1979, pp. 523–34) makes this situation even more complex and difficult to handle.

Finally, it would be naïve to think of the political authorities, political parties and politicians only as responsive and responsible actors, qualities that are absolutely instrumental in gaining political acceptance and legitimacy by the citizenry. Not only from a functionalist sociological perspective, but also from instrumental means-ends calculations of involved citizens, in many instances political violence may be a logical (de Nardo, 1985) and sometimes even a morally understandable choice. This, as a concluding thought, then points again at the *processual property* of political participation and violence. Turned around, this means that there are no easy answers and cures for such a complex phenomenon as political violence.

## Notes

1 Galtung (1969) p. 168.
2 For a detailed discussion of the rationale behind this conceptualization of violence, see Neiderhardt (1986).
3 For a more detailed presentation of these considerations, see Barnes, Kaase et al. (1979), pp. 27–56; see also Dalton, Beck and Flanagan (1984) and the two introductory chapters to Jennings and van Deth (1989).
4 Barnes, Kaase, et al. (1979), p. 148.
5 See also Allerbeck (1976).
6 Bürklin (1980); Preisert et al. (1987), p. 306; Noelle-Neumann and Ring (1985) p. 92.

## References

K.R. Allerbeck (1976) *Demokratisierung und sozialer Wandel in der Bundesrepublik Deutschland. Sekundäranalyse von Umfragedaten 1953-1974*, Opladen, Westdeutscher Verlag.

S.H. Barnes, M. Kaase et al. (1979) *Political Action. Mass Participation in Five Western Democracies*, Beverly Hills, Sage.

M.D. Blumenthal et al. (1972) *Justifying Violence: Attitudes of American Men*, Ann Arbor, University of Michigan Press.

W.P. Bürklin (1980) 'Links undoder demokratisch? Dimensionen studentischen Demokratieverständnisses', *Politische Vierteljarhesschrift*, 21, pp. 220–47.

P.E. Converse (1964) 'The Nature of Belief Systems in Mass Publics', in D.E. Apter (ed.), *Ideology and Discontent*, Glencoe, The Free Press.

R.J. Dalton (1988) *Citizen Politics in Western Democracies. Public Opinion and Political Parties in the United States, Great Britain, West Germany and France*, Chatham, Chatham House Publishers Inc.

R.J. Dalton, S.C. Flanagan and P.A. Beck (eds) (1984) *Electoral Change in Advanced Industrial Democracies. Realignment or Dealingment?*, Princeton, Princeton University Press.

P.R. Donati (1984) 'Organization between movement and institution', *Social Science Information*, 23, pp. 837–59.

D. Fuchs (1989) *Die Unterstützung des politischen Systems der Bundesrepublik Deutschland*, Opladen, Westdeutscher Verlag.

J. Galtung (1969) 'Violence, Peace and Peace Research', *Journal of Peace Research*, 6, pp. 167–92.

B. Guggenberger and C. Offe (eds) (1984) *An den Grenzen der Mehrheitsdemokratie. Politik und Soziologie der Mehrheitsregel*, Opladen, Westdeutscher Verlag.

K. Hildenbrandt and R.J. Dalton (1978) 'The New Politics: Political Change or Sunshine Politics', in M. Kaase and K. von Beyme (eds), *Elections and Parties. Socio-political Change and Participation in the West German Federal Election of 1976*, German Political Studies, London and Beverly Hills, Sage, 3, pp. 69–96.

S.P. Huntington (1974) 'Postindustrial Politics: how benign will it be?', *Comparative Politics*, 6, pp. 163–91.

Innenministerium (ed.) (1987) *Verfassungsbericht 1986*, Bonn.

R. Inglehart (1971) 'The Silent Revolution in Europe: Intergenerational Change in Post-Industrial Societies', *American Political Science Review*, 65, pp. 991–1017.

R. Inglehart (1988) 'The Rennaisance of Political Culture', *American Political Science Review*, pp. 1203–30.

R. Inglehart and H.-D. Klingemann (1976) 'Party Identification, Ideological Preference and the Left-Right Dimension among Western Mass Publics', in I. Budge, I. Crewe and D. Farlie (eds) *Party Identification and Beyond*, London, John Wiley, pp. 243–73.

M.K. Jennings, J. van Deth and S.H. Barnes (eds) (1989) *Continuities in Political Action: a Longitudinal Study of Political Orientations in Three Western Democracies*, New York, de Gruyter.

M. Kaase (1986) 'Massenkommunikation und politischer Prozeß', in Kaase (ed.) *Politischer Wissenschaft und politischer Ordnung – Analysen zu Theorie und Empirie demokratischer Regierungsweise*, Opladen, Westdeutscher Verlag, pp. 357–74.

M. Kaase (1990) 'Social Movements and Political Innovation', in R.J. Dalton and M. Kuechler (eds) *Challenging the Political Order: New Social and Political Movements in Western Democracies*, Cambridge, Polity Press.

H.-D. Klingemann (1979) 'Measuring Ideological Conceptualizations. The Background of Ideological Conceptualization', in S.H. Barnes and M. Kaase et al. *Political Action. Mass Participation in Five Western Democracies*, Beverly Hills, Sage, pp. 215–77.

A. Melucci (1980) 'The new social movements. A theoretical approach', *Social Science Information*, 19, pp. 199–226.

A. Melucci (1984) 'An end to social movements? Introductory paper to the sessions on "new social movements and change in organizational forms"', *Social Science Information*, 23, pp. 819–35.

J. de Nardo (1985) *Power in Numbers. The Political Strategy of Protest and Rebellion*, Princeton, Princeton University Press.

F. Neidhardt (1986) 'Gewalt – Soziale Bedeutungen und sozialwissenschaftliche Bestimmung des Begriffs', in Bundeskriminalamt (ed.) *Was ist Gewalt? Auseinandersetzungen mit einem Begriff*, Vol. 1, Wiesbaden, pp. 109–47.

E. Noelle-Neumann and E. Ring (1985) *Das Extremismus-Potential unter jungen Leuten in der Bundesrepublik Deutschland 1984*, Bundesminister des Inneren (ed.), Allensbach, Institut für Demoskopie.

H. Preisert et al. (1987) *Studiensituation und studentische Orientierungen an Universitaten und Fachhochschulen. 2. Erhebung zur Studiensituation im WS 1984/85*, unpublished manuscript from the Arbeitsgruppe Hochschulforschung at the University of Konstanz, Konstanz.

C.L. Taylor and A. Jodice (1983) *World Handbook of Political and Social Indicators*, (3rd edn.), Vols. 1–2, New Haven, Yale University Press.

H.-M. Uehlinger (1988) *Strukturen und Erklärungsmodelle politischer Partizipation in der Bundesrepublik Deutschland*, Opladen, Westdeutscher Verlag.

S. Verba, H. Nie and J. Kim (1978) *Participation and Political Equality*, Cambridge, Cambridge University Press.

# 2
# Violence and institutionalization after the Italian protest cycle

## Sidney Tarrow

Cycles of protest and violence produce divergent and highly selective visions of the recent past. We have seen such a phenomenon in the United States, where, for some, the image of the '1960s' represents a strange vision of utopia mixed with violence and drugs; for others, the decade is remembered as a time of creativity, joy and solidarity. These opposing visions, while they roughly coincide with preferences for 'order' and 'movement', do not always separate former participants from opponents of previous protest cycles: the bitterest memories are often found among disillusioned activists. In Italy, we also find a dual vision of the country's recent past. The memory of the creative explosion of *il sessantotto* is clouded by nightmares of the *anni di piombo* that followed. In their preoccupation with this later period of organized violence, many Italians have ignored the positive impact of the mass politics of the late 1960s, while many who participated in the movements of the earlier period bitterly remember that it lead to institutionalization, cooption and the restoration of the *status quo ante*.

Those Italians who remember violence as the main heritage of the Italian cycle do their country an injustice. In doing so they ignore the fact that many groups who had in the past been excluded gained increased access to politics in this period and that others who – while they were previously included in the political system – achieved inclusion only by according a heavy-handed delegation of powers to a political class that had not been renewed since the Liberation. Some go so far as to regard the broadening of the repertoire of participation that occurred in those years as unhealthy in itself; it is never comfortable having those who are born to subaltern positions demanding justice by uncivil means.

On the other hand, those who remember the period of mass protest as ending in cooption, institutionalization and the collapse of the dreams of *sessantotto*, do their country no less an injustice. An institutionalization of the movements of *sessantotto* certainly occurred, especially in the trade-union sector but also in the cities and in the professions. Institutionalization, however, means not only that a dream of liberation has been stifled; it also means that the changes made during a previous phase of politics gain a solid foundation. In the Italian case, it also meant that a movement to defend democracy against subversion from the extreme left and right could find popular roots. Those who see the 1970s exclusively in terms of the destruction of popular politics must explain why thousands of people were willing to leave their homes to demonstrate against violence, risking police truncheons and terrorist bombs.

Yet these two opposing visions of the end of mobilization are similar in one key way: they both characterize the years after 1969 in terms of a continuous and linear evolution. For proponents of the first school of thought (the heritage of violence), there was a single thread connecting the mass mobilization of 1967-8 to the organized terrorism of the late 1970s. For proponents of the second (the collapse of *il sessantotto*), the spirit of 1968 was subverted by groups who were essentially Leninist and who sought to smother its creativity and spontaneity with organization and ideology. Joseph LaPalombara gives a particularly compressed image of continuism in his book *Democracy Italian Style*:

> In its earliest phases, terrorism appeared as little more than an extension of the protest movements and the hundreds of more or less revolutionary groups that mushroomed in the universities in the late 1960s. Initially these groups talked and talked. Some then turned to kidnapping and kneecapping. Murder came later.[1]

LaPalombara does not claim to be an expert on terrorism but, together with many other observers of Republican Italy, the images he uses give the impression of a continuous and linear evolution from the mass movements of 1967-9 to the organized terrorism a decade later. For example, he is particularly harsh towards the radical professorate, whom he assumes grew out of the earlier movements. He blames the parties of the institutional left, a 'fair chunk of the Italian intellectual establishment', and the press for encouraging violence. Of university professors he writes:

> it is arguable that university students would scarcely have turned violent were it not for professors and writers who egged them on.[2]

A less-compressed and more-historical analysis of the years between 1967 and the years of organized terrorism suggests a more-differentiated and less-linear view. It suggests that violence developed not in a linear fashion out of the movements in the universities in 1967-8 but as part of a *competitive process of tactical innovation within the social-movement sector* that led some groups into the party of armed struggle but forced others to reject it and to join the institutional system. During this period, when many Italians were withdrawing from political activity into private life and a much larger group were moving into the political institutions in one form or another, the public for social-movement activity declined. This decline coincided with an increase in the number of groups seeking their support. This contradictory phenomenon increased the competition between the groups – who had emerged from 1967-9 – for support and created incentives for some of them to outbid one another through the use of ever more radical tactics. The extreme outcome of this spiral of competitive tactical innovation was terrorism, whose adoption was reinforced by the presence of a militant antiparliamentary extreme right on the streets. The shift of a fraction of the social-movement sector into clandestine organizations – although it is the opposite of the institutiona-lization of a cycle of protest – cannot be separated from it. For just as the formation of a mass movement of the extraparliamentary left was directed as much against the hegemony of the institutional left as against the system as a whole, the choice of armed struggle was directed as much at outdoing the extraparliamentary left as it was against the *PCI* (Italian Communist Party) and the trade unions. This provoked an inevitable reaction in both sectors; terrorism not only forced the parliamentary left to condemn violence and to join the efforts of the political class against it, but it forced the extraparliamentary left to choose between the extremes of an armed and an electoral strategy.

Moreover, terrorism produced a counterwave in public opinion against all forms of unconventional dissent, which enabled elites to isolate terrorist groups and defeat their opponents electorally in the extrapar-liamentary left. Isolation was most visibly accomplished by repression, but the ground for it was prepared by a process of ritualization, reconstruction and solidarity of the political class around the symbols of the regime. By collapsing these diverse sectors into a single *ammucchiata anti-istituzionale*, writers like LaPalombara make it impossible to understand how organized violence divided the extraparliamentary left and helped to unite the political class around a process of reconstitution. The term *ammucchiata istituzionale* is a pejorative reference to the artificial 'lumping together', or debased co-sociationalism between the parties in government and those in opposition; here I have used it in the inverse and ironic sense.

In the first section of this chapter, I shall illustrate these points by reconstructing the chain of events surrounding an emblematic occurrence – the Piazza Fontana massacre. Piazza Fontana and the events that followed marked the first major watershed between the movements of 1967-9 and the period of organized violence and institutionalization. This history shows how death and violence became contested symbolic terrain around which the political class reconstituted its unity and over which various elements of the extraparliamentary left competed for supremacy. In section 2.2, I shall assess some of the major arguments about the sources of and responsibility for terrorism and I shall formulate an approach that emphasizes the role of political competition and tactical innovation in the development of terrorism. In section 2.3, I shall turn to the institutionalization of the wave of protest. I shall argue that, from the outset, violence and institutionalization were symbolically linked and that, between them, they helped to bring the Italian cycle of protest to a close.[3]

## 2.1 A massacre[4]

Milan, 12 December 1969. It is market day in the city for the farmers of the Milan region. The *Banca dell'Agricoltura* in Piazza Fontana is crowded with people from the provinces, making deposits, negotiating loans, doing business and gossiping under the great rotunda. In a small brown satchel that has been secreted into the bank, a bomb explodes, killing sixteen people, wounding ninety and creating chaos. At almost the same time, similar devices explode in Rome.[5] For the first time since the protest cycle began, there are signs of an organized conspiracy. But by whom? The next day's headlines announced the bombings to a shocked country in large black letters.[6] President Saragat talked of the 'bestial lack of conscience' that could lead to a 'tragic chain of terroristic acts that must be broken at any cost' by the 'forces of democratic order'. His plea combined ritual condolences to the victims with a note of warning: if the Republic is to survive, it must be vigilant against subversion.

Death had been rare in the social movements that exploded on the scene from 1967 to mid-1969. But from the autumn of 1969 onward, death by violence increasingly accompanied – or was the object of – political conflict. The first turning point came three weeks before the Piazza Fontana bombing, when a policeman was killed when fighting broke out between students and the forces of order in Milan. When the extreme left responded by calling for 'working-class violence from the factory to the streets', the vindication of policeman Annarumma's death became a rallying cry for the right.[7]

Who actually committed the massacre of Piazza Fontana would not be untangled for years – and who actually planned it is an even stranger story.[8] The police quickly arrested twenty-seven leftists – mostly anarchists – of whom one – Giuseppe Pinelli – was suspected of having been in the vicinity of the bank on the morning in question.[9] Pinelli was hauled off to the *questura* (police main office) for questioning. There, after 'his alibi is broken', and in the presence of three police officials, the police announced that he had jumped from a fourth floor window into the courtyard below.[10] After he died in hospital an hour later, the police –

with amazing alacrity – publically declared him guilty of taking part in the bombing of the *Banca dell'Agricoltura*.

Until this time, the terrain contested by the social movements had been concrete and policy-related – albeit frequently radical. After Piazza Fontana and the suspicious death of Pinelli, however, death and mourning become contested terrain for both left and right. While the right claimed the Piazza Fontana massacre and the Rome bombings were the product of a left-wing plot, the left – particularly after Pinelli's death – saw these events as an organized provocation by the right and evidence of a growing 'fascistization' of the state. When a second anarchist, Pietro Valpreda, was arrested, the extreme left saw itself under general attack.[11] Repression soon went beyond Valpreda's arrest. In a classical pattern of using a highly visible outrage to justify general repression, the police began a general sweep of known left-wing groups and activists. In Genoa, they picked up six Maoists; in Milan, five more anarchists were arrested and the study of publisher Giangiacomo Feltrinelli was searched.[12] In the atmosphere of tension created by the bombings, the extreme left saw an attempt afoot to criminalize it.

In Milan, the mystery grew as Pinelli was revealed to be someone regarded – even by some of the police – as 'incapable of violent actions'.[13] His family denounced the *questore* (the police chief officer) of Milan in court for defamation of character.[14] The police – with their case against Pinelli's ghost dissolving and a new bird in the hand – began to focus on Valpreda's movements on the day of the massacre, but Valpreda continued to insist on his innocence,[15] and his aunt – in whose house he had been living – claimed he had been in bed at the time of the bombing.

For the extreme left, the Piazza Fontana massacre represented a serious threat of delegitimation. But it was also an opportunity to justify a vision of unified state-entrepreneurial-police domination that it had begun to formulate. At first, stunned by the bombings and by the swiftness of the police response, the groups on the extreme left began to use the suspicious circumstances of Pinelli's death to launch a campaign of militant anti-fascism that lasted through the parliamentary elections of 1972 up to the equally mysterious murder of police commissioner Calabresi in the same year. It used its two major resources – publication and mobilization – to counteract the campaign of repression launched by the police and the attacks made by the bourgeois press.

Propaganda efforts centred around the group *Lotta Continua*'s journal by the same name.[16] Unlike the American movements of the period, many of the groups that emerged from Italy's 1969 avoided being at the mercy of the bourgeois press (Gitlin, 1988) by building up their own press outlets. But a newspaper has to sell copies to survive and the classical publication of the extreme left – the 'little' journal engaging in theoretical debate – would never succeed as a national newspaper. *Lotta Continua* solved the problem by a brand of sensational and investigative journalism designed to attract a broad readership. The Piazza Fontana-

Valpreda case, with its overtones of unfair imprisonment and conspiracy, was ideal for catching the reader's attention. It kept Valpreda in the focus of the extreme-left public and *Lotta Continua* in the focus of the magistrates and the police.[17] *Lotta Continua*'s campaign was followed and reinforced by the publication of a remarkably successful book – *Strage di stato* – which presented a wealth of circumstantial evidence of right-wing collusion going back to the early 1960s (Anon. 1970).

The mobilization campaign began on a more sombre note at Pinelli's funeral on December 20. This became an occasion for a peaceful demonstration led by the anarchists.[18] The red flags of the marxist left and the red and black ones of the anarchists mingled as the entire extraparliamentary left closed ranks behind Pinelli's coffin. After the Christmas holidays, *Lotta Continua* launched a campaign against police commissioner Calabresi, who was quite simply characterized as Pinelli's assassin. From then on Bobbio notes:

> not a single demonstration fails to be dominated by slogans recalling Pinelli's death and the singing of a ballad that has been dedicated to him.[19]

The institutional left was far more cautious. But as suspicions spread that the Piazza Fontana massacre was the result of a plot involving parts of the security services with subversive elements from the extreme right, a series of mass demonstrations developed against repression, with *PCI*, *PSI* (Italian Socialist Party) and trade-union support.[20] As terrorism became public issue number one in the collective memory, these mass demonstrations against fascism, police repression and terrorism were largely forgotten; but for the political class in the early 1970s they constituted an important element of pressure.

It was not that the Communists and Socialists held a brief for anarchism or violence; but with the fear of a right-wing coup they revived the memory of the antifascist Resistance, when marxists, Catholics and the secular left were united against reaction. The official left was not above opportunism either; the unity that was shattered by the centre-left experiments of the 1960s could be recomposed by a common front against fascism. The combination of the threat of a resurgence of fascism and the left's need to restore its unity led it to array the glorious symbol of the unity of the Resistance to meet what it portrayed as a threat to the Republic.

The Piazza Fontana case was still not resolved and was moreover exacerbated by the assassination of Calabresi in April 1972. Although no one claimed responsibility for the murder, the inflammatory *Lotta Continua* headline the next day interpreted the murder as the revenge of the proletariat for Pinelli's death.[21] The murder marked the beginning of a period of kidnappings and political murders that culminated in the assassination of Aldo Moro five years later.

Stimulated by the Valpreda court case, which dragged on for years,

Piazza Fontana became the contested symbolic terrain for years to come. Even into the 1980s, the date of the massacre was marked by extreme left demonstrations recalling Pinelli's death and supporting Valpreda's innocence, followed by right-wing counter-demonstrations. The institutional left organized its own demonstrations, which skirted gingerly around the issue of a conspiracy involving the police, but which emphasized the need for democratic unity against a recrudescence of fascism and for solidarity with the families of the victims.

These demonstrations become occasions for democratic and anti-fascist solidarity. Veterans of the Resistance marched alongside workers, students and officials of the institutional parties. Each left-wing demonstration triggered counter-demonstrations by the extreme right, leading to street fights, clashes with the police – who tried to keep the groups apart – and further victims.[22] The violence of 12 December 1969 was destined to repeat itself interminably as new massacres occurred. Piazza Fontana, with its confusion of left- and right-wing subversion and its undertones of conspiracy, came to symbolize the shift from the relatively innocent mass politics of 1967-9 to the politics of organized terror.

Moreover, as the years passed, something else happened to the heritage of Piazza Fontana. As the passions of 1969 subsided and Valpreda's fate became little more than an uncomfortable memory, 12 December became the occasion for ritualized public mourning, moral rectification and for resoldering the unity of the political class. By reaction and evolution, violence gave rise to institutionalization.

A look at the 'repertoire' of collective action surrounding the anniversary of the massacre over the years gives some idea of this institutionalization.[23] In examining the sequence of public events occurring on the anniversary of Piazza Fontana, we find progressively fewer people participating in public marches and street fights and an increasing number of more formal meetings to remember the victims of massacres, and 'ecumenical' events, in which commemoration of the victims is combined with the defence of democracy. The date became an occasion for the country to lick its wounds and thread together a coalition of reconciliation, first in church services, then in public conferences and finally in meetings with the families of the victims. Politicians made ritual public appeals for peace and public order; a permanent anti-fascist committee was formed; the families of the victims organized themselves – and succeeded in gaining government compensation for their loss;[24] and a carapace of democratic reconciliation gradually formed over the painful memories of 1969 and in response to the demand for vigilance against fascism. As late as 1985, we could read in the daily press:

On the occasion of the sixteenth anniversary of the massacre of Piazza Fontana, the Permanent Antifascist Committee, in collaboration with the

Union of Family members of the Victims of Massacres, has organized a meeting today ... The discussion will centre on the theme: 'Institutions and democratic unity against massacres and subversion: from Piazza Fontana to San Benedetto Val di Sambro'.[25]

December 12 had become an annual democratic rite, transcending the cleavage that was driven into the political community by the massacre of Piazza Fontana. Figure 2.1 traces the number of violent and non-violent public events in Milan and elsewhere reported by *Corriere della Sera* on 12 December each year. The graph shows that in the tense atmosphere of the early 1970s, violent events were most common but declined rapidly by the time reconstitution was underway. By the late 1970s, the major proportion of 'Piazza Fontana' events were non-violent, ritualistic and solidaristic. Violence was a threat to Italian democracy but it was also a symbolic theme around which the regime was restored.

## 2.2 Social movements and violence

Like many others, Joseph LaPalombara's analysis draws a single blood-red line from the mass movements of 1967-9 to the organized violence of the late 1970s and from the university students of the earlier period to the hardened terrorists of the latter. He is wrong on both counts: although 1967-9 produced a ferociously violent rhetoric, the repertoire of collective action during this peak of mass mobilization was largely non-violent; as for the university students, most of their actions were non-violent and – like their professors – few of them were still active by the period of organized terrorism. Placing the blame for the violence of the late 1970s upon the children of 1968 is not very different from blaming Robespierre and the *terreur* on the Tennis Court Oath and the Third Estate.

### Violence and political violence

Before turning to these issues in Italy, we should first place the general phenomenon of violence in its international context. LaPalombara argues that it was terrorism that led to 'deserted streets of the major cities at hours when they ordinarily teem with human activity'.[26] This is an exaggeration; violence began to empty the streets in Italy's big cities even before terrorism became a serious threat to public order, simply because the decade was one of increasing violence in general. The 1970s were a period of increased criminality and delinquency in every industrial country in the West. For example, in England and Wales, 'serious offences' increased by 60 per cent from 1971 to 1981, and in the US, 'violent crime' increased by an equal proportion from 1970 to 1980.[27] Italy was no exception; violence was 'emptying the streets' even in areas

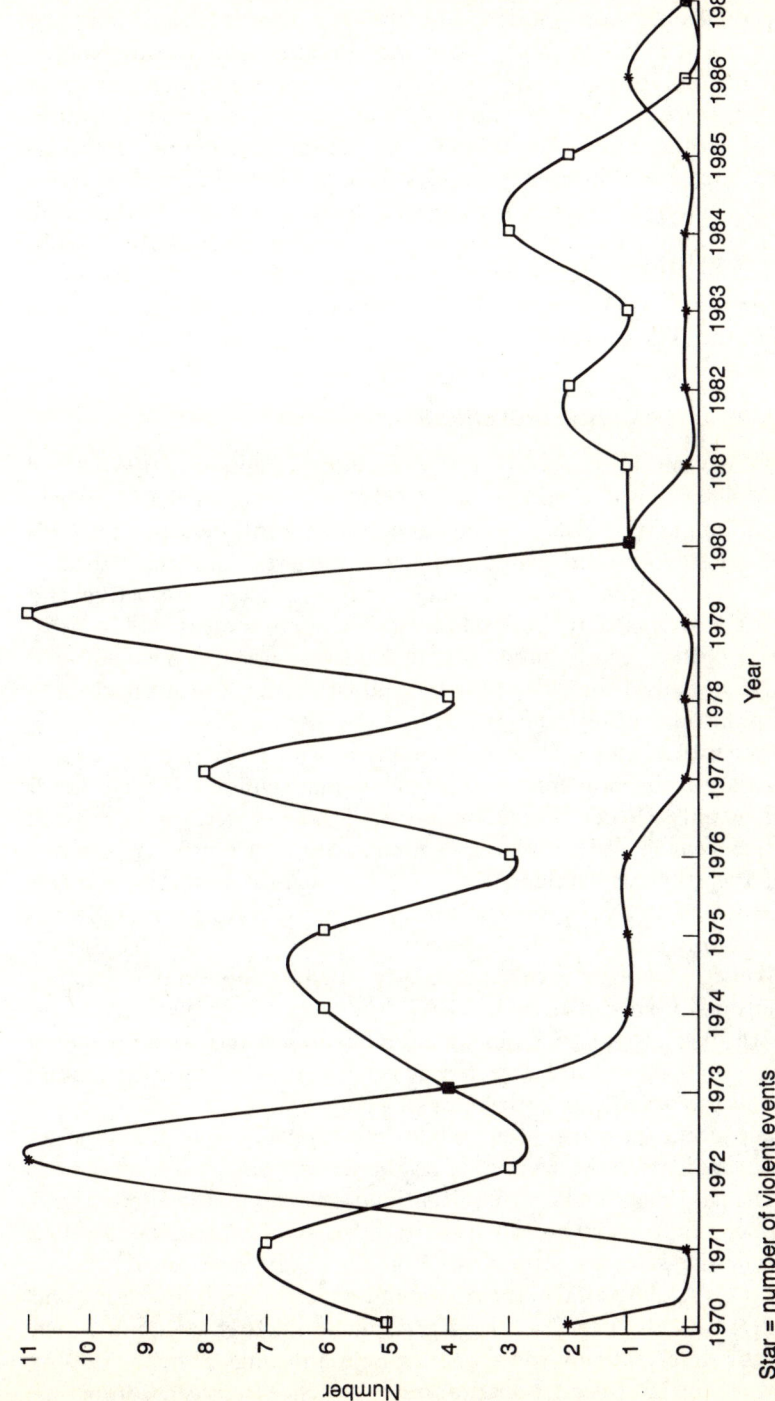

Star = number of violent events
Square = number of non-violent events

Figure 2.1 Violent and non-violent 'Piazza Fontana' events by year, 1970–87

where there was little or no political extremism. With respect to Italy, LaPalombara perhaps forgets that the 1970s was the period in which highly professional non-political kidnappings were perfected and the phenomenon of *lo scippo* (body-snatching) became widespread. Neither of these had anything to do with the student movement or with organized terrorism. These phenomena were most widespread in Milan, Turin and Rome, cities that would also become the major centres of organized terrorism. Figure 2.2 analyses the concurrence of violent crime and political violence in Milan using trial records; we can see that trials for ordinary criminal acts increased at the same time as trials for 'assaults on public officials', the latter being the usual charge made by the police when arresting demonstrators. There is a similar correlation for the data for Rome and Turin.

## The university students' movement

What of the 'continuism' between the student movement of 1967-9 and the political terrorism a decade later? Like many others, LaPalombara links the kidnappings, kneecappings and political murders of the 1970s and 1980s to the university-based protests in the late 1960s. But although the university students' protests were confrontational, combative and rhetorically extreme, they were seldom deliberately violent.[28] The main form of collective action used by the students was the occupation – which was notably peaceful – and the public march, the most classical form of political mobilization available.

From the protest events analysed in *Corriere della Sera* – hardly a source sympathetic to the students – it appears that violence of all kinds occurred in only 19 per cent of university students' actions, compared with 23 per cent in the sample of protest events as a whole. Moreover, much of the students' violence was directed against property and not against people. Table 2.1 gives the summary statistics on the main forms of action in universities and high-schools from 1967 to 1969. We can see that university students overwhelmingly used occupation and other confrontational forms; that high-school students used similar forms and were more likely to miss classes to attend marches and to hold public meetings; but that violence directed at others occurred in only a small minority in the schools in both kinds of protest.

Violence occurred most often when left-wing students encountered right-wing students in the schools or on the streets. The pattern was set as early as April 1966, when Paolo Rossi was set upon by fascist thugs during a peaceful demonstration at the University of Rome. Typically, a group of leftist students would occupy a school; subsequently fascist youth groups would attack them, defending the 'right to study' and bashing heads in the process. These groups would later encounter each other on the streets, disrupt each others' public meetings or lie in wait for one another outside their parents' homes. Violence between competing

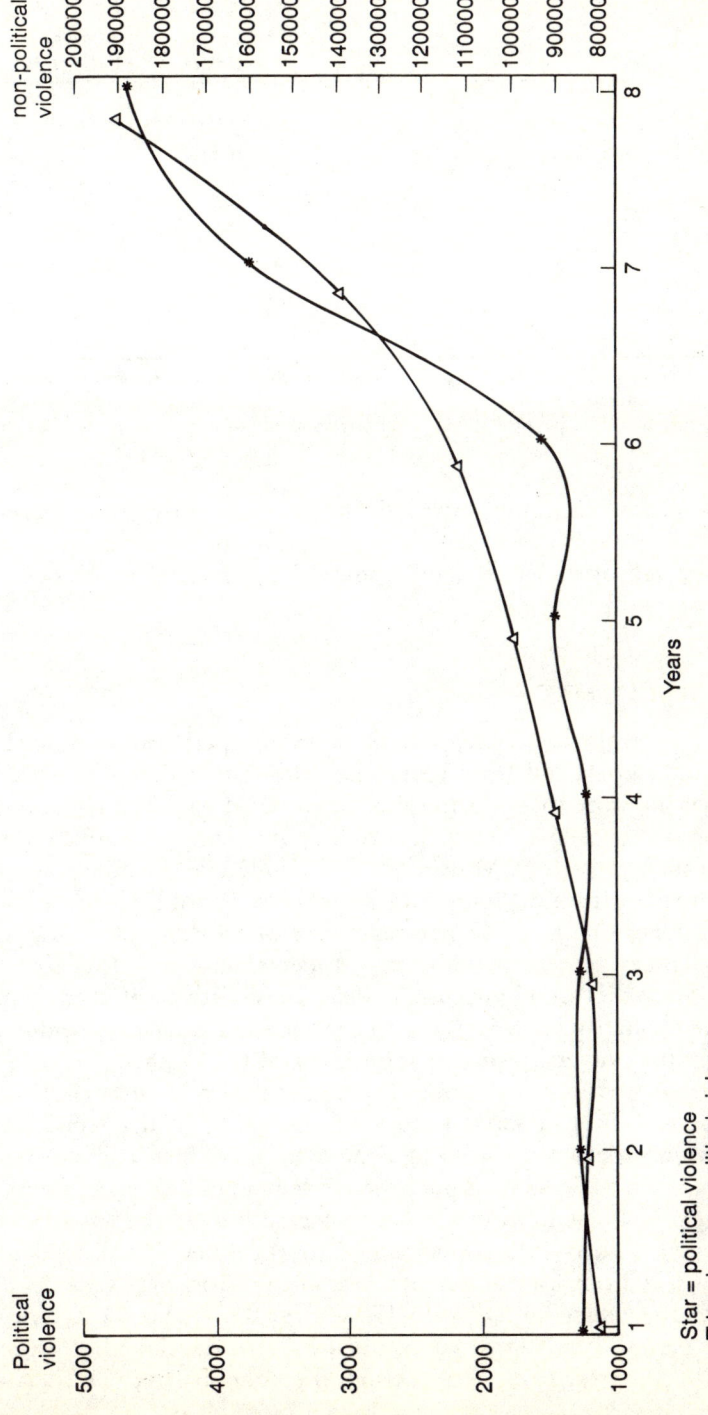

Star = political violence
Triangle = non-political violence

Figure 2.2   Trials for political and non-political violence in Milan, by year, 1965–72

Table 2.1 Forms of action used in university and high-school protests, 1967–9

| Action form | % of total protest events[*] | |
| --- | --- | --- |
| | Universities | High-schools |
| Routine forms | 4.3 | 21.8 |
| Assemblies | 28.8 | 30.0 |
| Marches and public meetings | 16.5 | 47.4 |
| Strikes | 2.8 | 45.9 |
| Confrontational forms | 45.3 | 49.6 |
| Symbolic actions | 3.6 | 3.7 |
| Damage to property | 5.8 | 4.8 |
| Violent encounter | 9.4 | 14.8 |
| Attack on persons [**] | 5.0 | 2.2 |

[*]University and high-school protests include only those in which the actors were students and the demands related to educational issues.

[**]Totals are not given as the same protest may frequently combine more than one form of action.

social movements made the streets dangerous and provided a background in violence for many future terrorists, but this is not the same as the deliberate use of violence against political targets that we associate with terrorism.

## Generations of violence

Not only was deliberate violence only a minor part of the student movements of 1967-9, but from Donatella della Porta's definitive study we learn that no more than a handful of them could have learned about armed struggle from the university-student movement or from the teachings of their professors. Most recruits to clandestine organizations in the 1970s came not from the university but directly out of high-school or from the factory. Of these, 43 per cent were of working-class origin, while only 11 per cent were university students, and only 6 per cent taught at universities or high-schools (della Porta, 1987). If there is a single source for Italian terrorism, it is to be found in the factories and the slums, not in the university-protest movement of the 1960s.

*Il sessantotto* was one of those fleeting, exuberant 'moments of madness' that we find in social history (Zolberg, 1972). It opened the gates to a wide variety of new social actors who developed a broadened repertoire of political action and put new social and political issues on the political agenda. In demonstrating the vulnerability of the system to pressure, it gave many the opportunity to use uncivil politics and violence but it did not lead in a linear fashion to terrorism.

Yet there *is* a connection between 1967-9 and the organized violence of the latter period. It relates to the competition that developed between groups who emerged from that period for support from a social-movement sector that had begun to shrink after Piazza Fontana. Terrorism was the product not of mass mobilization but of its decline (Pasquino and della Porta, (1982)).[29] It cannot be explained in terms of psychological or economic models. It developed out of the social-movement sector through competition, tactical innovation and differentiation, as I shall show below.

## The extraparliamentary groups and terrorism

Was terrorism no more than the extension of the extraparliamentary left, as LaPalombara and others have claimed? Once again, a closer historical reconstruction shows how partial and misleading such a conclusion can be. LaPalombara admits that initially most of the extraparliamentary groups 'just talked and talked', but what he fails to say is that most of them rarely did much else. Much of the activity of these groups took the form of words – words spoken at interminable party meetings, distributed in mountains of mimeographed pamphlets and published in hundreds of short-lived party journals.

The case that LaPalombara has in mind – a group that moved from propaganda of the word to that of deed – is *Potere Operaio*, some of whose leaders helped form the area of *autonomia* (the latter was a left-wing group which grew out of *Potere Operaio* and supported the autonomy of the working-class from its traditional representative, the PCI). The case of *Potere Operaio*, however, was not typical. Its theoreticians had bet so heavily on the revolutionary struggle in the factory that when mobilization declined in the early 1970s and the trade unions regained their hold on the working class, their members were left with little else but violence as a weapon. The fact that they called for a 'general insurrection' as the unions were making their greatest membership gains, and as their own mass support was slipping away, indicates the relationship between the decline of a social movement and the rise of terrorism.

The case of the *Il Manifesto* group, for example, was quite different – it seemed destined for a return to electoral politics even when its strategic line rejected it; so was that of *Avanguardia Operaia*, many of whose leaders became engaged in local politics through their role in the urban movements of the early 1970s; or *Lotta Continua*, which – for a time – was poised on the brink of 'vanguard violence', only to turn back from the precipice by 1973 (Bobbio, 1979). A number of trajectories came out of the 1967-9 period and most of them did not lead to the practice of organized violence. These groups were all part of a cycle of mass mobilization that began in 1967 and had essentially ended by the autumn of 1969. Piazza Fontana and the revelations and police searches that followed it marked the beginning of the end of this period of mass mobilization. The successful institutionalization of the factory councils continued the decline and the drain of a large number of former militants

into the PCI and the trade unions completed it. It had definitely come to
an end when the international oil shock, the coup in Chile and the
electoral recovery of the PCI led most of the extraparliamentary groups
either to abandon politics or to enter the party system. The cycle of
organized terrorism reached significant proportions only after 1972 and
peaked in 1978 when the 'old' extraparliamentary left was already a
memory.

Della Porta's study of the judicial records of convicted terrorists allows
us to assess the weight of extraparliamentary-group militants among
those who ended up in the camp of the armed struggle. Less than a
quarter of the 814 terrorists identified by della Porta came from these
groups. Of these, more than half came either from *Potere Operaio* or
from *Lotta Continua* (52 and 73 respectively). In the face of these
proportions, a linear argument about the extraparliamentary groups'
responsibility for terrorism is difficult to sustain. Where did the rest of
the terrorists come from? Della Porta's data again provide a clue. Of the
814 cases examined, 518 (almost two-thirds) came not from the
extraparliamentary organizations that had emerged from 1967-9, but
from a second generation of small, semi-clandestine associations that della
Porta collects under the rubric of 'autonomous collectives'. If the
extraparliamentary groups were the children of 1968, then the terrorist
generation – many of whom would have been too young to have
experienced *il sessantotto* – were its grandchildren.

Combining the data on the generational gap between mass mobilization and terrorism with that on the social and organizational origins of
the terrorists, we must conclude with Pasquino and della Porta that
terrorism was a function, not of the extension of mass politics, but of its
*collapse*. Organized violence did not become commonplace until the
mid-1970s, *when all the other forms of collective action had declined*. Figure
2.3 compares the data from the della Porta study of left-wing terrorism
with my own data on mass violence and small-group violence taken
from newspaper records in the period 1966-73.[30] It shows that the
beginning of organized terrorism coincided with the definitive decline of
mass protest and with the intensification of small-group violence.
Organized violence was not a property of the peak of mass protest; it was
a product of the end of mobilization.

## Politics as war

But *why* was it a product of the end of mobilization? The first reason
relates to the atmosphere of tension created by the presence on the streets
of militant, militaristic, extreme right-wing groups, some of which were
formed before the beginning of the cycle of protest. This is not to say
that terrorism was generated solely by a 'strategy of tension', but rather
that in Italy an organized counter-movement to the major movements
on the left was already active in the mid-1960s and provided a major

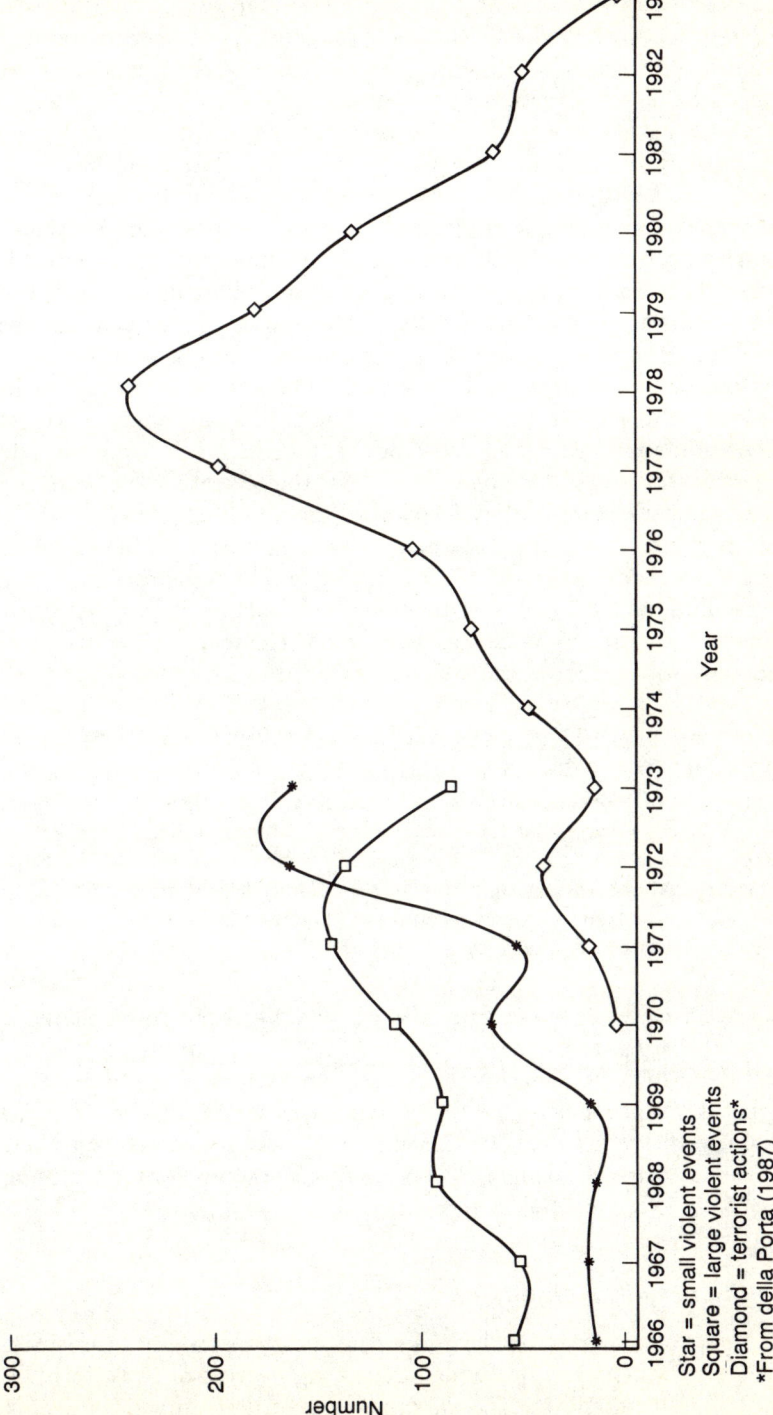

Star = small violent events
Square = large violent events
Diamond = terrorist actions*
*From della Porta (1987)

Figure 2.3   Large violent events, and small group violence, 1966–73, and terrorist actions, by year, 1970–83*

impetus for young people to be drawn into politics through street violence. As della Porta's study shows (1987), for the generation that entered politics after 1968, violence was perceived as a form of politics and politics as a form of warfare, precisely because of the presence of the extreme right on the streets.

There was an element of political opportunism in the extreme left's use of anti-fascism to build up support and demonstrate its prowess. Fascism – unlike capitalism – was a concrete and personified enemy against which young people could mobilize without prior knowledge of economics or a base in the factories. Instead of supporting their demands to reform the school system or sending them into difficult and probably fruitless attempts to rally the workers, the extraparliamentary groups could think of nothing more to do with their thousands of young recruits but to place them in their *servizi d'ordine*,[31] where they could learn about politics as a form of welfare. The complicity of the forces of order with the extreme right – self-evident to those on the opposite side – increased this sense of polarization on the extreme left and the conviction that the enemy they faced was 'the absolute enemy'.[32]

Even in the factories, the fight against fascism was a profitable arena for the extraparliamentary left, for it was one in which the parliamentary left's unwillingness to break constitutional rules placed it at a disadvantage. From 1971 to 1973, extraparliamentary elements in the factories tried to rally support from the workers by appeals such as these:

NO TO VAGUE ANTI-FASCISM; REAL OBJECTIVES FOR THE WORKING CLASS The strike called for Tuesday 24 October witnessed a great turnout of workers, but was unable to give a class answer to our needs ... We must say clearly that those responsible for the bombings from Piazza Fontana to the present day, are the *padroni* and their government ... We must say firmly that the calling of early elections (and the resulting right-wing government), the trade-union crisis (and the federative pact) are only to block the real needs of the working class ...[33]

If we wish to draw a line from the university-protest movements of 1967-9 to the organized terrorism of the late 1970s, it must pass through the intense period of physical conflict between extreme left and extreme right; that is, *the period when most of the future terrorists were being socialized into politics*. If we ignore this crucial phase and its effects on their formation, we are in danger of overlooking the major constitutive experience of left-wing Italian terrorism.

## Competition, radicalization and violence

The presence of the extreme right as a threat and an opportunity is not, however, the only way in which left-wing terrorism was formed. Violence against others was also an expression of the competition *within* the extreme left social movements for dwindling support from their constituency as the protest cycle diminished. What observers such as Angelo Ventura[34] fail to understand is the *politics* of the formation of terrorism. It was not the homogeneous product of the 'creative' phase of mass protest, but of the contradictory outcomes of the competition, conflict and decline in social-movement activity.

## Incentives to social-movement activity

Anglo-American researchers often treat social movements as if they were merely a form of interest group.[35] But the fundamental difference between interest groups and movements is that while the former can offer potential supporters 'selective incentives' (Olson, 1968) as well as ideological inspiration, the latter can only promise sacrifices to be made and risks to be taken in the name of collective goals. The fundamental problem that causes the characteristic cycles of rapid formation and decline of social movements is their absence of concrete incentives to participation.

How then do social movements solve this problem of incentives? In hospitable environments, they often find ways to glean resources from the system they oppose (McCarthy and Zald, 1977); when not facilitated by the system, they can build systems of internal reciprocity and mutual dependence that keeps militants active despite – or because of – the risks involved (della Porta, 1988). But the major concrete benefits that social movements can offer to potential participants are the solidarity, enthusiasm and pride that come from daring to challenge the system.[36]

As the history of any cycle of protest will show, mobilizing such a resource has disadvantages for any movement organization. First, it is certain to call down upon its supporters the wrath of the system and of the forces of order. This was evident in Italy as early as New Year's Eve 1988 when a protest at Viareggio's La Bussola nightclub led to the shooting of one young participant and to the arrest of a number of others.[37] Mobilization became increasingly costly as the police perfected their network of information and the effectiveness of their tactics in isolating organizers from their mass base.

Secondly, once a system has been challenged by people who dare, others quickly learn how simple such challenges are to mount. This leads first to an increased number of groups within the social-movement sector and then to tactical competition between them. In the broad sense, there was an abstract form of such competition in Italy between extreme left and right (abstract because they appealed to different constituencies). But more easily overlooked (and more important, because they appealed to the *same* constituency) was the competitive tactical innovation between groups within the extreme left who tried to outbid one another for mass support with the only resources they possessed – the courage and imagination to mount ever more radical challenges to the system.

Thirdly – and following on from the first two points – the spiral of tactical innovation, since it leads to increased disruption and thus to an increase in repression, produces a consequent decline in mass participation, as the costs of social-movement activity clearly became higher for participants. Police truncheons and arrests teach a hard lesson; kicks and chains wielded by fascist gangs are even tougher; and the fear and revulsion at the realization that we are involved with people who prefer violence to debate leads to an additional drain.[38] Most people who became involved in the movement during the exhilaration of mass strikes and faculty occupations were less likely to remain involved when the forms of action became increasingly extreme and violent.

In other words, once demonstrated, the ease of challenging the system through protest increases the number of movement organizations competing for support among a finite and ultimately shrinking constituency. These groups – with few concrete resources to offer supporters – compete for support through tactical innovation. And the larger the number of groups competing for a declining constituency, the greater the tendency to use radical actions to attract attention and gain support. This was particularly true of new and marginal groups, who can only gain attention away from more established, larger organizations through the use of extreme radical actions. The more radical their forms of action, the greater the risk of violence and the higher the level of repression. Once repression is triggered, the group has no alternative but to go underground, where the only tactical alternatives left to it are violent (della Porta, 1987).

To put this line of reasoning in political-economy terms: as the potential market for protest declines and the number of groups seeking a share of the same constituency increases, competition for support grows. This makes it more difficult to organize the kind of mass politics that the early movements know how to organize and it places a premium on forms of collective action that do not require a mass base to attract attention. This gives a tactical advantage to small, unknown groups on the margins of the existing mass movements, who can use their invisibility to escape police surveillance. The existing mass organizations may respond by adopting the tactics of their competitors to avoid being outflanked on the extremes; by condemning violence and moving towards the system; or both.

## The competitive spiral in Italy

We see such a sequence of formation of new groups, radicalization of tactics and resulting competition for support through tactical innovation and ultimately violence in Italy in the years after Piazza Fontana. I have already recalled how *Potere Operaio*, undergoing a crisis of militance in this period, adopted the strategy of a general insurrection in late 1971. Surely it is no accident that this occurred not long after the appearance of the *NAP* (*Nuclei Armati Proletari*, Armed Proletarian Nuclei) and the Red Brigades, and shortly before the kidnapping of engineer Macchiarini by the latter in March 1971? The veering of *Potere Operaio* towards armed struggle was the combined result of the decline of mass mobilization and of the competition of more radical organizations on its left. The spiral of radicalization, however, went beyond *Potere Operaio*. In response to its call for an insurrection, *Lotta Continua*, at a closed conference held in Rimini in April 1972, adopted the slogan of 'generalized struggle'.[39] At the theoretical level at least, the birth of a *partito armato* (armed party) set off a competitive spiral of radicalization between the two major extraparliamentary groups of the left.

What then of the level of practice? Faced by the dramatic actions of the Red Brigades and by the strategic radicalization of its competitor, *Lotta Continua* veered towards the acceptance of both mass and vanguard violence. The extent to which this strategy was put into practice in a systematic way is still controversial. For some, like Ventura, *Lotta Continua* was a militaristic group right from the beginning[40], while for others, such as Pasquino, it lived a double life from 1972 until the end;[41] but for a witness like Bobbio:

> *Lotta Continua* is, by its very nature 'movimentist', favouring a form of collective movement, [and] has always been quite alien to the choice of clandestinity.[42]

Violence was glorified in *Lotta Continua*'s publications: lists of enemies of the proletariat were compiled and published; cases of popular insubordination were glorified; and the public humiliation of personnel managers was described with approval. In this phase, the slogan 'kidnap the bosses' began to occur more and more often,[43] and Lotta Continua militants were often involved in incidents of violence against fascists. When police commissioner Calabresi was killed, the newspaper refused to deplore a murder 'in which the exploited realize their desire for justice'.[44] More recently, the group was accused of more direct involvement in this murder (see below).

Nevertheless, there was never a complete acceptance of 'vanguard violence' in *Lotta Continua* and it was soon rejected. For example, in a far less-often cited quotation than the one above, when Calabresi was killed, *Lotta Continua* cautiously pointed out that political homicide was 'not the decisive weapon for the emancipation of the masses'. In an important article published in another journal, Luciano Pero criticized the 'left opportunism' of 'those who are willing to leave it to the masses to decide, on a case by case basis, on whether acts of violence are legitimate' (Pero, 1972). By late 1972, Sofri himself had steered the group towards the strategy that led to its electoral involvements in 1975 and 1976.[45] As terrorist outrages began to affect the appeal of the extreme left as a whole, opposition to terrorism gained ground in the organization and

*Lotta Continua* condemned 'vanguard violence', warning that 'to treat the problem of force as a separate problem [separate from that of the mass line] means putting the rifle in the command post'.[46]

However, many of *Lotta Continua*'s militants may have carried out in practice what the party never officially accepted in theory; the role played by political competition in forcing the group to choose between violence and institutionalization is still very much an open issue. It is exemplary, for example, that the magistrate's accusation against Sofri and Pietrostefani for complicity in the murder of Calabresi claimed that:

> *Lotta Continua* militants killed Calabresi, [who was] considered by them as the assassin of the anarchist Pinelli, to give a proof of their strength the militant and more extreme wing of the left that is the BR.[47]

According to the magistrate, Sofri and Pietrostefani had 'ordered' the murder of Calabresi to stem the drain of militants from *Lotta Continua* to the new and clandestine groups forming to its left.

The ultimate choice of an institutional strategy by the three major groups of the extraparliamentary left produced a void into which a number of collectives, action committees and factory vanguards remained. United only by opposition to the institutional left and by the desire to contest the 'leap into politics' that the 'old' extraparliamentary left was taking, these groups were practically *born* in clandestinity. With the decline of mass mobilization of the early- and mid-1970s, the only way for them to gain the attention of the workers was through violence.

## Linear and competitive evolution

Thus we can only link the terrorism of the late 1970s back to the mass movements a decade earlier by tracing a two-step process of competition, outbidding and separation within the social-movement sector. In the first stage, the extraparliamentary left competed for support with the PCI and the trade unions by proposing radical – but mass – forms of collective action to the workers. In the second, a new generation of autonomous groups, collectives and terrorist organizations competed for support with the extraparliamentary groups by proposing more radical, sectarian forms of collective action which – in the absence of a mass base – had to be violent to gain attention.

In the first stage, the one constant in the period 1967-72 was the attempt by the various formations of the extraparliamentary left to convince the workers that the PCI had deserted them and that the trade unions were in league with management. Ferocious rhetoric, expressive slogans and extreme ideological appeals were some of the tactics available to them. But workers are more impressed with deeds than words – or so these groups supposed. In the end, the major resource that the extraparliamentary groups had to outflank the official left and to impress the workers with their prowess was their power to disrupt. This was a fruitful strategy as long as mobilization was increasing and the unions were on the defensive, as was illustrated in cases like Porto Marghera in 1968 and Fiat in 1969. But after the union successes of the 'hot autumn' and the successful institutionalization of the councils of delegates, the constituency for mass mobilization declined. It was at precisely this time – between 1968 and the end of 1969 – that the number and variety of extraparliamentary groups trying to appeal to the workers increased. An ever-increasing number of groups were competing for the support of the workers, who had less and less incentive to follow their lead.

The effect of the worker's demobilization was devastating for organizations that had built their appeals around the hypothesis of continued factory militance. Some, like *Potere Operaio*, collapsed by 1973; others became essentially publicists for a revolutionary hypothesis that seemed more and more illusory; a larger number of individuals than is usually admitted ended up in the ranks of the PCI (Lange, Tarrow and Irvin, 1988), while others – such as *Lotta Continua* – leapt from the factory to successive sectors of Italian society – the cities, the prisons, the south – in a furious attempt to find new 'internal vanguards' to keep the struggle alive.

What links the extraparliamentary groups to the terrorists a decade later is that both tried to attract the support of the workers by outbidding those who had arrived earlier: the extraparliamentary groups used mass forms of collective action to outflank the unions and the PCI; the terrorists used violence to outbid the extraparliamentary groups. In the words of Bobbio:

> the prospective of a mass revolt was increasingly distant, while acts of rupture, proletarian expropriations, illegal actions, accompanied by a verbose exaltation of the armed struggle, leapt to centre stage.[48]

## 2.3 Institutionalization and violence

The story of Piazza Fontana illustrated the beginnings of the spiral of violence that was ultimately to end in mass imprisonments, *pentitismo* and the denunciation of former comrades and friends. But this story also shows how the violence in the Italian protest cycle led to the institutionalization of protest. I would like to close this chapter by turning to the complex issue of the relationship between the two. In his essay on *The Politics of Disorder*, Theodore Lowi observes that:

> When movements act on the government or any of its parts, there tends to be action with very little interaction – that is, very little bargaining. But this is not violence ... The effect of the movement is of another sort altogether: *the*

*demands and activities of a movement tend to activate the mechanism of
formal decision-making.*[49]

Critics of Italian politics have stressed how poorly institutionalized it
is. Giuseppe Di Palma, for example, notes that the Italian parliament has
not gained the degree of legitimacy that his colleague, Nelson Polsby,
found in the American Congress.[50] But the institutions of one country
will seldom function like those of another. If we are to understand the
institutionalization of protest, we shall have to do so in terms of Italy's
political culture, which is informal, conflictual and uses the language of
ideas even to describe a well-worn political game.[51] Political scientists
usually see institutionalization in greater organization and routinization,
in the shift from confrontation to bargaining and in a greater
specialization of function. Using these criteria, we find a number of ways
in which the protest movements of the late 1960s and early 1970s
activated mechanisms of formal decision-making and brought about an
institutionalization of protest in Italy.

Elsewhere, I have shown how in the course of its protest cycle, Italy
developed a broader repertoire of participation than it possessed when
the cycle began.[52] If some people were using violence by its end, there
were many more who were organizing marches and public meetings,
using assemblies to develop their demands and to plan their course of
action, and forming grassroots bodies like neighbourhood councils or
feminist collectives.

In a number of sectors, new institutions and practices developed,
reversing the disruptiveness of the early phase of the cycle but also
providing social actors with more solid resources with which to advance
their goals. In industrial relations, new institutions were developed and
new roles were imposed on old ones; in the cities, militant urban
movements turned towards the politics of planning and municipal
politics; in the professions, authority roles were scrutinized and
hierarchies challenged; among the social-movement organizations, some
became more specialized in representing particular social groups or
policy publics, while others turned into community organizations.

Where observers like Lowi see protest cycles as fated to end in
institutionalization and others like LaPalombara have emphasized their
legacy of violence, the hypothesis I should like to put forward is that the
cycle of Italian protest ended in a combination of the two, to some extent
through their symbiosis. For although the violence of the Red Brigades
was light years away from a factory council, from the door-to-door
organization of a tenants union, or from the policy-oriented mobilization
of the women's movement, there were connections between the two
kinds of phenomena that helped to bring about the close of the cycle.

On the one hand, if extremists were adopting increasingly violent
tactics, it was their violence that drove many of the veterans of 1968 off
the streets and led the extraparliamentary groups into electoral politics.

On the other hand, if the political parties temporized in condemning terrorism, they also absorbed a large number of former movement militants into the 'constitutional arc' (Lange, Tarrow and Irvin, 1988). At each turn of the spiral of violence the gap between movements and institutions widened, forcing participants in the social-movement sector to choose either one direction or the other, as *Lotta Continua* did between 1972 and 1975.

The effect of these processes was cumulative. For example, although the defection of the less militant from the extreme left gave a clearer field to the extremists, it also deprived them of the social base they needed to renew themselves. And although the entry of groups like the NAP and the Red Brigades into the armed struggle left the extraparliamentary groups more homogeneous than before, each terrorist outrage pushed them further into proclaiming their loyalty to the rules of institutional politics.

This bifurcation of the movement sector produced two types of groups: highly-structured 'new' parties with national programmes and memberships on the one hand, and small cells of militants using street violence, industrial sabotage and clandestine organizing on the other. The hard work of repressing terrorism was done by the police and the judiciary and many paid for it with their lives; but it was the internal dynamic of the cycle of protest and the bifurcation of the social-movement sector into institutional and anti-institutional branches that made it possible.

The coincidence of violence and institutionalization can be illustrated by comparing my data on union-sponsored peaceful public events in Milan with the curve of violence in the same city. The conferences, debates, policy discussions and attempts to lobby public officials that the *CGIL* (Communist and Socialist Trade Union) and *CISL* (Christian Democratic Trade Union) were organizing constituted an important sign of the institutionalization of industrial conflict locally, just as the efforts of the unions to negotiate national wage agreements were signs of institutionalization at the national level. Perhaps in a well-ordered society, such a process would have occurred only after the definitive stifling of dissent. But as Figure 2.4 indicates, in Milan these apparently contradictory trends were present at the same time. Figure 2.4 shows that the number of publicly organized non-disruptive events organized by the two main union confederations coincided almost exactly in time with the increase in violence. Behind the headlines that were painting a stark picture of a society going down the drain, a slow and patient institutionalization of protest was building up.

## Conclusion

In the wake of the years of terrorism, some argued that the Italian state

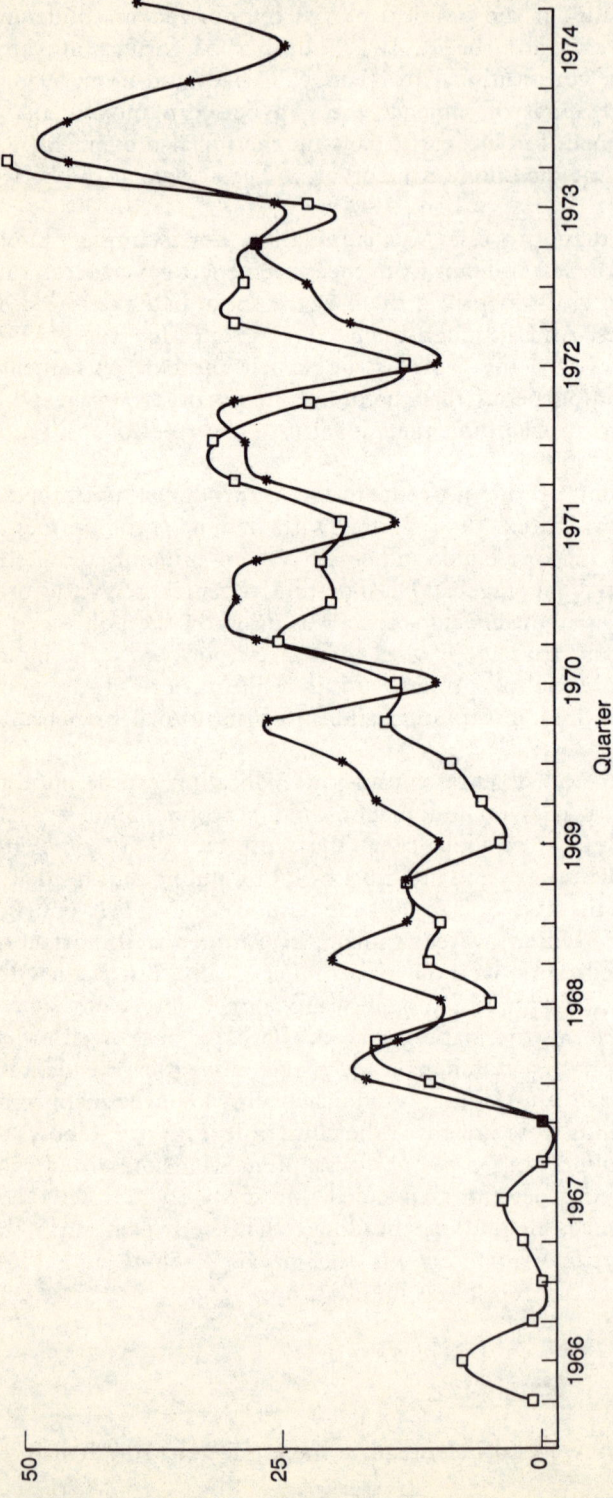

Star = trade union federations
Square = violent events

Figure 2.4 Violence in Milan, 1966–73 and public events of Milanese union confederations, by quarter, 1968–74

should have followed the example of the former Federal Republic of Germany in controlling the press more tightly and rooting subversives out of the public services and the schools. West Germany's experience also teaches us a lesson about the suffocation of popular politics that they would do well to contemplate. For these were not only years of increasing political violence in West Germany; they were also years of exploding popular participation, neighbourhood councils, *Burgerinitiativen*, cooperatives and autonomous communities. The draconian measures taken against dissent in the FRG not only put a cap on terrorism; they helped to smother many of the new forms of political activity that grew out of the 1968-70 period, leaving the country in the hands of the right-wing of the SPD.

American observers like LaPalombara would also do well to contemplate the history of their own country before blaming the Italian state for excessive permissiveness in fighting subversion. In the McCarthy years, Americans could see the results of repression in a country with a much stronger tradition of civil liberties than in Italy. Italy's not adopting such policies may have been costly, but the risks of curtailing basic civil liberties in the fight against terrorism would have been greater. As it is, many people spent years in preventive detention as the government searched for evidence on which to try them; others still suffer the threat of judicial harassment which cannot be beneficial to encouraging citizens to speak their minds.

The mass politics of the 1967-9 period in Italy had two effects that critics of Italian 'permissiveness' would do well to ponder. First, it opened Italy up to new and expanded forms of political participation that rejected the *delega* the major parties had impressed upon mass politics since the Liberation. Not even critics of *sessantotto* would deny that this is a virtue for a political system that many of the same critics accuse of *partitocrazia* (the degeneration of the political system). Secondly, during the *anni di piombo*, it was not only, or even primarily, repression that created a consensus against subversion. Popular politics, in the form of mass, organized demonstrations against fascism, terrorism and repression played a role in creating a constituency for support of the republican constitution and insuring that Italy would combat terrorism without destroying that framework. Terrorism was indeed a danger to Italian democracy. But the critics' obsession with it has clouded over one of the richest and most fruitful periods of democratic growth of the Italian Republic. Italian democracy survived attacks from both left and right, not only, or even primarily, because governments learned to repress terrorism. It also survived because organized violence came at the *end* of a period of mobilization and as part of a competitive process whose major outcome was institutionalization. By this time, the mass base was lacking for an assault on the state and terrorism helped to reunite people around the symbols of democracy.

## Notes

1 Citations are from the English-language version (1987), *Democracy Italian Style*, New Haven, Yale University Press, pp. 169-70. For the Italian version see (1988), *Democrazia all'italiana*, Milan, Mondadori. Italian readers should note that the title of the original English-language version does not convey the ironic tone in the phrase 'democrazia all'italiana'. It is not clear why LaPalombara – or his publishers – chose to give such an ironic tone to the title, when the message of the book is that democracy in Italy is alive and well. A roundtable discussion of the book, organized by the Conference Group on Italian Politics and Society at the American Political Science Association annual meetings in 1987, is reproduced in *Polis* (1988) 1, pp.199-216, April.

2 Ibid., p. 177.

3 The data used in this analysis come mainly from a large empirical study of the Italian cycle of protest, published in 1989 in its entirety as *Democracy and Disorder. Protest and Politics in Italy, 1965-1975*, Oxford, Clarendon Press. Other reports from the project will be found in Tarrow (1982), della Porta and Tarrow (1986), and Stefanizzi and Tarrow (1989).

4 I am grateful to Tom Zamora, whose PhD thesis at Cornell helped me to reconstruct the story of Piazza Fontana and the events that followed.

5 *Corriere della Sera*, 13 December 1969, p.3.

6 *Corriere della Sera*, 13 December 1969, p.1.

7 L. Bobbio (1979) *Lotta Continua: storia di una organizzazione rivoluzionaria*, Milan, Savelli, p. 52.

8 Through most of 1970 and 1971, the bourgeois press continued to assume a left-wing origin for the massacre of Piazza Fontana. But by 12 December 1972, *Corriere della Sera* was reporting that the delay of the Valpreda trial might be due to the magistrates' pursuit of a 'pista nera'. This trail eventually led to the two right-wing extremists, Freda and Ventura (12 December 1973). By the following year, the newspaper recognized that there indeed existed what the left had been calling a 'strategy of tension' (*Corriere della Sera*, 13 December 1970).

9 *Corriere della Sera*, 15 December 1969, p.2.

10 *Corriere della Sera*, 16 December 1969, p.1.

11 *Corriere della Sera*, 17 December 1969, p.1.

12 *Corriere della Sera*, 20 December 1969, p.1.

13 *Corriere della Sera*, 17 December 1969, p.3.

14 *Corriere della Sera*, 28 December 1969, p.8.

15 *Corriere della Sera*, 17 December 1969, p.3; *Corriere della Sera*, 18 December 1969, p.2.

16 Founded in the autumn of 1969, soon after *Lotta Continua*'s formation, the newspaper was at first a bi-weekly, then became a weekly and finally a daily newspaper. Although it had pretensions of becoming a general organ of the extreme left like *Il Manifesto*, its line was too sectarian to serve as an organ of information and its circulation was largely dependent on its simple tone, sensational headlines and investigative reporting.

17 And not without cost: the editor responsible for *Lotta Continua* was soon hauled up before the court on charges of defamation (Bobbio, op. cit., (1979) p.55.

18 *Corriere della Sera*, 21 December 1969, p.8.

19 Bobbio, op.cit. (1979), p.55.

20 Corriere della Sera, 19 December 1969, p.8.

21 Sixteen years later, one of the presumed assassins came forward to confess to having driven the murder vehicle, named the presumed trigger man and put the blame on Adriano Sofri and Giorgio Pietrostefani, leaders of *Lotta Continua*, for having 'ordered' the murder. See the press reports following Sofri's and Pietrostefani's arrests on July 28 1988.

22 In 1970, as the fascists made gains in the local elections, the anniversary became the scene of three separate demonstrations in Milan – one fascist, one by the ANPI and one by the Movimento Studentesco. The official demonstration by the extreme right was cancelled but a group of young fascists congregated in Piazza San Babila looking for trouble (*Corriere della Sera*, 13 December 1970). The ANPI demonstration came off peacefully, but the fascists and the extreme left clashed and more than fifty people were arrested. A young man, Saltarelli, was killed when a police teargas grenade pierced his chest. The police first claimed he died of a heart attack, but an autopsy proved their responsibility (*Corriere della Sera*, 15 December 1970).

23 The concept of the 'repertoire' is laid out by Tilly (1978). For an application to the Italian case, see Tarrow (1989) and della Porta and Tarrow (1986).

24 *Corriere della Sera*, 13 December 1981.

25 *Corriere della Sera*, 13 December 1985, p. 13. San Benedetto Val di Sambro is the place on the rail route between Florence and Bologna where during the night of 23 December 1984 a bomb exploded on the inter-city Naples-Milan train. Thirteen people died and many others were injured.

26 LaPalombara, op.cit., p. 167.

27 For the British data, see (1981) *Social Trends*, p. 205. For the American data, see United States Federal Bureau of Investigation (1979) *Crime in the United States*, p. 37.

28 Tarrow (1989) Chapter 3.

29 Pasquino and della Porta (1982) p. 30 define terrorism as 'the outcome of the degeneration and decomposition of collective movements'. For other evidence on the relationships between left-wing terrorism and the social movements in Italy see della Porta (1987), della Porta (ed.) (1984) and Pasquino (1983).

30 'Mass violence' is defined as violence that occurred in the course of a protest event including more than 500 participants; 'small-group violence' is defined as violence carried out by a group of fewer than twenty people or by an unknown group. For a more detailed presentation of these findings, see della Porta and Tarrow (1986) and Tarrow (1989), Chapter 12.

31 For an explanation of *servizi d'ordine*, see Chapter 6, note 15.

32 See Manconi, Chapter 4, in this volume.

33 From a manifesto of the *consiglio di fabbrica* of Motori Bassani, Lodi, 27 October 1972, found in the personal archive of Giovanni Arrighi, to whom I wish to express my thanks. These democratically run trade union factory councils were first set in the 1970s and allowed more direct worker-participation in factory decision-making.

34 In della Porta (ed.) (1984) p. 75.

35 This approach is most easily recognized among the so-called 'resource mobilization' school of social-movement theory. For the best research in this tradition, see Zald and McCarthy (1987). For a critique and analysis, see

Klandermans, Kriesi and Tarrow (1988). This view is not unknown among political scientists, one of whom – only half in jest – was heard to remark that 'a social movement is an interest goup that you like'.

36 Tarrow, (1989) Chapter 3.

37 Tarrow, (1989), Chapter 6.

38 This was particularly true of young women. Almost ignored in the literature on the movements of 1967-9 was the negative effect of violence upon them, many of whom defected – not only into feminist groups – but away from political activity in general as the result of the violence. This was remarked upon by every woman interviewed in the course of the study cited above (Tarrow, 1989).

39 Bobbio, op.cit. (1979) p. 98.

40 *Corriere della Sera*, 29 July 1988, p. 1.

41 Pasquino (1983) p. 252.

42 Bobbio, op.cit. (1979) p. 103.

43 Ibid., p. 81.

44 Ibid., pp. 113-16.

45 Ibid., pp. 113-16.

46 *Lotta Continua* (1975) pp. 122–3.

47 At the time of writing Sofri and Pietrostefani have been sentenced in the first instance. Pietrostefani has since appealed while Sofri has not – despite this juridically unusual non-application for an appeal, the public prosecutor has applied on his behalf. For an interesting insight into the trial, see also the recently published book by Carlo Ginzburg (1991) *Il giudice e lo storico: considerazioni in margine al processo Sofri*, Turin, Einaudi.

48 Bobbio, op.cit. (1979) p. 140.

49 Lowi (1971) p. 54.

50 Di Palma (1977) p. 187; see also Polsby (1968).

51 LaPalombara (1987) Chapter 3.

52 Tarrow, 1989, Chapter 3.

## References

Anon. (1970) *Strage di stato*, Milan, Samonà and Savelli.

L. Bobbio (1979) *Lotta Continua: storia di una organizzazione rivoluzionaria*, Milan, Savelli.

D. della Porta (1987) 'Organizzazioni politiche clandestine: Il terrorismo di sinistra in Italia durante gli anni settanta', Ph.D thesis, European University Institute. Published 1990 *Il terrorismo di sinistra*, Bologna, Il Mulino.

D. della Porta (1988) 'Recruitment Processes in Clandestine Political Organizations: the Case of Italian Left-Wing Terrorism', in Klandermans, Kriesi and Tarrow (eds) *From Structure to Action. Comparing Movement Participation Across Cultures*, Greenwich, Conneticut, JAI.

D. della Porta (ed.) (1984) *Terrorismi in Italia*, Bologna, Il Mulino.

D. della Porta and G. Pasquino (eds) (1983) *Terrorismo e violenza politica. Tre casi a confronto*, Bologna, Il Mulino.

D. della Porta and S. Tarrow (1986) 'Unwanted Children: Political Violence and the Cycle of Protest in Italy, 1966-1973', *European Journal of Political Research*, 14, pp. 607-32.

G. Di Palma (1977) *Surviving without Governing: the Italian Parties in Parliament*, Berkeley and Los Angeles, University of California Press.

C. Ginzburg (1991) *Il giudice e lo storico: considerazioni in margine al processo Sofri*, Turin, Einaudi.

T. Gitlin (1988) *The Whole world is Watching*, Berkeley and Los Angeles, University of California Press.

B. Klandermans, H.-P. Kiriesi and S. Tarrow (eds) (1988) *From Structure to Action: Comparing Movement Participation Across Cultures*, Greenwich, Conneticut, JAI.

P. Lange, S. Tarrow and C. Irvin (1988) 'Phases of Mobilization: Social Movements and Political Party Recruitment', unpublished paper.

J. LaPalombara (1987) *Democracy, Italian Style*, New Haven, Yale University Press.

Lotta Continua (1975) *Le tesi, le relazioni politiche, lo statuto approvato al I congresso nazionale di Lotta Continua*, Rome, Edizioni Lotta Continua.

T.J. Lowi (1971) *The Politics of Disorder*, New York, Basic Books.

J.D. McCarthy and M.N. Zald (1977) 'Resource Mobilization and Social Movements: a Partial Theory', *American Journal of Sociology*, 82, pp. 1212-41.

M. Olson (1968) *The Logic of Collective Action*, New York, Schocken.

G. Pasquino (1983) 'Differenze e somiglianze: per una ricerca sul terrorismo italiano', in della Porta and Pasquino (eds), *Terrorismo e violenza politica: tre casi a confronto*, Bologna, Il Mulino.

G. Pasquino and D. della Porta (1982) 'Interpretations of Italian Left-Wing Terrorism', paper presented to the XII World Congress of IPSA, Rio de Janeiro, August 9-14.

*Polis* (ed.) (1988) 'A proposito di ...', *Democrazia all'italiana*, pp. 199-216.

N. Polsby (1968) 'The Institutionalization of the US House of Representatives', *American Political Science Review*, pp. 144-68.

S. Stefanizzi (1989) 'The Regulation of Protest: the Interaction of State and Social Regulation in the Cycle of 1966-73', in P. Lange and M. Regini (eds), *State, Market, and Social Regulation: New Perspectives on Italy*, Cambridge, Cambridge University Press.

S. Tarrow (1982) 'Le organizzazioni dei movimenti sociali; cosa sono? quando riescono?', *Laboratorio Politico*, 2.

S. Tarrow (1989) *Democracy and disorder. Social Protest and Politics in Italy, 1965-1975*, Oxford, Clarendon Press.

C. Tilly (1978) *From Mobilization to Revolution*, Englewood Cliffs, Prentice Hall.

A. Venturi (1984) 'Il problema delle origini del terrorismo di sinistra', in della Porta (ed.), *Terrorismi in Italia*, op. cit.

M.N. Zald and J. McCarthy (eds) (1987) *Social Movements in an Organizational Society*, New Brunswick, N.J., Transaction Books.

A. Zolberg, (1972) 'Moments of Madness', *Politics and Society*, winter edition, pp. 183-207.

# 3
# The history of the Red Brigades: organizational structures and strategies of action (1970–82)

## *Gian Carlo Caselli and Donatella della Porta*

## Introduction

If we look at the recent history of industrial democracies, leftist political terrorism does not appear to be a particularly Italian phenomenon. Nevertheless, Italy is the country where it has been responsible for the largest offensives and has lasted longest. After an initial period of embarrassed or negligent silence, the media and intellectuals have now focused on the affairs of underground organizations. Our knowledge of leftist terrorism in Italy has been enriched by dozens of essays on different specific objects: the life histories of militant members of underground organizations; political interaction in the cities where the phenomenon was most developed; the ideological roots of the armed struggle; the institutional conditions that facilitated the emergence of violence and so forth. The available literature, although vast, is also extremely heterogeneous from a scientific point of view.

In organizing our work, we have concentrated on a single underground organization – the Red Brigades (BR) – and reconstructed its history using secondary sources and primary trial material no longer covered by judicial secrets. Rather than offering a mere chronological presentation of the events, we intend to organize the available data around some variables in order to identify a coherent periodization of the phenomenon. In dealing with the analysis of the evolutionary dynamic of underground organizations we have started from the hypothesis that violent action – even where it has characteristics that make it a criminal phenomenon – follows the logic of the pursuit of ends common to other types of collective behaviour.[1] We shall concentrate on the way in which resources are gathered and mobilized by the group in relation to its objectives, the characteristics of its potential recruitment base and the conditions of the external environment.

Using the theoretical material of the organization as an instrument to understand the meaning of terrorist actions,[2] each section will be divided into three parts: organizational structure, strategy of action and lines of interpretation. In particular, as far as the organization is concerned, we shall examine the available information relative to: organizational model (that is, degree of articulation and centralization, systems of recruitment and existence of internal factions); type of membership (size, level of organizational commitment, socio-geographic origin and political origins); socio-geographic location of the organization (with regard to the cities and social structures where terrorism has had the greatest following throughout the various periods). As far as terrorist action is concerned we shall attempt to identify and distinguish by period: its strategic aims, targets (and in relation to this, the population target of the actions), forms and location.[3] At the end of each section we shall attempt to analyse the possible interpretation of terrorism in relation to its characteristics and to the conditions of the social actors, the political system and the repressive state apparatus of that particular period.

In the study presented here we have identified four distinct periods in the history of the BR: (1) the period of 'armed propaganda' (1970–4); (2) the 'attack on the heart of the state' (1974–6); (3) the 'strategy of destruction' (1977–8); and (4) the military confrontation with the state for survival of the organization (1979–82). It is important to stress that the periodization is primarily in relation to the internal characteristics of the underground group (organization and action); and only some hypotheses are put forward with regard to the relationship between internal development and external conditions. In the presentation we shall try to focus on the important questions for which no answers have yet been found and the most important directions that historical and sociological investigation should take.

## 3.1 The period of 'armed propaganda' (1970–3/4)

In the first phase of their existence – 1970–3/4 – the activity of the Red Brigades was limited to the two major industrial cities of northern Italy, Milan and Turin. The actions of the organization – as regards objectives and interventions – appear to reveal the intention to maintain a constant link with the interests of a broader political and trade-union movement that was developing during the period. In this sense the BR presented themselves as the extreme fringe of a broad – but certainly not homogeneous – collective protest.

### 3.1.1 The organization: opting for clandestinity

The first actions attributable to the BR date back to the autumn of 1970 but – in the opinion of the scholars working in this area – the history of the main terrorist organization is rooted in the students' movement of the 'hot autumn' of 1968 and 1969. Without dwelling too much on what is already well-known,[4] we should nevertheless recall that the origins of the BR are to be found in the *Collettivo Politico Metropolitano* (Political Metropolitan Collective (CPM)), formed in Milan in September 1969 with the support of – among others – Trent University students and members of various grassroots worker organizations (in particular, those of the big factories Pirelli, Sit Siemens and Alfa Romeo). It is widely believed to have been an assembly organized by the CPM at Chiavari in 1969 that led to the decision to make the 'operational transition' to the armed struggle. Until the summer of 1970, however, the political interventions of the group apparently remained within the limits common to many collectives generated by the events of 1968. In fact, with the aim of extending the conflicts originating from within the factories and educational institutions to the entire society, the CPM faced – initially without any particular emphasis – the issues of 'insurrection' and of the use of violent forms of action. The debate on the armed struggle became more important and even started to be translated into concrete choices when some militants of the CPM united with a group of ex-members *(fuoriusciti)* of the Reggio Emilia section of the FGCI *(Federazione Giovanile Comunista Italiana)*, to found *Sinistra proletaria* (Proletarian Left). In January 1971, a newspaper of the same name proclaimed the need to 'entrench the principle that there is no political power without military power in the fighting proletarian masses, to educate the proletarian and revolutionary left to the resistance through partisan action, to the armed struggle'.[5] The publication of *Sinistra proletaria* subsequently ceased, but in April of 1971 another periodical traceable to the group *Nuova resistenza* (New Resistence) started to publish interviews with Palestinian and Latin American guerrillas, articles on armed European groups and communiques from the BR and the *Gruppi Armati Proletari* (Proletarian Armed Groups, (GAP)). By the time that this newspaper too ceased to exist – little more than a month later – the BR had already become an autonomously structured organization.

BR activity was initially concentrated in Milan and focused primarily on the major factories, where the contradictions were more manifest and the conflicts more acute. The choice of the location for intervention is explicitly motivated in the first of the organization's documents. In contrast to the GAP which referred to partisan resistance in the mountains, the BR declared that their aim was the 'constitution of worker nuclei in the factories and neighbourhoods of the industrial poles and in the metropolitan areas where insurrection and exploitation are most concentrated'.[6]

Meanwhile in Rome a short-lived spontaneous group was set up – which carried out various actions aimed at neo-fascist targets in the name of the BR between 1970 and 1971 – the BR attempted to extend their sphere of influence on the national territory. In 1972 it established a base in Turin. It was obviously Fiat that – with the symbolic importance of the revolt of young immigrant workers – attracted the particular attention of terrorists. Significantly, BR activity was then extended to another major industrial pole, Mestre.[7]

Given the need to find receptive ground for the initial wave of recruitment, the BR concentrated on those factories in which autonomous groups had most developed during the preceding years and where criticisms of the trade-union leadership had been most harsh. It was not by chance that the first distribution of leaflets took place at the Pirelli plant where the radical *Comitato Unitario di Base* had a certain following and at Sit Siemens where the *Gruppo di studio operai-impiegati* was set up on the extreme positions of *Gruppo di Studio Impiegati,* which had organized the first strike of technical employees.[8]

It is clear that the organizational structure of the BR changed over this period, the main transformation being the transition from semi-clandestinity to complete clandestinity. The initial practice of 'double militancy' *(doppia militanza)* – a clandestine organization coupled with the public political activity of its members – did not survive the first tests. In May 1972 the group was subject to arrests and searches. The *brigatisti* were forced to recognize the impossibility of simultaneously carrying out 'double level' activity, i.e. mass political work and underground work. The clandestinity of some members became a concrete problem at this time. Whereas until that time, only the 'tactical' and 'defensive' aspects of clandestinity had been taken into consideration, the BR now began to talk of the 'strategic scope' of clandestinity. Thus, an internal BR document written during this period states that:

Clandestinity is a necessary condition for the survival of the military offensive of the political organization that operates within the imperialist *metropoli.* Operating underground allows a marked tactical advantage over the class enemy who is instead exposed in his person and in his installations.[9]

At this point the distinction between 'regular forces' and 'irregular forces' becomes fundamental. Regular militants are those who 'work' full-time for the organization and live in clandestinity under false names even when they are not wanted by the police. Irregular militants are those whose clandestinity is limited to being a member of the organization and who live – apparently – lawfully, are normally employed and carry out lawful political activity.

On the logistic level, after the 1972 arrests, the BR were structured according to totally new criteria, seeking a better level of 'cover' and operational security. The organization acquired various properties and equipped them as 'bases'. Around each base revolved a group of people responsible for studying the various local situations, for information-gathering and for the formulation and implementation of criminal plans as they were decided upon.

Given the limited size of the BR until 1974 and the scarce territorial diffusion of action, we can say that the organizational model at this stage was still rough and experimental.[10] Nevertheless, we cannot deny the constant force within the organization to adapt such structures to changing circumstances. Thus, in addition to the *colonne* (territorial organizations linked to various *brigate*), the *fronti* were founded with the aim of politically centralizing the various sectors of intervention. First of all there was the 'logistic front' – with specific responsibility for the provision of arms, bases, car number-plates and documents – and the 'large factory front' or *fronte di massa* (mass front).[11] In fact, the control of the organization remained in the hands of its founders; in the meantime (1972–3) a new organism was set up in the form of the Executive Committee, responsible for directing and coordinating the activity of the *fronte* and the *colonne*.

A last important element in the analysis of the organization is the sociological characteristics of its members. Many *brigatisti* were recruited from within groups on the extreme left. The founders come from – as we have said – the Milan collective, *Sinistra proletaria* and from a group of ex-members of the Reggio Emilia FGCI. Among the Milan members, many – including Renato Curcio and Margherita Cagol – had been part of Marxist-Leninist groups, whereas the Emilians often came from a militant background in the PCI (such as Prospero Gallinari and Alberto Franceschini), or trade-union movement (Tonino Paroli). As regards social background, BR members do not seem to be very different from those of other political groups on the extreme left. Some militants did come from the middle or upper classes or the petit bourgeoisie, but many members of the historic nucleus *(nucleo storico)* came from working-class families or from a modest social background.

One interesting aspect of the BR is the organization's recruitment process. In this first phase particular attention was paid to small groups of the extreme left that seemed a more 'promising' source of 'proselytes'. Thus it is also thanks to the contacts made with the *Collettivo di Borgomanero* (Borgomanero Collective) that a nucleus of *brigatisti* was formed which then operated within the Turin *colonna*. The *Sinistra Proletaria del Lodigiano* – which then set itself up as *Collettivo Politico La Comune del Lodigiano* (based in Casalpusterlengo) – provided other recruits to the Milan *colonna*.[12] Useful for understanding the process of expansion of the BR during this period is therefore the reconstruction of contacts (often based on personal ties) that the terrorist group managed to make with political collectives which – on the basis of their ideology and theory of action – were not very different from many similar organizations born in the same period.

### 3.1.2 Action: the focus on factory problems

The type of actions carried out by the BR in the period under examination mirrors the needs of an organization that has to face up to the initial problems of establishing itself. Thus they avoided forms of excessively violent action that might have provoked an immediate rejection by the base to be won over. Interventions were most often where the chance of recruiting militants was greatest, i.e. large factories in industrial cities of the north. During this phase there were also numerous actions against extreme right-wing targets. It is probable that (beyond the ideological motivations) this choice was oriented to the need to justify the use of violent forms of action with a social base more willing to accept less-orthodox instruments of intervention in the anti-fascist battle rather than in factory negotiations.

The choice of the armed struggle was initially justified, primarily as a need to defend the organization against the threat of authoritarian reactions. This theme was accompanied and eventually substituted by that of the massive restructuring by which capital – according to the BR – would attempt to reabsorb the converted worker. Faced with the rejection of reformism by the proletariat on the one hand and the contradictions inherent in the development of imperialism on the other, wrote the *brigatisti,* the bourgeoisie had to 'reorganize the entire power apparatus to the right',[13] seeking to regain control over the labour force by means of the 'growing despotism of capital, a progressive militarization of the state and class conflict, and the intensification of repression as a strategic fact'.[14] In the factory the reactionary plan was expressed by 'the interweaving of two long-established and coexisting tactics: the technical restructuring of production and political perse-cution'.[15]

In this situation BR actions were oriented toward a sort of armed support of the trade-union battle. The organization sought to intervene in major factory summits, with provocative actions and 'exemplary' gestures intended to demonstrate that 'the *padroni* are vulnerable as individuals' and that the 'armed workers' can defend their victories while the hesitations of the PCI would only lead to defeat. In relation to these functions the BR defined themselves as:

> groups of armed propaganda whose fundamental task is to gain the solidarity and support of the proletarian masses for the Communist revolution ... to reveal the most hidden power structures and the conniving between power groups and/or apparently separate institutions.[16]

It is moreover stressed – and it is a characteristic peculiar to the first phase – that:

> the action of the BR is therefore always in relation to the inescapable objectives of the mass movement ... It is therefore necessary to pay the utmost attention so that the BR do not tend to constitute themselves as the 'military wing of the masses', [so that] they do not substitute themselves for them [the masses] during the struggle. Their task is in fact to stimulate the movement with action, forcing it to channel itself within the strategic prospect of the people's war, developing its strength, restoring security and renewing trust in its capacities.[17]

Simultaneously, however, the BR supported the belief that soon became 'official' BR policy: 'that class autonomy is aggregated within the armed struggle and not the other way around, because only the armed struggle expresses class power'. In the *Autointervista* (self-interview) of September 1971, the BR presented a sort of general programme in which – without denying the belief that some forms of struggle would emerge spontaneously from the 'class movement' ('organization of self-defence, initial underground work, direct action, etc.') – the need to pass from this 'necessary tactical phase' to the 'strategic phase of the armed struggle' is established. In order to make this transition the BR needed to 'realize two fundamental conditions: (1) to compete with power at all levels (freeing political prisoners, carrying out death sentences against the police, proletarian expropriations, etc.) and to show that they knew how to survive these levels of conflict; (2) to generate an alternative form of power in the factories and the working-class neighbourhoods'.[18] The history and documents of the BR in the successive years demonstrate the constant effort of the group to realize these two conditions, with the slogans on the need to 'carry forward the attack on the heart of the state' and to construct the armed party (*Partito Comunista Combattente*, PCC) as a structure of 'alternative power'.

The desire of the BR to link themselves to a broader level of social conflict is demonstrated in the choice of the targets and the forms of intervention. The targets of the main actions are all in some way connected to the factory. The first series of actions attributable to the BR took place in 1970 at the Pirelli works, while the first BR attack took place at the Sit Siemens plant – where the initial contacts were probably greater. It was at the time of the negotiation of the annual employment contract in the autumn of 1972 that the terrorist group moved from Milan to Turin. BR targets were primarily the managers most in contact with the working-class base and right-wing trade unions. Attacks were often carried out against personnel managers, security staff and heads of sections whose 'responsibility' for the repression of the workers' struggle was more immediately identifiable. In the autumn of 1970, for example, attacks were made on the cars of the central personnel manager at Sit Siemens and on the head of security and head of personnel at Pirelli Bicocca. This sort of activity continued throughout the period. Numerous arson attacks were carried out on the cars of exponents of *SIDA,* the *giallo* trade-union in the car industry,[19] and raids on the headquarters of the association. Given that the restructuring in the factory took place – according to documents distributed by the BR – using fascists as instruments of repression in the workers' struggle, the activity of the terrorist group was directed in particular against the right-wing trade-union, CISNAL. It was subsequently extended in general to include individuals and organizations of the extreme right.[20] In this way the BR were also able to pursue their objective of spreading propaganda to a broader social stratum.

With regard to the choice of objective, we should stress that in order to maximize the positive response of the group at which the propaganda was directed, the terrorists paid great attention to levelling accusations against the victims for their supposed 'crimes'. This is clear if we examine the four kidnappings carried out by the BR between 1972 and 1973. The first kidnap victim was the director of Sit Siemens, Idalgo Macchiarini, who was accused of a 'particular anti-worker rigidity' in factory negotiations. The second kidnap victim was the provincial secretary of the metalworkers' section of CISNAL of Turin, Bruno Labate, who was charged with employing right-wing thugs at Fiat. An internal document listed the 'anti-worker responsibilities' of the third kidnap victim, the director of Alfa Romeo, Michele Mincuzzi. The last kidnap victim was the head of personnel at Fiat, Ettore Amerio, who was named by Labate – or at least so the BR claimed – as the person responsible for keeping records on trade-union militants at the Turin factory. The actions were moreover justified by a practical objective: the 'trials' of kidnap victims and the documents stolen during raids, explained the *brigatisti,* helped the BR to amass information on the structure of repression in the factory, the restructuring processes and the instigators of various episodes defined by the BR as acts of provocation. Information extorted in this way was immediately 'exposed' to the unaware working class in the form of leaflets and documents.

We should finally point out that the development of the BR towards the adoption of more specifically terrorist forms of action (which go beyond the threshold – common to other groups of the extreme left operating during the same period – of generic commitment to violent techniques) came about gradually. In fact in its first two years of action, BR violence was directed exclusively against property. Arson was the most widespread form of action, while the BR indignantly rejected the accusation of destroying finished products. Between 1972 and 1974 raids took place – generally lasting only a few minutes – on the headquarters of the MSI, CISNAL and *Unione Cristiana Imprenditori e Dirigenti,* (UCID), a pressure group of managers and entrepreneurs. The first attack directed against an individual took place in the spring of 1972 with the kidnapping of Macchiarini, followed in 1973 by the three other kidnappings referred to above.

In other words, in the period under review the BR went through a preparatory stage, 'in view of the strategic phase of the armed struggle'[21] of which the Amerio kidnapping (lasting eight days) was a first example. With this crime the organization appeared to be pursuing more ambitious objectives. At this point in time we are faced with a criminal enterprise able to diffuse its message at the national level and beyond. The message was no longer aimed at a limited circle: now the interlocutors were Fiat (that is to say the summits of economic–political power as far as Italy is concerned) and the entire working class. The leaflets avenging the Amerio kidnapping, already spread by the mass media, were in fact distributed clandestinely in the factories of many cities: Turin obviously, but also Milan, Genoa, Venice, Porto Marghera, Bologna, Piacenza and Florence. The Amerio kidnapping, moreover, does not fall into the category of 'exemplary' actions that have no additional relevance once committed. It was a prolonged action with which the organization wanted (or claimed to want) to obtain something else – the suspension of the *cassa integrazione guadagni* (wage guarantee fund) then used by Fiat.

### 3.1.3 Lines of interpretation: the escalation of violence

Among the interpretations put forward to explain the birth of terrorism in Italy, three deserve consideration in relation to this first period of BR activity.

The first links the emergence of terrorism to the history of collective movements. The birth and the first actions of the BR took place during the life of a protest movement that was certainly not yet declining. Although it is true that the movement – considered as a studentesque utopia – tended towards crisis, the student protest during this period spread from one city to another, reaching the south of Italy and being reinforced in the secondary schools. The activities of the student groups soon extended to take in the 'workers' struggle'. Thus, between 1969 and 1970 groups emerged which sought to generalize the specific conflicts and to transform 'anti-authoritarian impulses' into 'anti-capitalistic actions'. Conflict in the factories went through a particularly bitter period. In many factories the 'hot autumn' broke down the barriers after years of repression. New, often radical forms of struggle also appeared.

The growth of terrorist groups at this point during the life of the protest movement may represent one of the outcomes (certainly greatly distorted) of collective tensions. During this phase the BR resembled many other groups that had been created – in other countries – on the fringes of the protest movements at the end of the 1960s: the German *Rote Armee Fraktion* (RAF), the Japanese Red Army, the US Weather

Underground and *Nouvelle Resistence Populaire* in France. Like these groups the BR were clandestine organizations generated from within a protest movement. It was this protest movement that inspired them – at least at the beginning of their activity – to establish the targets to be attacked and to adopt forms of action they then took to their extremes. Like the other groups, the choice of the armed struggle taken by the BR led to a progressive separation from the collective movements that had generated them and to a gradual, definitive abandoning of the logic of political intervention in favour of more extreme forms of the militarization of conflict.

The second hypothesis emphasizes the inability of the state to provide adequate solutions to the protest. The cry (frequently made in BR documents, but also found – albeit with different characteristics – in the ideology of the GAP) to defend against the reorganization of the apparatus of state repression is mixed with the fear of a possible *coup d'état*. Over and above the frequent references to the Piazza Fontana bombing, the writings of the BR often refer to plots for authoritarian *coup d'état (complotti golpisti):* the attempted *coup* by Valerio Borghese and the *Rosa dei Venti*.[22] The destructive manoeuvres of the right are often cited to justify the need for the armed struggle. Street demonstrations often became bloody battles with the forces of law and order and the radicalization of the clashes facilitated the diffusion of the ideology of violence. On the other hand, the Rumor government and the centre-right governments of Andreotti and Malagodi appeared unable to guarantee or reinforce public trust in state institutions.

The third hypothesis is that in this period the state apparatus was unable to deal with the struggle against terrorism on the basis of a sufficient knowledge of the phenomenon in all its components. While we still discuss the entity of the repressive pressure exercised on groups of the extreme left, the BR – practically up until 1974 – were in fact undervalued. However insufficient it may be in explaining the diffusion of terrorism in its multiple origins, it is certain that the greater or lesser efficacy of the state response was a determining factor in the reinforcement of the phenomenon.

## 3.2 The attack on the heart of the state (1974–6)

Three important characteristics emerge during this period that began with the kidnapping of Mario Sossi and finished at the end of 1976: the terrorist organization sought a national dimension; the actions against targets outside the factory became more frequent and revealing; and the development of forms of action using typically terrorist instruments was accentuated and perfected.

### 3.2.1 The organization: the national dimension

The first improvement – indispensable for a terrorist organization that has set itself the task of transforming the entire state structure – was the acquisition of a national dimension. In the Sossi kidnapping the BR, employing a tactic already used in the management of the Amerio kidnapping, sought to demonstrate they were entrenched in different territorial contexts: the action was avenged and propagandized in various central and northern Italian cities. As regards duration and characteristics, the action took on as its interlocutor the entire national public opinion.

In reality, the organization was still substantially centred on the Milan and Turin *colonne*,[23] while the structures created in the Veneto were being reinforced: but not even in Genoa was there a *real colonna* (and in fact the Sossi kidnapping was the work of militants brought in from other cities, given that *in situ* the BR at that time could only rely on the support of a few individuals). Only after the abduction of the Genoan judge (to face the 'problem of the state' better in the future) was the decision taken to 'start up an intervention' in Rome.[24] In the meantime the fusion of the BR and the *Nuclei armati proletari* (Armed Proletarian Nuclei, (NAP)) – whose actions were aimed at the poorest sections of the southern population – was going ahead (it was almost complete at the beginning of 1976). Soon, however, the rapid defeat of the latter slowed down BR's ambitions to extend the process of armed propaganda to central and southern Italy. In particular, expansion in central Italy,[25] (where small industry and the service sector predominate) and the south (where the proletariat is mostly made up of the socially marginal strata of the big cities) seemed hardly feasible for an organization 'conceived' in terms of the major industrial zones of the north.

The desire of the *brigatisti* to entrench their activity in a broader territorial context is mirrored in a greater centralization and compartmentalization of the organization. It is probable that the development of clandestine groups inevitably pushed them towards this type of organizational transformation. The 1975 'Resolution' made by the Strategic Direction stressed the need to move toward the construction of the *partito combattente,* defined as a 'party of fighting cadres ... [the] advanced division of the working class and thus a distinct and organic part of it'.[26] As explained in another document:

> In the immediate future, the fundamental aspect of the question is the construction of the fighting party as a real interpreter of the political and military needs of the 'objectively' revolutionary class stratum and the articulation of fighting organisms at the level of classes on the various fronts of the revolutionary war.[27]

The structure adopted by the organization during this phase is described in a leaflet found in a BR hideout in Piacenza in October 1974 and entitled, 'Some questions for the organizational debate'. It reaffirmed the need for clandestinity and the distinction between 'regular' and 'irregular' forces in that the former 'consist of the most aware and willing cadres produced by the armed struggle', while the basic task of the 'irregulars' is to 'win popular support for the organization, to construct the centres of articulation of revolutionary power'. Nevertheless, the relationship between the two components was not hierarchical.[28] Subsequently the Strategic Direction was proposed – a sign that it had not been previously realized[29] – in the 1974 document cited, where we read that:

> At the beginning of our history there was a nucleus of comrades who, operating revolutionary choices in the battle, won an undisputable vanguard role. This historic nucleus brought the organization to this point, subjecting – as far as possible – every basic choice, victories and defeats, to discussion among the comrades of the regular and irregular forces. Now, with the growth of the organization [in terms of] its influence, complexity and political and military responsibilities, this historic nucleus is not enough. We have had to redefine and broaden the total executive cadres of the organization. It is proposed that, following discussion with the comrades, a revolutionary council will be formed that gathers together and represents all the pressures and revolutionary energies developed in the *fronti,* the *colonne* and the irregular forces. This council will be the highest authority of the BR.[30]

The Strategic Direction thus took on tasks such as the formulation of political policy line, the passing and application of the laws governing the internal life of the group and budget management. It also named the Executive Committee, which was responsible for the day-to-day government of the organization.[31]

During this period a third *fronte* ('for the struggle against the counter-revolution') was added to the two existing ones (factory and logistic). This front was created to bring the BR offensive to the 'heart of the state' (the Sossi kidnapping represents the first action in this new direction).

At this point, the organizational structure of the BR appeared to be well-defined according to a precise model: but we must immediately stress the gap that existed in reality between theory and praxis. In theory, the organization was supposed to consist of an *hierarchically organized vertical structure (brigata-colonna-esecutivo)* and a *horizontal structure* (the *fronti*), characterized with respect to the specific competences of individual militants (factories, etc.). Again, in theory the work of the *fronti* should have been continually to analyse the sectors within their competence and to transform this knowledge into possible proposals for 'politically and socially motivated campaigns'. It was then the responsibility of the Executive Committee to make this information executive by organizing the campaigns concretely and delegating them (on the organizational level) to the individual *colonne*.[32]

In practice, however, this type of functioning was blocked by internal friction and resistance. In fact, the theoretical model of the *fronte* (on the basis of which the worker *brigatista* at Fiat was supposed to discuss and decide with the worker *brigatista* at Alfa, etc.) turned out to be irreconcilable with the dominating hierarchical structure based on the *colonne*. Above all, this conflicted with the principle of the compartmentalization of organization into *brigate* and *colonne*. The outcome was that the logistic front was limited to being a mere branch specializing in the service problems and no longer functioning as a proper front; while the mass front ended up by only existing on paper. To sum up, the organization was increasingly characterized by the imposition of a centralized and oligarchic bureaucracy. It was precisely these issues (allowing the withering away of the *fronti* and the imposition of a suffocating 'bureaucratic centralism') that gave rise to the bitter controversy that broke out at the end of the 1970s (see section 3.4.1) between the executives of the organization, on the one side, and the 'imprisoned comrades' who made up the so-called 'historic nucleus' and the various dissident groups that emerged within the BR, on the other.

The limited number of new militants recruited by the BR in this period came from small groups of the extreme left, some of them based in the big factories in the north where the BR concentrated their propaganda activity.[33] Such transitions occurred in the context of the crisis of some groups of the New Left such as *Potere Operaio* and *Lotta Continua* – and of the strengthening of the area of *Autonomia Operaia* (Worker Autonomy, (AutOp)), as a result of the process of 'autonomization' of the base committees and worker collectives in the big factories from the management of the New Left.[34] It was partly in this climate of growth, or at least improved organization, for the most radical components of the workers' movement that the BR found the right conditions for a new wave of recruitment. It is useful to remember that a substantial quota of BR recruits were workers.

A final point to be taken into consideration in evaluating the potential force of the organization during this period is the action of the state apparatuses in the struggle against terrorism. If the management of the Sossi kidnapping, according to many, increased the area of 'non-rejection' toward the BR,[35] it was, however, precisely following this episode that the state began to perceive the full force of the terrorist threat and coordinated the anti-terrorist structures in the struggle against the BR. The energy with which the repressive apparatus of the state faced the struggle against terrorism had two effects: on the one hand it pushed the BR toward an accentuation of the military aspects of defence, noticeably lowering the chances of the latter to expand its contacts in the factories; on the other hand, the ranks of the regular militants were upset by a series of arrests that brought the organization to the verge of collapse. The infiltration of a covert agent (*frate mitra* 'brother machinegun') and controls carried out on house occupant-owner registration led to the discovery of many BR hideouts and to the arrest of a great many militants.[36] It is a known fact that in the first half of 1976 the BR could only count on around ten effective members still at liberty, leaving the organization to face a profound period of crisis that could have been definitive. It was precisely at this time, however, that the restructuring of the repressive apparatus of the state, which had been organized following the Sossi kidnapping, substantially reduced the state's ability to deal with terrorism.[37]

### 3.2.2 Action: the confrontation with the state

During this period the activity of BR terrorist groups was subject to important changes: targets became more 'political', and a 'militaristic' tendency – in stark contrast to the alleged 'populist' orientation of support for the mass struggle – began to predominate in the management of BR actions. We also witnessed the progressive barbarization of the forms of action. Important innovations primarily concern the guiding 'logic' underlying terrorist action: interventions shifted from the factory to more directly political objectives, and away from 'armed defence' against an alleged 'authoritarian regression' to an attack against the so-called 'neo-golliste authoritarian attempts to change democracy',[38] while a substantial amount of organizational resources were monopolized in the confrontation with the repressive apparatus of the state.

In this period, the greater part of the victims were still chosen from the milieu of the factory; in avenging such actions the BR stressed (often with an unscrupulous twisting of the truth) those aspects that best lent themselves to the theme of struggle against the exploitation of the working class. During this period, attacks struck – among others – Vincenzo Casabona, director of personnel at Ansaldo, 'accused' of having organized the restructuring of the company; Luigi Solera, a doctor working at Fiat, 'suspected' of having allowed questionable dismissals on the pretext of absenteeism; a head of personnel at Fiat Mirafiori, Giuseppe Borello, 'responsible' for having endorsed dismissals for bad performance; and the director of Singer, Enrico Boffa, 'defined' as the main instigator of the decision to close the Leini plant. Actions were also carried out against trade unionists of *CISNAL* (right-wing trade union) and members of the *SIDA* with the clear objective of gathering consensus; the dates of the actions were often chosen to coincide with the crucial periods or deadlines in the trade-union struggle.[39] More than in the past, however, the action began to take into consideration the 'political' level of the capitalist system.

The BR tried to give an ideological justification to the shift of attention to more directly political targets. State intervention in the economy was defined as an attempt to combat the lowering of the profit rate: in the face of the crisis, state institutions would be assigned the task of raking-in the social value added for the multinationals. In the 1975 Strategic Resolution the BR wrote that:

The state takes on in the economic field the functions of a large bank in the service of great imperialistic multinational groups. It is the direct expression of the big imperialist multinational groups, with a national pole. The state becomes, that is, the specific function of the capitalist development in the multinational phase; it is the imperialist state of the multinationals.[40]

The pursuit of new and more 'political' objectives was presented as a response to the manoeuvres of the owners:

> If in the factories *Autonomia Operaia* is sufficiently strong and organized to be able to maintain a permanent state of insubordination and to win a permanent space for power as it grows, outside the factory it is still weak to the point of being unable to put up resistance to the forces of counter-revolution. For this reason the forces of the counter-revolution tend to shift the main contradictions [to] outside the factory. One must respond to the strategic encircling of the workers' struggle by extending the revolutionary initiative to the vital centres of the state; this is not a voluntary choice, but an indispensible choice to maintain the offensive in the factory too.[41]

Outside the factory, the target of action was frequently the *DC* (*Democrazia Cristiana,* Christian Democratic Party): held to be the body primarily responsible for the authoritarian *neo-gollista* plan for institutional reform, of which the BR talk at length in their documents. 'This plan,' they wrote again taking up a theme much discussed at the time, 'aims at the transformation of the republic born out of the Resistance in the sense of the creation of a presidential republic'.[42] Given that the realization of this programme would have implied a 'rigid control of social forces' and a 'growing militarization of power', the BR talked of a 'counter-revolutionary adjustment': 'the counter-revolutionary initiative' – they maintained – 'is today taken on in the first person by a power bloc within the state: it is above all against this force that we must launch our hardest attacks'.[43]

Activity planned to 'counter' *neo-gollista* plans included the raids on the headquarters of the *Centro Resistenza Democratica* of the right-winger Edgardo Sogno and the *Centro Studi Don Sturzo of Turin,* headed by a political figure from the right of the *DC,* Giuseppe Costamagna. The BR also injured the leader of the *DC* councillor group in Milan, Massimo De Carolis.

Besides the objective to 'beat the *DC,* organized centre of reaction', the resolution of the directive organism stressed the need to 'attack the state at its weakest links, dislocate its centres, free the comrades in prison, carry out reprisals against the judiciary of the regime'. Hence the BR planned and carried out the kidnapping of the magistrate, Mario Sossi. But the well-placed blows that the forces of law and order began to inflict on the BR forced the organization to defend itself. The BR were forced to plan activity connected with problems inside the organization, which did not reflect the needs of the social struggle and the level of awareness of the working-class base they wanted to influence. In addition to premeditated actions (attacks on *carabinieri* barracks, raids on the offices of the district inspectorate of the Institutions of Prevention and Punishment in Milan and the Sossi kidnapping) we must add, to complete the balance of this type of activity, the deadly gun battles that members of the BR engaged in with the forces of law and order to avoid arrest.[44]

Finally, the forms of action were subject to major transformation. On the one hand they continued to use types of intervention already experimented with in the preceding period: attacks on the cars of intermediate company cadres and members of the rightist trade-union hierarchy; raids on the headquarters of political and professional organizations (presented as information-gathering activity to uncover the hidden articulation of repression); political kidnappings (such as those of Sossi and Casabona) that served simultaneously to gather information and to 'punish' the most exposed 'reactionaries'. On the other hand, in addition to these elements of continuity, there is a major innovation linked to the use of arms. In the preceding period, machine-guns and pistols were only used as a means of intimidation to immobilize the public during a raid or to threaten the victims during a kidnapping. Whereas in this second period, arms were used directly against individuals in order to wound and kill. The BR carried out and claimed responsibility for five actions of premeditated injury.[45] The use of arms against individuals was probably a threshold beyond which BR fanaticism no longer recognized possible limits to striking the good of physical integrity. The first cases of woundings are recorded alongside the first assassinations. In Padua on 17 June 1974 a raid on the provincial headquarters of the *MSI (Movimento Sociale Italiano*, a right-wing neo-fascist party) ended with the killing of two right-wing militants. Responsibility for the assassination was claimed by the BR but it was presented as a simple 'work accident'. Nevertheless, in the leaflet claiming responsibility for the two homicides, the BR wrote that 'the revolutionary forces from Brescia onwards are legitimate to respond to fascist brutality with the armed justice of the proletariat'.[46]

In addition, until the assassination of the General Public Prosecutor of Genoa, Francesco Coco, and two members of his bodyguard, the killings had not been premeditated but took place – as we have seen – during clashes with the forces of law and order in the attempt to avoid arrest. The June 1976 terrorist attacks in Genoa are a watershed as regards overcoming a further threshold in the unstoppable brutalizing process of the shift to more typical forms of terrorist violence. Far from being proof of the concrete force of the clandestine organization, the triple assassination constituted a criminal 'bet' as to the organizational ability of the BR to concentrate the forces of all regular militants who had avoided arrest (around ten) in the execution of an undertaking so sensational as to 'relaunch' the BR, making it appear still firmly in place and growing, regardless of the imprisonment of its 'historic leaders' (who were simultaneously on trial at the Turin Assize Court). Unfortunately, the BR plan was successful, thanks also to the conspicuous self-financing obtained by the kidnapping of the industrialist Costa. The already-noted restructuring of the repressive apparatus of the state (with respect to the patterns of intervention adopted after the Sossi kidnapping) constituted objective causes of delay in the struggle against the newly-emerging BR.

### 3.2.3 Lines of interpretation: terrorism in the economic crisis

In order to analyse the development of the BR in this period we need to look at variables that are external to the organization and variables that are internal to it.

As regards the first type of variable, it is possible that the crisis of the protest movements that emerged in the preceding period reflected on the affairs of the BR. The protest slackened off in the universities; the fragile organizations that made up the panorama of the extraparliamentary left disappeared after a few attempts at short-lived alliances; the electoral deadline was met without success; the 'petrol crisis' of 1973 and the politics of austerity that followed constituted difficult new problems for the trade unions – inflation, the *cassa integrazione* and the decentralization of production. The low level of mobilization produced an 'excess of militancy':[47] that is, it freed an area of ex-militants, who had lost faith in legal forms of collective behaviour and who consequently constituted a possible source of recruits for clandestine organizations.

Another element that could have contributed to broadening the area of those who had lost faith in traditional politics, potential context of reference of the subversive organizations, was singled out by some in the line of the 'historic compromise' adopted by the PCI. According to this hypothesis, terrorist violence would emerge as a reaction to the social pact as a sort of 'symbolic surrogate to [the] class struggle'.[48] Once again in relation to the problems posed by the 'historic compromise', others have reflected on the peculiar activation of the BR every time the power relations in Italy tend to change in any way that differs from the traditional one.[49] Given this hypothesis, the suggestion has been made to examine terrorism as the product of external – foreign – forces: a question that is still open but beyond the scope of this essay.[50]

Even considering the enormous importance of contextual variables, we believe that the evolutionary process of the BR in this phase cannot be fully understood without a reconstruction of the internal dynamics of the clandestine organization. The path followed by the BR – and in an even more rapid way by the NAP (Armed Proletarian Nuclei)[51] whose existence did not last for more than a couple of years – is similar to that of other armed groups in the industrial democracies. Because of the very logic of clandestine action, the terrorist organization gradually lost all contact, both material and ideological, with reality. Because of the need to withdraw from state repression, the BR became separated from the places of collective action. For example, many militants recruited in factories were forced to leave their jobs for fear of being arrested. This consequently lowered the ability and ambition of the underground organization to carry out 'political agitation' and to influence the choices of the mass movement. To compensate for the organizational weakness, the BR accentuated their utilization of terrorist violence, with the result that they were stigmatized by the very social strata from which they expected support. Gradually as the survival of the organization increasingly tended to depend on the outcome of direct clashes with the forces of law and order, the fate of the groups seemed to be sealed. We shall consider this point in more detail in the last part of the chapter. For the time being it is enough to point out that by this time there were already signs of this sort of development, despite the relaunching of the organization apparently caused by the Genoa attacks in 1976.

## 3.3 The strategy of destruction (1977–8)

The fresh outbursts of violence in 1977 and 1978 essentially set Italian terrorism apart from – initially analogous – phenomena present in other industrial democracies in the same decade.[52] The violent generation of some collective phenomena emerging between the end of 1976 and the beginning of 1977 supply a new base potential to the clandestine organizations that seemed – at the end of the preceding period – in a phase of decline. The emergence of a new area of recruitment produced broad changes both in the organizational structure and in the extent and type of terrorist action.

### 3.3.1 The organization: the Partito Comunista Combattente

At the beginning of this period the objective of BR activists was the organization of the broad but dishomogeneous and dislocated area of those who were willing to carry out armed action. With this end in mind, the plan to create the *Partito Comunista Combattente* (PCC) was launched. In April 1977, the BR wrote that a vanguard had developed within the proletarian strata, and that this vanguard had 'adopted the armed struggle for communism as its focus of action [and] thus has formed a true – albeit dispersed – movement of struggle, [which] due to its intensity and political maturity has made the preliminary steps toward civil war and the people's war'.[53] In June of the same year the organization stressed the need for the struggle to take a more revolutionary direction:

> Together with this richness and complexity there is still a marked dispersion of forces, caused by the particularistic placing of many armed vanguards

which basically fight within the narrow limits of the specific situations of which they are an expression.[54]

It is this function of guide party that the BR would like to achieve; and the document goes on to state that:

> to transform the oblique process of a diffused and disorganized civil war, into a general direct offensive of a unitary plan, it is necessary to develop and unify the *Movimento Proletario di Resistenza Offensiva* constructing a fighting party.[55]

While the emergent terrorist organizations attempted – in contrast to the NAP – to give themselves an alternative structure to that experimented by the armed groups in the past, for the realization of the plan outlined above, the *brigatisti* substantially reproposed the same organizational model already expressed in the document found in the Piacenza hideout four years before.[56] There were nevertheless some changes; the principles appear to be the following:

1) There was a clarification of the distinction between regular and irregular members: this was no longer exclusively linked to the clandestine condition of individuals and the division between the two types of militants increasingly reflected the difference between those who dedicated themselves totally to the organization and those who only carried out occasional tasks; there was also the introduction of a new figure, the 'legal regular': that is, a militant who continued to live using his own personal particulars (name, date of birth, etc.), but who 'worked' full-time in the organization.
2) The territorial articulation acquired more precise referents, now being able to count on five *colonne:* beyond those 'traditional' ones in Milan, Turin and the Veneto, the by now autonomous Genoa *colonna* and the new *colonna* set up in Rome.
3) The BR sought to react to the striking discrepancy between theory and praxis that had in the past prevented the *fronti* from functioning coherently with a decentralized vision of the organization. But the solution was a mere mechanical reproposition of previous models: the only variation was that the *fronti* were reduced to two (logistic and mass, the latter also referred to as the *Fronte della controrivoluzione*). The growing number of militants in prison and their tendency to organize themselves in the so-called *brigate di campo* pushed the BR to build up a 'prison front'.[57]

Once again, however, the oligarchic and centralized formulation predominated in the end: in fact the power was concentrated above all in the Executive Committee, while the fronts were reduced to a sort of 'under-executive', without really being able to run the organization along horizontal lines. It is clearly not sufficient to write that 'the *fronti* are the vehicles of the political policy of the organization, that link up with the poles of intervention *(colonne),* where these [the latter] adopt a class role which is intermediated with the general line and articulated with the reality of the movement'.[58] In reality, the BR increasingly resembled an absolute monarchy, where the executive controlled, coordinated and directed everything.

Even if in this phase the BR were unable to accomplish the objective of centralizing and coordinating different instances of the *Movimento Proletario di Resistenza Offensiva (MPRO)* toward the constitution of the *PCC,* in the middle period the *brigatisti* nevertheless gathered the fruits of their improved organizational structures, surviving longer than other scattered terrorist groups.[59] In this period, however, the frequency and territorial diffusion of actions for which the BR claimed responsibility already testify to a marked reinforcement of the terrorist organization. While in the two preceding phases terrorist activity had been sporadic – being concentrated in the winter months and with long silences between one action and another – from the beginning of 1977 it resumed with continuity and virulence, with only very brief pauses between the end of July and the beginning of September. Sporadic interventions were replaced by 'campaigns': actions carried out simultaneously by different *colonne* against the same type of target.

At this point it would be interesting to find out where the *brigatisti* managed to recruit members in this period and how they were able to reconstruct an organization that appeared to be compromised. A commonplace that often emerges in the analyses on the 'second wave' of terrorism is the difference between the 'historical' *brigatisti* and those of the new generation. The assertion does not seem refutable. Since, as various witnesses confirm, between 1975 and 1976 police and *carabinieri* succeeded in inflicting severe blows on the organization of the BR, and less than ten regular *brigatisti* were still at large at the end of 1976, we can assert that the membership of the main terrorist organization of the left underwent a radical transformation immediately afterwards. Almost all the terrorists of the 'first generation' were in prison.[60] Even if, at the beginning of the period, the *brigatisti* of the oldest militancy maintained the key posts in the organization, they shared the leadership with subsequently recruited militants.[61] Moreover, the composition of the 'base' militants was greatly renewed and some of their characteristics were changing. It is above all obvious that the *brigatisti* that joined the organization during this period are nearly always younger: while in the previous period the main defendants in the BR trials were born in the period 1945–50, the new recruits were born between 1950 and 1955.

Only more specific research on the political courses taken by militant members of the armed struggle can tell us what weight the already mentioned crises of some New Left groups (above all, *Potere Operaio* and *Lotta Continua*) had in the recruitment of the terrorist organizations. To cite just a few examples, Walter Alasia, who died in a gun battle with the police at the end of 1976 as well as many of the militants of the NAP and *Prima Linea* (PL), not to mention those left over from the autonomous factory collectives and the degeneration of the most violent groups of the 1977 university movement, had belonged to *Lotta Continua*.

### 3.3.2 Action: the 'dislocation of the system'

Under the impact of external events, and partially as a consequence of some internal developments, the BR transformed (at times accentuating a process already in action) their strategy (from 'armed propaganda' to 'unleashing civil war'); their targets (the factory to the 'heart of the state'); their definition of the enemy (from *neo-gollismo* to social democracy); their tactics (from 'hit-and-run' to 'dislocation of the apparatus'); and their forms of intervention (from 'punitive actions' to 'destruction').[62]

The assassination of the General Public Prosecutor, Coco – though this took place in the previous phase – represented a tragic 'bridge' in the transition from actions of armed propaganda to actions intended to 'dislocate' the state structures. The objective was no longer the mere 'exposure' of the hidden manoeuvrings of power or the 'punishment' of enemies of the collective movement; the terrorist organization set itself the task of attacking and destroying capitalist power itself. The image of the enemy also changed. At the beginning of their history the BR had sought to take on the role of vanguard of the movement, also comprising the institutional components of the left. Starting in the mid-1970s, trade-union leaders and *Berlingueriani* (followers of the general secretary of the PCI, Enrico Berlinguer) were considered as the enemies to be beaten. The bourgeois state, we read in the resolution of the Strategic Direction in 1978, alternatively utilizes fascism or social democracy. Where in the past the state had made attempts at authoritarian actions, the present plan was instead a neo-corporatist pact that assigned the task of controlling the working class to the trade unions: in this situation, the armed struggle was the only possible instrument of insurrection against the system. The painstaking ideological work carried out by the BR was partly mirrored by some transformations in the political order. Above all, the ideological shifts served to rationalize the isolation with respect to the social strata to which the organization referred.

The transition from armed propaganda to the logic of 'destruction' implied a transformation in the forms of action. In actions targeting the factory the contrast with respect to the initial activity is clear: in the beginning the choice of each victim was meticulously 'justified' with the listing of the personal 'crimes' of which – according to the BR – he was guilty, but in this period the BR instead attacked at random among the thousands of executives and intermediate cadres of the largest firms. During this two-year period (1977–8) the BR thus carried out eighteen woundings and one assassination among the personnel at Fiat and Lancia in Turin, Sit Siemens, Alfa Romeo, Breda and Pirelli in Milan, Italsider and Ansaldo in Genoa. Two industrialists were moreover injured by the *brigatisti*. In none of these actions were the BR concerned to stress – even if only for the sake of propaganda – the 'responsibility' of the victims.

Individuals came under attack merely because, in carrying out a task in a complex mechanism, they were symbols of the system that the BR wanted to destroy.[63] By striking indiscriminately the members of certain social groups, the terrorists aimed to promote a generalized sense of terror in order to block at various points the functioning of some 'command systems'.

With the 'cooling-off' of the factory conflicts, the terrorist organization cut itself off from the objectives of the trade-union struggle and its actions tended to be more frequently directed against political objectives. To this end, the BR pursued a pattern of action that differed from the one carried out by the scattered terrorist groups. Where the latter attacked the symbols of a diffused power that penetrated the private spheres of the individual's life – striking gynaecologists, psychiatrists and drug dealers, for example – the BR focused on the DC, singled out as the 'national expression' of the agreement between the capitalist regimes towards the constitution of the 'imperialist state of multinationals'. In this period the actions against the largest government party followed two separate logics. On one hand, a good twelve municipal and regional DC councillors were injured, which demonstrates the will of the BR to persevere in their programme of dislocating the state apparatus by means of a detailed action of intimidation of political personnel at the intermediate level.[64] This first tactic was exemplified in the well-known slogan of the day 'strike one to educate a hundred'. On the other hand, actions were directed, with a greater logic of 'direct confrontation', at the physical elimination of those political opponents considered to pose the greatest threat to the terrorist plan. This was the logic of the most serious and emblematic crime of the entire period: the abduction of the president of the DC, Aldo Moro, that cost the life of five of his bodyguards and – after a long and dramatic kidnapping – his own death.[65] Heedless of their isolation – or perhaps in an extreme attempt to react to it – the BR attempted to engage in a confrontation with the state based on the military logic of the maximization of the real losses of the enemy. The abduction by the BR had had a double objective: to mobilize the various armed groups working in Italy, pushing them to intensify their actions and to 'raise the level of attack', and to provoke a climate of civil war that would facilitate some form of legitimation of the underground organization by the state institutions. Given the enormous disproportion between the forces employed, this ambitious plan failed and the outcome of Aldo Moro's kidnapping was – quite the opposite – an explosive factor of crisis. Not only did the BR fail to obtain any type of recognition from the institutions, but the decision to kill the hostage also produced strong controversy both among the militants of other clandestine groups and within the organization itself.

With their ambitions to find new recruits, the BR, we shall see more clearly in the following period, turned their attention to new groups that had taken the strategy of violent action on board, especially the groups of the so-called *terrorismo diffuso* (see Note 59). In the documents of this period, the BR talked about subjects – partially outside the factory – who had already chosen the road to civil war.[66] To lend theoretical dignity to the redefinition of their potential base, the resolution of the Strategic Direction of 1978 contained a long section dedicated to the analysis of the class structure in the society of mature capitalism. According to what the *brigatisti* wrote, in the large industry only the unskilled worker would have revolutionary interests, while the professional workers would have reformist ambitions. The best allies of the mass worker would thus be found outside the factory: among the manual-service workers, the 'industrial reserve army' and the marginal proletariat. According to the BR, from these groups would emerge those armed but dispersed struggles that the *Partito Comunista Combattente* hoped to unify. Various actions were aimed at influencing these social groups and at 'hegemonizing' the clandestine groups born after the 1977 movement. The most emblematic of them was probably the wounding of the Dean of the Faculty of Economy and Commerce at the University of Rome, which took place during the worst phase of disorder at the university. In addition, the campaign against journalists carried out at the beginning of June 1977, which led to the tragic and fatal attack on the vice-director of *La Stampa,* Carlo Casalegno, probably aimed at building up 'prestige' to impress the members of the small clandestine groups.[67]

Finally, there was an increase in the number of actions that expressed the war declared against the repressive apparatus of the state. The BR were responsible for a number of assassinations against the police and the judiciary, which during this period paid the tragic price of fifteen human lives. In this respect we should also mention the appalling series of crimes carried out by the BR to prevent the carrying out of the Turin trial against the so-called historical heads – or 'founding fathers' – of the organization. The assassination of the General Public Prosecutor Coco in June 1976 had prevented the continuation of the trial. In April 1977, the assassination of the Turin lawyer, Fulvio Croce, prevented the formation of a jury and the trial was postponed for a second time. In March 1978, the Assize Court of Turin was reconvened for a third time. The new trial session was accompanied, outside the court, by attacks programmed with inexorable cynicism: the homicide of Marshal Berardi, precisely at the beginning of the trial; the tragic events connected with the kidnapping of Moro; and the killing of Commissario Esposito, which was 'placed' in such a way as to coincide with the time of the court's final decision. This time, however, the trial took place and the BR suffered a heavy political defeat. The terrorist group claimed that the Turin trial was not 'a' trial but *the* trial of the armed struggle: and that the armed struggle could not – in reality – be tried. The BR then set themselves two objectives: to intimidate those (judges, juries and court-defence lawyers) responsible for carrying out the trial; and to demonstrate that the state would only be able to finish the trial if it rejected the application of democratic rules, thus revealing the 'true' authoritarian nature of a state based on the arbitrary repression of 'dissent'. The painstaking respect for democratic legality, instead, made a considerable contribution to instilling elements of crisis into the terrorist groups.

The attempt at 'dislocation' was moreover directed against the Ministry of Justice and the prisons. Forced by the creation of the maximum-security prisons to put aside any plan to free their imprisoned comrades, the brigatisti fell back on an alarming series of kidnappings and serious crimes against members of the judiciary and prison officers.[68] This ended with an attack that was an emblematic example of the BR's new 'logic': the killing, in an attack under the walls of Carceri Nuove in Turin, of two policemen on external-security duty.

The attempt to influence the area of the armed struggle with such actions and the increasing physical confrontation with the repressive apparatus of the state converged in bringing about more and more violent forms of action. This transformation in the forms of action was ideologically justified as a transition from 'armed peace' to 'unfurling civil war':

Dislocating the forces of the enemy means an attack whose main objective is still that of the propaganda of the armed struggle and its need, but in it already begins to work also the tactical principle of the next phase: the destruction of enemy forces ... Dislocating the enemy forces is therefore [the logic of action in] the last period of the phase of armed propaganda [which will] progressively usher in that of the revolutionary civil war.[69]

In a tragically coherent way this new phase heralded — with respect to previous years — the increasing violence of the tactics employed. Various reasons could explain this progressive barbarization. In the first place, the woundings and the assassinations probably aimed at demonstrating technical efficiency in order to hegemonize an area already inclined toward the armed struggle. Secondly, the assassinations allowed the BR to keep public attention focused on terrorist activity. Thirdly — and particularly in the subsequent phase — the increasing brutality derived from the 'anger' generated by the incipient political crisis within the organization and from the belief that such a crisis could be hidden by repeatedly raising the 'military' level of confrontation. We should finally remember that the plan for greater military 'efficiency' in the actions has been explicitly theorized in the documents of the organization. In an attempt ideologically to rationalize the escalation of terror, the BR wrote that:

At the beginning and because we were forced to do so, we operated in small nuclei and carried out small actions. Then, as the guerrilla warfare became stronger and better established, we went on to more complex actions that simultaneously employed — but always in small actions — more nuclei. [The stage] beyond guerrilla warfare [directed] the use of campaigns, that is, [the organization of actions] simultaneously in more poles on the same line of battle. This is a guiding principle for the growth of guerrilla warfare. A second guiding principle was that of the transition from quick actions *('mordi e fuggi')* to 'prolonged actions' (Amerio, Sossi, Costa). That allowed us to carry out more incisive armed propaganda and to demonstrate to the movement of resistance the levels reached by guerrilla warfare in the organization of proletarian power. It moreover allowed us to multiply the contradictions within the state. A third guiding principle, finally, was that of the rapid concentration of numerous forces to attack the enemy in small battles (Casale, Coco). The restructuring of the Imperialist State of the Multinationals is characterized by its militarization and by the concentration of military forces in defence of its vital organs. Developing the revolutionary initiative to [bring about] the political and military dislocation of this apparatus involves the adoption of new combat techniques that foresee and make present from now on, the fundamental aspect of the civil war: the destruction of the imperialist forces.[70]

### 3.3.3 Lines of interpretation: political violence and the 1977 movement

The reorganization of the BR after the serious crisis of the preceding period was undoubtedly connected to the emergence of new collective, and quite soon, violent unrest. Hence the debate on the history of Italy's main terrorist group partly coincides with that of the origins of the 1977 protest and the reasons for its degeneration.

According to one interpretation, the deviation of the protest movement at the beginning of the period toward violent forms of action was not so much linked to the 'intrinsic nature' of the protest but rather to its destructive dynamics. The factor that sparked off protest was the proposal for university reform, which the students defined as the reactionary attempt to destroy a series of victories won from 1968 onwards. In the movement, however, we find flowing together – from the first phase of its existence – a series of political initiatives that took place outside the school and the factory: the circles of the young proletariat, the *consultori* (advisory health centres for women) born out of the feminist movement, the patrols against drug dealers, the committees for the 'self-reduction' of electricity bills or cinema tickets and the first 'free radio stations'. The ideology of the new protest was more open to the issues of the post-industrial society – the extension of the dominion of the (state) apparatus over the most private spheres of individual life and the reappropriation of the repressed needs of physical and personal subjectivity – and critical of the so-called *economicismo* (strictly economic interpretation of Marxism) of the New Left. The new political groups refused the organizational model of the Marxist-Leninist group, and mistrusted some of the more traditional forms of protest.

Two solutions were adopted in the search for more effective instruments of intervention. One part of the movement – which took the form of the 'metropolitan indians' at the height of the protest,[71] but whose precursors must be looked for in the women's movement – stressed spontaneity and imagination. Another component of the movement was influenced by the escalation of violence that began with the street clashes with police and fascists (from car-jack attacks to molotov cocktails and from molotovs to the use of high firepower pistols, like P-38). The presence of terrorist groups also helped this escalation by providing the justifications for the use of violence. Some episodes of repression in the spring of 1977 probably had an impact on the radicalization of the protest.[72] With the movement's inability to find intermediate objectives on which to develop the protest, and in isolation from other political and social forces, it was the most violent wings of the collectives of *Autonomia* that came to dominate the other components. After a few months of life the movement was already irremediably split: meetings became impossible when the more violent elements began to deal with internal clashes by physical violence and all attempts to propagandize the reasons for the protest externally were abandoned. By 1978 the movement was in full crisis: if one component gave up political involvement and returned to private life or more cultural forms of action, other fringes took the road of no return into clandestinity. As already stated, it was to these groups, which were already well-disposed towards the illegal practice of political intervention, that the BR turned their attention for recruits. The new *brigatista* thesis of the transition from armed propaganda to civil war came from the growth of what the BR defined as the *movimento di resistenza proletario offensivo*:[73] that is:

> the area of antagonistic class behaviour caused by the worsening of the economic and political crisis ... the area of the forces, groups and revolutionary nuclei that give a political-military content to their initiatives of anti-capitalist, anti-imperialist, anti-revisionist and pro-communist struggle.[74]

The rapid degeneration of the collective movement of 1977 was also analysed in reference to the conditions of the political system; we have already mentioned the thesis of a 'blocked' political system and the absence of an institutional opposition. The Italian political class was accused of being 'unable to carry out its tasks if not in a repetitive way, [or] to renew itself conforming to new needs or new stimuli, to develop and to regulate itself'.[75] Moreover, the PCI (engaged in the politics of 'institutional inclusion'), the trade unions (forced to cope with the difficulties of managing an economic crisis), and the political formations of the New Left were all politically unable to organize the new social groups and to represent their interests.

This interpretation, however, needs to be more carefully examined. In this case, the protest takes on violent characteristics because of the very characteristics of its social base. The 1977 movement was often described as a movement of the *Lumpenproletariat* – that is, of those who were socially alienated or in insecure employment. Sometimes the most specifically economic aspects of these definitions are uppermost; at other times there is an emphasis on the appearance of new value systems. An initial analysis of the characteristics of the *brigatisti* arrested after 1977 does not confirm the hypothesis of an 'entrenching' of terrorism among socially alienated groups.[76] While the percentage of unemployed among the arrested is irrelevant, from the data available it turns out that, before the final transition to clandestinity, many *brigatisti* were part of the central work-market (employed in large factories or the public sector), with manual workers, but also intellectuals (teachers, technicians, etc.) and professionals. As far as the participation of students is concerned (this group constituted a considerable if not the main component of the membership of the organization) and the appearance of new collective protagonists (carriers of alternative value systems with respect to both those proposed by bourgeois culture and those widespread in working-class culture), we limit ourselves to observing that the phenomena of intellectual unemployment and the rejection of industrial society are not peculiar to the Italian situation. The theories that attempt to explain terrorism as the mechanical effect of social marginality are hence unable to offer any explanation of the specific consequences this phenomenon has produced in Italy.

## 3.4 The 'military' confrontation with the state for the survival of the organization (1979–82)

This period began with the murder of the trade unionist Guido Rossa in January 1979; it witnesses the second and more marked political and, subsequently, organizational collapse of the BR. While the political plan to involve the working class in the armed conflict clearly failed, state repression began to inflict incisive defeats on the clandestine organization. The terrorist groups found themselves even more isolated by the crisis of the youth protest and increasingly concentrated their resources on the military defence of their members and the survival of the organization. If in 1979 the BR – regardless of their political defeats – managed to maintain a certain organizational force, from 1980 the drop in their offensive capacity was vertical. The isolation and the defeats accentuated the internal divisions and multiplied the number of defections. In spite of some successful actions from the military point of view and the consistent recruitment among the survivors of scattered terrorist groups, the BR were unable to halt their own crisis.

### 3.4.1 The organization: internal factions and inter-group war

Up until the preceding period, the organization had more or less remained intact (and had made great efforts to appear so), but in the period beginning in 1979 we see a series of internal splits and divisions, with long-lasting reciprocal antagonisms that sometimes ended in death threats and in the rather pathetic invitation to adopt a sort of federalism of armed groups that was not followed up. While it formally maintained the compartmentalized and centralized structure that had characterized it in the past, the old organization of the BR broke down under the blows of exacerbated internal divisions. With the rapid decline of the 1977 movement and the equally rapid decline of the scattered terrorist groups, the hopes of a generalized guerrilla war vanished. At the same time, the BR found themselves confronted with a certain number of militants but without any political reference point for action. The solution adopted was to define the armed struggle as autonomous with respect to other forms of 'class struggle', up to the point where it was considered the only possible form of the defence of the proletarian masses. The roots of the marked internal divisions during this period are certainly to be found in the situation of open political crises the BR had already begun to experience in the period immediately preceding the murder of Aldo Moro. The conflicts that shattered the group – apart from personal struggles for leadership[77] – were symptoms of dissatisfaction with the manifest isolation of the organization. A common element among the splinter groups was – probably not incidentally – the reciprocal accusation of *militarismo,* understood as a separation-off from the political logic of intervention i.e. the extremist tendency to use exclusively military arguments to justify the armed struggle.

The first split within the organization appeared in 1979. In a document published in July by the New Left daily, *Lotta Continua,* a group of dissenters – the most well-known being Adriana Faranda and Valerio Morucci, both ex-members of *Potere Operaio* – accused the historical leaders (nearly all imprisoned in Asinara) of having broken off all contact with the reference base. These dissenters, defined by the press as *movimentisti* (favouring collective movements irrespective of its political contents), levelled the criticism of *vetero-stalinismo* (outdated-Stalinism) and *vetero-operaismo* (outdated emphasis on the 'worker tradition') against the orthodox BR, the first because of its conception of the party as an external vanguard and the second because of its mechanical deduction of the central importance of the worker from the notion of productive work. The group headed by Faranda and Morucci deplored the fact that the *fronte di massa* did not function properly; they stressed the need for involvement in the 'new sectors of political intervention which are developing beyond the big factories and the hegemonic figure of the "mass worker"', sectors in which Communism 'already exists as an affirmation of the 'socialized individual' against all forms of delegation, [and which is] rich in critical ability and the willingness to enjoy the riches provided by the development of productive forces'.[78] According to this splinter group, the armed struggle needed to follow the rhythms of growth and development of the new social subject, while the assassination of Moro had represented instead the breaking-off of the focus on the work among the masses.

The response of the orthodox BR to the criticisms of 'young master Morucci and Miss Faranda' was severe. In a document dated July 1979 the *brigatisti* in prison in Asinara hotly restated criticisms of the groups belonging to *Autonomia,* reaffirmed the centrality of the factory worker against the thesis of the 'socialized worker' and stressed the need for the party to unite against 'armed spontaneity'. Despite this, only a few months later, it was precisely the main exponents of the first-generation *brigatisti* who began to argue with the external group led by Mario Moretti. In the autumn of 1979, the imprisoned first-generation members of the BR demanded the dismissal of the standing Executive Committee. It was accused of bureaucratic and military deviation, of being unable to mediate with the masses (particularly at Fiat), of the bad management of the Moro kidnapping and of excluding imprisoned militants from participating in the internal debate on the future of the organization. After the initial clash the fracture was diplomatically patched up, but the *brigatisti* of the historic nucleus nevertheless became willing to support the setting up of other breakaway groups within the organization.

The group headed by Curcio and Franceschini in some way favoured the setting up of the *colonna* Walter Alasia in Milan as an autonomous clandestine group in contrast to the official BR. In the meeting of the Strategic Direction of 1980, a nucleus of the Walter Alasia *colonna* called for the resignation of 'Moretti and company' – as the first-generation *brigatisti* had done beforehand – accusing the leaders of being responsible for the loss of contacts with the workplace and with the working class. The appearance of the first symptoms of insubordination constituted a serious risk for a military-type organization such as the BR. The leaders of the organization certainly realized this and after the expulsion of the rebel *colonna* an entire document was dedicated to the episode, significantly entitled 'Beat liquidationist opportunism and defeatist ideology'. While the Executive Committee criticized the Walter Alasia group for its 'theoretical incompetence' and 'negative attitude', it interpreted the split within the organization as the consequence of the difficulties of managing the transition from the armed propaganda to civil war. The orthodox BR defined the split as:

> the infantile reaction of [those] who, faced with the tactical difficulties of the revolution, stop reasoning. In this way the political struggle is reduced to the confrontation of banally personalized power.[79]

Finally, the historic nucleus also supported the last and most serious splinter group, founded in the spring-summer of 1981: that of the *Fronte carceri* of Senzani, which generated the *Partito della Guerriglia del*

*Proletariato Metropolitano* (Guerrilla Party of the Metropolitan Working Class). Here again, the main accusation made by the group against the leadership concerned the loss of any sort of contact with the protest movement. This line of argument, which helps to explain the conflict of power at the top leadership level, probably mirrored – as in other cases – a widespread unease over the unstoppable loss of any hope of influencing a broader protest movement. Its ambition to find a new base of reference pushed the *Partito-Guerriglia* into turning its attention to the marginal proletariat of the great southern metropoli. In concrete terms – as for the Walter Alasia group – this ambition only produced an accentuation of the savageness of the actions carried out. A document formulated by ex-terrorists states that:

> this struggle between factions within the BR highlights how the populist tendency of the OCC *(Organizzazioni Comuniste Combattenti)* to try to obtain the solidarity of the masses, gaining their solidarity with actions supporting the class struggle, and the militaristic tendency to attack the political and military structures of power, in a sort of private war, are nothing other than two sides of the same coin; they are used at different times by the same organization or faction, or the various organizations or factions are counterposed on the two choices in a game of constantly inverting roles.[80]

Factionism, however, was not the only result of the political crisis of the organization. Many *brigatisti,* mistrusting what remained of the collapse of the initial plan that had motivated their choice of the armed struggle and encouraged by the concessions that a law approved *ad hoc* afforded those collaborating with justice or who publicly renounced their past as terrorists, broke their pact of association with the terrorist organization. The confessions of the *pentiti* brought about the arrest of terrorists and supporters and the discovery of a series of hideouts.

From 1980 (the year of the arrest and subsequent confession of the first 'big repentant', Patrizio Peci) the erosion of the BR structure – whatever the name assumed by the various splinter groups – became constant and unstoppable all over Italy. Despite the occasional – and sometimes savage – renewal of the criminal offensive,[81] between the end of 1981 and the beginning of 1982 the failure of the campaign to kidnap Fiat manager, Cesare Romiti, and the freeing of the Nato general, James Lee Dozier, confirmed a further collapse of the *Partito-Guerriglia* and of the rival BR faction in the shape of the *Partito Comunista Combattente* (PCC).

Moreover, the collapse of the web of solidarity within the organization had a deleterious effect on the network of external supporters who had in the past supplied the important logistic support. The image of the BR deteriorated and the area of the so-called 'non-rejection' towards terrorism, where the *brigatisti* had found hiding places and cover, tended to dissolve.

The separateness of the class movements that reduces the recruitment and the support bases of the OCC in the ghetto-milieu well-known in counter-guerrilla work is translated in a chronic logistic weakness, seen then that the clandestine apparatus of the OCC are getting progressively heavier.[82]

The multiplication of the organizational 'events' and the proliferation of splinter groups appear to be an attempt to fill the vacuum left by the wave of arrests that took place at the end of 1982.[83] Moreover, a significant percentage of the 'last recruits' of *brigatismo* was made up of ex-prisoners, relations of imprisoned terrorists, old contacts or old militants who had been recycled even after a considerable length of time after 'freezing' or disaffection.

### 3.4.2 Action: a 'private' war for survival

This period witnessed the exponential concentration of the BR's resources on the struggle for the survival of the organization.[84] Most of the actions were aimed at acquiring material guarantees (e.g. self-financing by means of bank robberies) and reconstructing the psycho-logical pact of solidarity among the members of the various fringes into which the clandestine formation was divided; the latter also included the violent intimidation of and retaliation against those who took an openly hostile position to terrorism. Thus, the murder of the Genoan worker Guido Rossa – who testified to the judiciary against a *brigatista* – was followed by a ruthless punitive campaign against the repented *(pentiti)* comrades and those suspected of *pentimento*.[85] Among the most tragic episodes of this campaign was the kidnapping and assassination of Roberto Peci, the brother of the *pentito,* Patrizio, carried out by the Senzani group in the summer of 1981. Equally savage were the murders of the two Mondiapol policemen carried out in Turin in October 1982, with the aim to propagandize the presumed betrayal (subsequently recognized to have been non-existent) of the BR leader, Natalia Ligas. Peculiar to this phase were the actions carried out against the army. These were intended simultaneously to demonstrate the level of 'class war' reached in the conflict and to obtain arms. The most serious action of the series was the attack at Salerno on an army truck, which caused the death of three policemen and left many injured.

The inevitable consequence of the deterioration of the private confrontation between the clandestine organization and the state was then the growth of the frequency of direct confrontations between terrorists and the forces of law and order. The number of members of the *polizia* or *carabinieri* who lost their lives or were seriously injured in *brigatisti* attacks or in gun battles that often preceded the arrests or followed criminal actions was high. BR commando groups also attacked – consistently with the logic of open war in which the objective is to inflict heavy losses on the enemy – the highest levels of the

law-enforcement hierarchy: during this period we witness the assassinations of the *tenente colonnello* of the *carabinieri,* Varisco, the Commissario police chief of Venice, Albanese, and the head of the 'Flying Squad'
of Naples, Ammaturo. At the beginning of 1982 the deputy head of the
Rome section of the anti-terrorist police group (Digos), De Simone, was
wounded.

There were also many attacks against the judiciary. In the period
February–March 1980 these included the assassinations of the vice-
president of the Higher Judicial Council (*Consiglio Superiore della
Magistratura,* CSM), Vittorio Bachelet, and the ex-head of the Secretary
for Prisons, Girolamo Minervini.[86] Once again, the prison sector was
singled out as the target. The campaign against the high-security prisons
included two revolts of political prisoners in Trani and Asinara; in
December 1980 the kidnapping of a senior magistrate working for the
Ministry of Justice, Giovanni D'Urso; and the murder of General
Galvaligi who was one of those responsible for security in the special
prisons.

Notwithstanding this concentration of organizational resources on
survival, actions apparently aimed at political propaganda continued to
take place, at least in the first two years of the period (1979–80). The
splinter groups 'specialized' in different types of targets: the Walter Alasia
group focused on various Milan factories; the 'historic nucleus'
concentrated on objectives connected with the prisons; the Senzani group
tried to gain support from the movement of the unemployed in Naples
and the *veneti* sought international support with the abduction and
kidnapping of the NATO General Dozier, who was freed after a few
days by the special police squads.

Even after having proved to be ineffective, the actions of 'disarticulation of the intermediate cadres' persisted, both in the factories and
against the DC. The victims within the factories were chosen at a higher
level of the hierarchy with respect to the past, but were less numerous. In
1979 (which was, as we have said, a 'bridging' year) and at the beginning
of 1980 the 'orthodox' BR still appeared to focus some attention on the
factory – as testified by the bloody actions at Fiat in Turin and at
Meccanica Generale Navale in Genoa. After the destruction of the Turin
and Genoan *colonne* the factory target was more or less monopolized by
the Walter Alasia group and by the *colonna* of the Veneto.[87]

Actions carried out against the political forces – concentrated against
the DC, the only exception being a Communist assessor wounded in
Naples – were also quite numerous at the beginning of the period but
tended to drop as the pressure of the state apparatus against terrorist
groups increased. In the period 1979–80, the DC continued to be the
target of numerous actions,[88] but in the successive two-year period there
were only two criminal episodes carried out against the party of the
relative majority: both took place in Naples and both were particularly
serious.[89]

A weak attempt was made, moreover, at propaganda directed at the 'new emerging subjects'. The rebel *brigatisti* of the Walter Alasia group turned their attention to the service proletariat with some actions at the Milan Policlinico: the most serious of these was the murder of the health director of the Marangoni hospital. In the spring of 1980, the Rome *colonna* concentrated various interventions against presumed 'exploitation' of workers with insecure employment or working in the 'black' economy: for example, the woundings of an official from the Ministry of Employment, of three members of a cooperative of porters and of the owner of the Sales Offices of a publishing house. The abduction of General Dozier was, moreover, interpreted as an attempt to gather solidarity from the newly-born peace movement. Finally, using populist demagogy, the *brigatisti* of the Neapolitan *colonna* led by Senzani demanded, in exchange for the freeing of the abducted DC politician Cirillo, the requisitioning of housing for those made homeless by the earthquake in Irpinia in 1980 and unemployment benefit for all those registered as unemployed.

These apparently propagandistic actions were prompted, nevertheless, by a strategy that differed from that of previous periods. If the actions against the DC, all of which occurred in pre-electoral periods, respected in a certain sense the rules of 'timeliness', in this period the aim of maintaining some formal link with the mass movement disappeared altogether; the latter in many ways manifested its desire definitively to reject any form of terroristic violence.[90]

It seems to us, however, that the real motivation for many of the terrorist crimes carried out during this period can be traced to the struggle among the various factions fighting over the hegemony of the leftovers of the organization. The kidnapping of D'Urso and the murder of Galvaligi could have been motivated by the choice of the BR's leaders to meet some of the demands made by the 'historic nucleus' in prison.[91] The assassinations of the industrial managers Briano and Mazzanti were (according to some witnesses) organized by the Walter Alasia group to reinforce its prestige in the conflict with the Executive Committee. The simultaneous kidnapping of the two industrialists, Taliercio and Sandrucci (the first carried out by a sort of breakaway section of the BR operating in the Veneto and the second by the Walter Alasia group) seem to be a further expression of the competition between the two branches of the organization.

For all those factions into which the BR was divided, criminal action – ever less rationalizable in terms of the expression of political and social conflict – expressed the desperate search to testify to the survival of the group and, with it, to the group's existential identity. This need also conditioned the choice of the forms of action; the terrorists' ambition was increasingly concentrated on the military success of the action. Increasingly bloody crimes were carried out to maintain faith in the choice of the armed struggle among the members of the group.

Moreover, in order to keep the attention of the media concentrated on their activity during this period, the *brigatisti* carried out six kidnappings – which lasted from one to three months – and which were often accompanied by tragic events. The way of making interventions became so savage as to provoke (see, for example, the case of the two prison-guards murdered in Turin) condemnation from within the terrorist organization itself. While the number of attacks on property, with its limited instrumental use, were reduced, the number of murders for which the BR claimed responsibility remained relatively high; eleven in 1979, eight in 1980, eight in 1981 and fourteen in 1982.

As we have said, the number of deaths was not accompanied by a reinforcing of the organization and the military success of the campaign in the summer of 1981 (four simultaneous kidnappings) did not translate into political success. Threatened from within by the series of dissociations and constantly under attack from outside by the forces of law and order, the remaining groups of *brigatisti,* in order to deny defeat, were forced to construct a new image of the armed struggle as autonomous and self-sufficient. The most recent documents presented – much more emphatically than in the past – a completely unreal image of reality: the language is cryptic and the guiding logic for actions of blind fury is quite incomprehensible to the outsider (and was at times rejected even within the organization). One of the documents written by 'dissociated' terrorists states:

With the *Partito della Guerriglia del Proletariato Metropolitano* and the actions of the last months, the long phase in which the fighting praxis was seen in function of the activation of a revolutionary process on the battlefield or ... in the real interests of the proletariat, has come to an end. Now there is a phase of war among bands as an end unto itself, as a praxis of liberation. The recent theoretical syntheses of the *Partito della Guerriglia,* are the most coherent ideological base. These are not limited, as were the old documents, to analysing the reality in a more or less mystified way, drawing lines of tendency in which to insert their own action: the new theorization does not propose an analysis, but rather a new vision and way of living, a reality beginning from the existential condition of metropolitan guerrilla warfare. One no longer speaks, as before, of civil war as an historical phase of the class struggle to be promoted [by means of] guerrilla warfare, one speaks of 'war' as a dimension until now neglected by reality, the only complete expression of conscience and the political struggle of the proletariat to the present level of the development of capital, [the] expression of a new 'absolute enmity between classes'. Guerrilla warfare is then the only way to break the total social control that is first of all control of the conscience, only expression of conscience and class struggle to which is counterposed the state of somnambulism and madness into which the non-fighting proletariat (the so-called schizophrenic metropolitan proletariat) would fall. It is not necessary to win civil war, but only to witness it taking place in the daily reality. From this war as a hallucinated vision of the social reality, one passes then to the actions of guerrilla warfare which contain their own justification in the form of a simple activation of a conjectured social potential.[92]

A final observation refers to the force of terrorism throughout the period. If 1979 and 1980 were still years when virulent terrorist actions in many Italian provinces persisted, from 1981 the pace and frequency of *brigatista* activity slackened off and was mainly concentrated in Rome with some actions taking place in Naples.

### 3.4.3 Lines of interpretation: the crisis of the clandestine organization

Without doubt, various elements had an impact on the crisis of the BR: the affairs of the scattered terrorist groups, the growing and irreversible isolation of the BR in public opinion, the law on the *pentiti* passed in 1981 and the greater efficiency of the state apparatus in the repression of clandestine groups.[93] Nevertheless, the collapse of the terrorist organization also appears to follow internal dynamics, already experienced by clandestine groups in other countries.[94]

During its evolution, the terrorist organization moved away from its action of political propaganda and concentrated instead on its 'private' war with the apparatus of the state. The process of development of the BR evolved towards an *impasse*. Crushed by the contradictions between the need to prepare for a long battle and the need to maintain conditions of clandestinity, the BR were forced to reject the instruments of propaganda guaranteed to collective actors in democratic regimes. The terrorist organization then accentuated its isolation when the logic of the planned actions forced the confrontation with the repressive apparatus of the state. Trapped between state repression on one hand, and progressive reduction of possible initial sympathies on the other, the BR found themselves increasingly entrapped in actions to defend the organization. The need for financing forced the terrorists to take part in acts of petty *banditismo*, which exposed them to armed clashes with the police and dangerous competition with the *malavita* (when it was not actually colluding with organized crime), further discrediting the image of the organization. The contacts with common criminal elements was accentuated in the prisons, where terrorists were sometimes forced to enter into alliances (or pacts of 'non-belligerance') with the rival bands governing relations among prisoners. Forced by the pressure of the forces of law and order, the contacts with the outside were limited to the urgent demand for logistic support.

The BR's direct confrontation with the repressive apparatus of the state took place in two different periods. The different size of the force reached by terrorism in these two cycles of its existence is evident in the different efforts made by the state institutions to defeat the clandestine organizations. In the first phase (1975–6) the organization of the BR –

stable but reduced in size – was damaged in little more than a year by a series of arrests. In contrast, nearly four years were needed (1979–82) to make the terrorist organization – already politically on the decline – collapse under the blows of military defeats. In the second cycle of the defeat of the organization, the BR experienced the collapse of solidarity from within. At a time when terrorism was already in a state of political crisis, the Italian state introduced the already-mentioned law on *pentiti,* which stipulated the reductions of sentences for terrorists who collaborated with the state and special treatment for those who publicly dissociated themselves from the armed struggle. These two factors contributed to breaking the bonds of solidarity within the organization, markedly reduced the possibility of external help, established a climate of reciprocal suspicion among members of the band and led to the long chain of subsequent arrests that enabled the state to accomplish the organizational defeat of the BR.

## Notes

1 For a definition of the category 'terrorism' and an analysis of the international literature on the subject, see della Porta (1983).

2 For the 'culture of terrorism', which is not dealt with in this work, see Dalla Chiesa (1981), Dini and Manconi (1981) and Marletti (1979).

3 For a comparison with data on other clandestine organizations, of both the left and right, see della Porta and Rossi (1983).

4 The history of the BR has been reconstructed by, among others, Agostini (1980), Barbato (1980), Bello (1981), Bocca (1978a, 1978b), Galleni (1981), Manzini (1979), Pansa (1980), Papa (1979), *Soccorso rosso* (1976), Silj (1977), Sole (1979), Tessandori (1977) and Weinberg (1982). Direct sources have also been used from *Tribunale di Torino* (1975a, 1978, 1979).

5 Cited in Silj, (1977) p. 89.

6 *Brigate rosse,* (1971a).

7 In the period under review BR also attempted to establish a base in Emilia but without success; the militants stationed there were subsequently transferred to the Veneto.

8 Information on the recruitment of terrorists in factories can be found in Cavallini (1978).

9 Presented in *Soccorso rosso* (1976) p. 125.

10 During this phase, many of the things written in the documents of the organization were no more than forecasts or programmes, rather than actual working situations.

11 The term 'mass front' is used because the 'factory front' – in contrast to the 'logistic' front – had an external 'referent' outside the organization.

12 It has been discovered, for example, that there were double versions of some texts for congresses organized by this *collettivo:* militants received one or other of the two versions depending on their supposed attitude towards the armed struggle.

13 *Brigate rosse* (1971a).

14 Ibid.

15 *Brigate rosse* (1973).

16 *Brigate rosse* (1971b).

17 Ibid.

18 *Brigate rosse* (1971a).

19 Corporatist-type trade unions set up by factory owners to avoid the formation of left-wing trade unions.

20 A document on the structure of neo-fascist groups in Milan is contained in *Brigate rosse* (1971c).

21 *Brigate rosse* (1971a).

22 The Piazza Fontana bombing took place in a Milan bank on 12 December 1969, causing the death of sixteen people and wounding ninety. In December 1970, *Principe* Valerio Borghese, an ex-official of the fascist Republic of Salò, attempted a right-wing coup with the occupation of part of the *Ministero degli Interni* in Rome. See also the affair of the *Rosa dei Venti,* an organization working 'parallel' to the intelligence body, SID. For both cases, see G. Viglietti (1986) in Borracetti (ed.), *Eversione di destra, terrorismo, stragi,* Milan, Angeli.

23 Important, with regard to the Turin *colonna,* was the construction of a logistic hinterland in the small town of Biella. Here many militants were recruited but none of them were ever used in action. In fact, the Biella structures were only used to deposit material or to find refuge outside the operational zones.

24 Transferring one of the founders of the organization, Alberto Franceschini, who was arrested shortly afterwards.

25 In the Marches and Tuscany the BR only established regional committees. These were structures whose scope was markedly inferior to that of the *colonne,* precisely because of the lack of an *in situ* 'referent' that would allow a more conspicuous presence.

26 *Brigate rosse* (1974) p. 25.

27 A BR document reproduced in *Soccorso rosso* (1976) p. 277.

28 The document continues, 'From a political point of view there is no difference between militants in the regular forces and irregular forces. Both contribute with parity of rights and obligations to ensure the general political line of the organization'. The document found in the hideout at Piacenza is reproduced in full in *Tribunale di Torino* (1975a).

29 The first meeting of the Strategic Direction took place at the end of 1974 in the Veneto after the arrest of Curcio and Franceschini on 8 September of that year.

30 *Tribunale di Torino* (1975a).

31 The Strategic Direction was a type of parliament of the organization, which used the papers written by the various *colonne* and by imprisoned comrades as a basis for discussion. Finally, the Strategic Direction sums up the argument and sets down the political line chosen in a special document that becomes valid in the long-term.

32 The proposal to intervene in particular sectors could obviously also start 'from below', on the basis of communications by the *brigate* about current needs.

33 With regard to propaganda activity, we should note the BR's experience with the publication *Controinformazione,* which involved – at the compilation and diffusion stages – militants from other groups whose relationship with the BR thus became rather close. In later years, the diffusion of the

ideological message, in the form of their own publications, took place by means of normal commercial channels: it is enough to remember the text that caused greatest scandal, *Collettivo prigionieri comunisti delle Brigate rosse* (1980).

34 On this hypothesis, see the sentence issued by the investigating judge Palombarini, *Tribunale di Padova* (1981), which is partially published in Palombarini (1982), and Scarpari (1981). For a discussion on the direct transition from *Potere Operaio* to the BR, see the Assistant Public Prosecutor of the Republic, Calogero, Procura della Repubblica di Padova (1981), Galante (1981) and Ventura (1980).

35 In contrast to the state's advocacy of the outright rejection as the proper civil response to terrorism, a part of the radical left and some left-wing intellectuals espoused the line of 'non-rejection'. During this period a common slogan expressing this attitude was 'Neither with the state nor with the Red Brigades'.

36 Of the members of the first Executive Committee – Curcio, Franceschini, Morlacchi and Moretti – only the last managed to escape arrest in this period. Moreover, by the end of 1976 the greater part of the 'historical' militants both from Milan and Reggio Emilia had been imprisoned. Renato Curcio escaped from Casale prison in February 1975 but was recaptured in January 1976. Margherita Cagol died in a gun battle with the *carabinieri* in June 1976.

37 On this point see Rodotà (1984a) and Caselli (1979).

38 This term is a reference to the institutional reform introduced by De Gaulle in France.

39 The document that claimed responsibility for the Sossi kidnapping stressed, for example, that the action took place on the day of Gianni Agnelli's inauguration as President of the Confindustria.

40 Document cited in *Soccorso rosso* (1976) p. 270.

41 *Brigate rosse* (1974).

42 Ibid. p. 180.

43 Ibid. The document cited continues: 'It is time to break through the web of the past and to overcome the traditional definition of militant anti-fascism. To strike the fascists with every means and in every place is both just and necessary. But today the main contradiction is that posed by the forces of the counter-revolution.'

44 The following are among the most tragic assassinations: Marshal Maritano in the hideout of Robbiano of Mediglia; a lance-corporal of the *carabinieri*, D'Alfonso, during the rescue of the industrialist Valerino Gancia at Acqui Terme; the policeman Niedda at Ponte di Brenta; Commander Cusano at Biella; Deputy Police Superintendent, Padovani and Marshal Bazzega in Milan during the raid on the home of a young *brigatista*, Walter Alasia.

45 In the period preceding the assassination of the Public Prosecutor of the Republic for Genoa and his bodyguards, the BR carried out four woundings against targets connected with the large factory: Enrico Boffa, head of personnel at Singer; Valerio Di Marco, head of personnel at Leyland-Innocenti; Luigi Solera, doctor at Fiat Mirafiori; and Matteo Palmieri, head of the security forces at Magneti Marelli. A wounding, already noted, of councillor Massimo De Carolis, strikes a political exponent of the DC.

46 Cited in *Soccorso rosso* (1976) p. 253. Brescia had been the scene of a neo-fascist bombing three weeks earlier.

47 The hypothesis is illustrated by Alessandro Pizzorno in *Mondoperaio* (1978).

48 See Ferrajoli (1979). For some starting points on the relationship between the rise of terrorism and the degeneration of collective movements, see Melucci (1978) and Stame (1979).

49 Some observations in this direction are in Caselli (1979).

50 On this issue see Violante (1984a).

51 The history of the NAP has been reconstructed in *Soccorso rosso napoletano* (1976).

52 For more exhaustive information on the history of terrorism in West Germany, the USA and Japan, between the end of the 1960s and the beginning of the 1970s, we refer respectively to the work of Irving Fetscher, Ted R. Gurr and Hiroshi Kawahara, in della Porta and Pasquino (1983). For some comparative observations of the three historical cases cited and the Italian case, see Chapter 6 by Gianfranco Pasquino in the same volume (1983).

53 *Brigate rosse* (1977) p. 1.

54 Ibid., p.4.

55 Ibid.

56 The organizational structure is set out in *Brigate rosse* (1978).

57 The BR had already discussed this point in 1975, but the proposal had no concrete consequence.

58 *Brigate rosse* (1978) p. 57.

59 The term 'terrorismo diffuso' was used to indicate the splintered nature of the phenomenon, with various small and unconnected groups active throughout Italy in the period. The term also refers to the indiscriminate nature of the actions carried out by these groups against targets with no precise objectives.

60 Only Moretti, Micaletto, Azzolini, Bonisoli and Gallinari (who escaped from prison in January 1976) were still at large.

61 Raffaele Fiore, Riccardo Dura, Luca Nicolotti and Cristoforo Piancone, among others.

62 For a reconstruction of the activity of the BR in this phase, we have used Alberti and Caselli (1980); Barbano, Andruetto, Costanzo and Monticelli (1980) and Galleni (1981). We have also referred to the trial records included in *Tribunale di Torino* (1980 and 1982), *Tribunale di Roma* (1981) and *Tribunale di Venezia* (1982).

63 In Turin, the sensational case of the wounding of Ghirotto, where the wrong person was wounded by mistake ('guilty' only in so far as he was the twin of the chosen victim), the BR wrote – in the leaflet claiming responsibility for the action – that the mistake made no difference because (as he was still an employee at Fiat) one twin was worth another, even 'politically'.

64 We must recall the attack on Galloni, a member of parliament for the DC, and the wounding of two of his bodyguards, which took place at the end of the period.

65 Much has been written on the BR's most dramatic crime. See, *inter alia* Bocca (1978) and Moss (1981).

66 This ideological shift was directly conditioned by the progressive strengthening of the Rome *colonna*. For example, the 'intervention' in the tertiary sector and in the marginal and alienated proletariat, are pushed for by the entry in the BR of a strong 'spontaneista' component (previously involved in *Autonomia*).

67 Among the actions carried out in this period, we should recall the woundings

of Bruno, the Assistant Editor of *Il Secolo XIX* of Genoa; Montanelli, the editor of *Il Giornale Nuovo* of Milan; and Rossi, the director of television news on the first channel of the RAI.

68 From the wounding of Traversi and the killing of Palma and Tartaglione (judges working at the Ministry) to the murders of Cutugno in Turin, De Cataldo in Milan and Santoro in Udine (who all belonged to the prison guard).

69 *Brigate rosse* (1978) pp. 41–2.

70 Ibid., pp. 42–3 *passim*.

71 The Metropolitan Indians, so-called because they identified with and used the symbols of dispossessed American Indians, were a youth sub-culture that emerged in the second half of the 1970s. They were non-violent but carried out 'provocative' public actions.

72 Among the events most often referred to by the media at the time are the death of two young people – Francesco Lo Russo and Giorgiana Masi – during police intervention at public marches; and the incidents which took place at the public meeting held by trade-unionist leader Luciano Lama at the Roman university, La Sapienza (of which there are various contradictory versions). On the dynamics of the transition from political violence to militancy in clandestine groups, see Calvi (1982), Stajano (1982) and Chapter 6 in this volume.

73 See for example, Acquaviva (1979a).

74 *Brigate rosse* (1978) p. 44.

75 Bonanate (1979a) p. 177.

76 A connection between terrorism and alienation was established in Ferrarotti (1979). In other cases the hypothesis is put forward of a relationship between the discontent produced by the increase in youth unemployment and the development of political terrorism: see, for example, Cavalli (1977). Neither of the two interpretations, with respect to the available data, is able to give an exhaustive explanation for a phenomenon peculiar to Italy and whose origins must, therefore, be sought in the specific interweaving of preconditions and causal factors of the last twenty years or so of Italian history.

77 A good description of the reality of the fights inside the 'tormented archipelago of subversion' is given by one of its protagonists: 'the risk, and at the same time the limit [of this reconstruction] is that there was, or there is, something which brings together, structures, has moments of coordination: but this often passes through conflicts, power struggles, perhaps even the 'worst things'. I mean to say that these aggregations are processes which are not at all linear or painless. They are tiring processes, the power struggle is inherent to them, not only among different organizations, but sometimes also within the same organization: rivalry between 'chiefs', sometimes of a personal nature, under the cover of the language of politics.'

78 In the analysis of Cacciari (1980) p. 67.

79 *Brigate rosse* (1980) p. 6.

80 *Detenuti del carcere di Brescia* (1982) p. 6.

81 Note between the spring and summer of 1981, the four kidnappings, carried out simultaneously, of the regional assessor, Ciro Cirillo, the head of Montedison, Giuseppe Taliercio, an Alfa Romeo manager, Renzo Sandrucci and Roberto Peci, the brother of the *brigatista pentito*.

82 *Detenuti del carcere di Brescia* (1982) p. 6. A wide range of political, social and

cultural forces carried out a series of initiatives designed to reduce the area of indifference or sometimes of support for the armed struggle. Among them were the hundreds of meetings on terrorism organized at Turin in the factories, the neighbourhoods and in the schools (see Caselli (1981)). The action of these forces contributed to the isolation of the terrorist organization.

83 What remained of the Partito-guerriglia after the arrest of its leader, Giovanni Senzani, set up, for example, a *fronte della guerra alla controrivoluzione globale armata* (sub-divided into the following sectors: armed institutions, logistics, SIM-DC/national-international imperialistic politics), and a *fronte di massa* (sub/divided into the following sectors: factory proletariat, tertiary sector proletariat and extra-legal proletariat). In fact the *fronte della guerra* was made up of only two militants, a Milanese and a Sardinian; the latter had been suspended for 'deviation'.

84 The information on the criminal activity of the BR in the course of this last period has been taken, apart from the sources already cited, from two documents of the PCI Direction-Section for State Problems (1981 and 1982) and from the daily press for the last two years (1981 and 1982).

85 The *brigatista* Liburno was attacked by his ex-companions during a trial in the spring of 1981. In December 1981 a *Prima Linea* militant, Giorgio Soldati, was assassinated in Cuneo prison by the group *Terrore rosso*. The *brigatista* Gargiulo was wounded by other prisoners in Palmi prison at the beginning of 1982. In July 1982, the *brigatista,* Ennio di Rocco, was killed in Trani prison. In December 1982, the *brigatista* Anna Maria Massa was wounded in Voghera prison.

86 The murder of Giacumbi, the *procuratore della Repubblica* of Salerno, appears to have been the work of a criminal group that was not yet part of the BR.

87 In the period 1980–1, the Walter Alasia group was responsible for three woundings of members of the Alfa Romeo management; the kidnapping of Sandrucci, a director of the Alfa Romeo office for the organization of work; the assassination of Briano, the personnel director of Magneti Morelli and Mazzanti, the technical director of Falck. *Brigatisti* belonging to the Veneto *colonna* were responsible for the murder of two industrial managers from Porto Marghera, the deputy technical director of Petrolchimico, Gori, and the director of Montedison, Taliercio.

88 The DC was attacked repeatedly both for its representatives (note the woundings in Genoa, Milan and Rome and the assassinations of the provincial councillor of Rome, Schettini and the regional assessor for Campania, Amato) and its premises (the break-in at the offices of the Rome committee of the DC in piazza Nicosia).

89 Note the kidnapping (with the murder of the bodyguard) of the regional assessor for Campania, Cirillo, in 1981, and the double assassination – once again in Naples – of the regional assessor, Delcogliano, and his driver in 1982.

90 'It is significant,' continues the document written by former terrorists 'that in the hot days of the 1979 contract at Fiat [the Turin *colonna* of the BR was still intact] and in the dramatic struggle in 1980 against the sackings and the *cassa integrazione,* the OCC did not have anything to say,' *Detenuti del carcere di Brescia* (1982) p. 5.

91 The request for intervention of the imprisoned companions became increasingly pressing. It is sufficient to remember *Comunicato No. 21* of 7 December 1979, issued at the end of the Turin appeal hearing of the *capi*

*storici* of the organization, and which, with a truculence inversely proportional to the actual residual potential of the organization, promised 'a proletarian class war which [will be] war without quarter, that must be carried on twenty-four hours a day and without the respite of the weekend. Wherever the enemy is, in the factory or in the home, in army barracks or out walking, he must feel himself trapped, spied upon, exposed to the most fantastic and irreversible traps and ambushes.' More immediately, the imprisoned *brigatisti* requested – as has emerged in the memoirs of the ex-militant terrorist Fenzi – their companions to intervene on the *fronte delle carceri*.

92 *Detenuti del carcere di Brescia* (1982) p. 8.
93 It has been noted that the drop of efficiency in the struggle against terrorism was due to the substantial disbanding of the special squads of *carabinieri* and the police after the arrest of the *capi storici* of the BR (see Caselli (1979) p. 241 and 244 *passim*). Only from September 1978, with the creation of an inter-force investigative organism led by General Carlo Alberto dalla Chiesa, do we see a recovery of professionality and concentration in the fight against terrorism.
94 See the considerations of three German ex-terrorists: Baumann (1976), Klein (1980), and Mahler (1980). See also della Porta (1982).

## References

S. Acquaviva (1979) *Guerriglia e guerra rivoluzionaria in Italia. Ideologia, fatti, prospettive*, Milan, Rizzoli.
P. Agostini (1980) *Mara Cagol, una donna nelle prime Brigate Rosse*, Padua, Marsilio.
P. Alberti and G.C. Caselli (1980) *Il terrorismo rosso*, paper presented at the conference 'Perché la barbarie non uccida la democrazia', Turin.
R. Alquati, M. Boato, M. Cacciari, S. Rodotà and L. Violante (1980) *Terrorismo: verso la seconda Repubblica?*, Turin, Stampatori.
F. Barbano, A. Andruetto, S. Costanzo and A. Monticelli (1980) *Gli obiettivi attuali del terrorismo secondo i documenti e le azioni dei gruppi eversivi*, paper presented at the conference 'Perché la barbarie non uccida la democrazia', Turin.
T. Barbato (1980) *Il terrorismo in Italia*, Milan, Bibliografica.
B. Baumann (1976) *Tupamaros Berlin-Ouest*, Paris, La Presse d'aujourd'hui.
A. Bello (1981) *L'idea armata*, Rome, L'Opinione.
G. Bocca (1978a) *Moro, una tragedia italiana*, Milan, Bompiani.
G. Bocca (1978b) *Il terrorismo italiano 1970–1978*, Milan, Rizzoli.
L. Bonanate (1979b) 'Dimensioni del terrorismo politico', in L. Bonanate (ed.) *Dimensioni del terrorismo politico*, Milan, Angeli.
V. Borracetti (ed.) (1986) *Eversione di destra, terrorismo, stragi: I fatti, l'intervento giudiziario*, Milan, Angeli.
*Brigate rosse* (1971a) 'Autointervista'.
*Brigate rosse* (1971b) 'Classe contro classe, guerra di classe'.
*Brigate rosse* (1971c) 'Organizziamo un grande processo popolare'.
*Brigate rosse* (1973) 'La crisi è uno strumento usato dalla reazione per battere la classe operaia'.
*Brigate rosse* (1974) 'Contro il neogollismo portare l'attacco al cuore dello stato'.

*Brigate rosse* (1975) 'Risoluzione della Direzione Strategica', April; *Controinformazione* (1976) 7–8 June.

*Brigate rosse* (1977) 'Portare l'attacco allo Stato Imperialista delle Multinazionali'.

*Brigate rosse* (1978) 'Risoluzione della Direzione Strategica', February; *Controinformazione* (1978) 11–12 July 1978.

*Brigate rosse* (1980) 'Battere l'opportunismo liquidazionista e l'ideologia della sconfitta'.

M. Cacciari (1980), 'Per una de-costruzione dell'immagine monolitica del terrorismo', in Alquati, Boato, Cacciari, Rodotá and Violante, op.cit., pp. 60–83.

F. Calvi (1982) *Camarade P38*, Paris, Grasset.

G.C. Caselli (1979) 'Criminalità politica organizzata e problemi di risposta dello Stato', in R. Villa (ed.) *La violenza interpretata*, Bologna, Il Mulino.

G.C. Caselli (1981) 'La questione dei pentiti', *Quaderni della giustizia*, No. 4.

L. Cavalli (1977) 'La violenza politica', *Città e regione*, Vol. III, Nos. 10–11, pp. 7–45.

M. Cavallini (1978) *Terrorismo in fabbrica*, Rome, Editori Riuniti.

Collettivo prigionieri comunisti delle Brigate rosse (1980) 'L'ape e il comunista', *Corrispondenza internazionale*, Vol. VI, Nos. 16–17.

N. dalla Chiesa (1981) 'Del sessantotto e del terrorismo: cultura politica tra continuità e rottura', *Il Mulino*, Vol. XXX, No. 273, pp. 53–94.

D. della Porta (1982) 'Violenza politica e terrorismo ideologico nelle società contemporanee. Note a margine di un convegno', *Cattaneo*, Vol. II, No. 2, pp. 25–36.

D. della Porta (1983) 'Le cause del terrorismo nelle società contemporanee. Riflessioni sulla letteratura', in della Porta and Pasquino (eds), *Terrorismo e violenza politica. Tre casi a confronto: Stati Uniti, Germania e Giappone*, Bologna, Il Mulino, pp.11–47.

D. della Porta and G. Pasquino (1986) 'Interpretations of Italian Left-wing Terrorism', in P. Merkl (ed.) *Political Violence in Contemporary Society*, Berkeley and Los Angeles, University of California Press, pp. 169–90.

D. della Porta and M. Rossi (1983) 'I terrorismi in Italia tra il 1969 e il 1982', *Cattaneo*, Vol. III, No. 1, pp. 1–44.

Detenuti del carcere di Brescia (1982) 'Documento'.

V. Dini and L. Manconi (1981) *Il discorso delle armi*, Rome, Savelli.

L. Ferrajoli (1979) 'Critica della violenza come critica della politica', in L. Manconi (ed.) *La violenza e la politica*, Rome, Savelli, pp. 36–69.

F. Ferrarotti (1979) *Alle radici della violenza*, Milan, Rizzoli.

S. Galante (1981) 'Alle origini del partito', *Il Mulino*, Vol. XXX, No. 275, pp. 447–87.

M. Galleni (ed.) (1981) *Rapporto sul terrorismo italiano*, Milan, Rizzoli.

H. Klein (1980) *La morte mércenaire*, Paris, Seuil.

H. Mahler (1980) *Per la critica del terrorismo*, Bari, De Donato.

L. Manconi (ed.) (1979) *La violenza e la politica*, Rome, Savelli.

G. Manzini (1979) *Indagine su un brigatista rosso*, Turin, Einaudi.

C. Marletti (1979) 'Immagine pubblica e ideologia del terrorismo', in Bonante (ed.) op.cit., pp. 181–253.

A. Melucci (1978) 'Appunti su movimenti, terrorismo, società italiana', *Il Mulino*, Vol. XXVII, No. 256, pp. 253–67.

*Mondoperaio* (1978) 'Terrorismo e quadro politico', debate between F. Cicchitto,

L. Colletti, F. Mancini, A. Minucci and A. Pizzorno, Vol. XXXI, No. 14, pp. 5–18.

D. Moss (1981) 'The Kidnapping and Murder of Aldo Moro', *Archives européennes de sociologie*, Vol. XXII, No. 2, pp. 265–95.

G. Palombarini (1982) *Il 7 aprile: il processo e la sua storia*, Venice, Arsenale.

G. Pansa (1980) *Storie italiane di violenza e terrorismo*, Bari, Laterza.

E.R. Papa (1979) *Il processo alle BR*, Turin, Giappichelli.

Partito Comunista Italiano–Sezione problemi dello Stato (1981) 'Attentati e violenze in Italia', (pamphlet).

Partito Comunista Italiano–Sezione problemi dello Stato (1982) 'Attentati e violenze in Italia', (pamphlet).

G. Pasquino (1983) 'Differenze e somiglianze: per una ricerca sul terrorismo italiano', in della Porta and Pasquino (eds) op. cit.

G. Pasquino (1984a) 'Sistema politico bloccato e insorgenza del terrorismo. Ipotesi e prime verifiche', in Pasquino (ed.) *La prova delle armi*, Bologna, Il Mulino, pp. 185–220.

Procura della Repubblica di Padova (1981) Requisitoria del sostituto procuratore Pietro Calogero in the proceedings against *Autonomia*, 18 May.

S. Rodotà (1984a) 'La risposta dello Stato ai terrorismi: gli apparati', in Pasquino, op.cit., pp. 77–93.

G. Scapari (1981) 'Processo a mezzo stampa: il '7 aprile''', *Quale giustizia*, No. 51, pp. 228–92.

A. Silj (1977) *'Mai più senza fucile!' Alle origini dei Nap e delle Br*, Florence, Vallecchi.

Soccorso rosso (1976) *Brigate rosse. Che cosa hanno fatto, che cosa hanno detto, che cosa se ne è detto*, Milan, Feltrinelli.

Soccorso rosso napoletano (1976) *I Nap. Storia politica dei Nuclei Armati Proletari e requisitoria del Tribunale di Napoli*, Milan, Collettivo editoriale Libri rossi.

R. Sole (1979) *Le défi terroriste: lecon italienne à l'usage de l'Europe*, Paris, Seuil.

C. Stajano (1979) 'Terrorismo e crisi dello Stato', in Manconi (ed.) pp. 22–32.

C. Stajano (1982) *L'Italia nichilista. Il caso di Marco Donat Cattin, la rivolta, il potere*, Milan, Mondadori.

V. Tessandori (1977) *Br. Imputazione banda armata. Cronaca e documentazione Brigate Rosse*, Milan, Garzanti.

N. Tranfaglia (1981) 'La crisi italiana e il problema storico del terrorismo', in Galleni (ed.) pp. 477–544.

Tribunale di Padova (1981) *Ordinanza sentenza* of the investigating judge Giovanni Palombarini in proceedings No. 183/79, 28 September.

Tribunale di Roma (1981) *Ordinanza sentenza* of the investigating judge Ernesto Cudillo in proceedings No. 18/78, 15 January.

Tribunale di Torino (1975a) *Ordinanza-sentenza* of the investigating judge Gian Carlo Caselli in proceedings No. 595/74, 31 October.

Tribunale di Torino (1978) *Sentenza* of the Assize Court, 23 June.

Tribunale di Torino (1979) *Sentenza* of the Assize Appeal Court, 8 December.

Tribunale di Torino (1980) *Ordinanza-sentenza* of the *consigliere istruttore* Mario Carassi in proceedings No. 6587/79, 9 December.

Tribunale di Torino (1982) *Ordinanza-sentenza* of the *consigliere istruttore* Antonino Polaja in proceedings No. 918/80, 9 December.

Tribunale di Venezia (1982) *Ordinanza-sentenza* of the investigating judge Carlo Nordio in proceedings No. 274/80, 3 February.

A. Ventura (1980) 'Il problema storico del terrorismo italiano', *Rivista storica italiana,* Vol. XXCII, No. 1, pp. 141–7.

R. Villa (ed.) (1979) *La violenza interpretata,* Bologna, Il Mulino.

L. Violante (1984a) 'Politica della sicurezza, relazioni internazionali e terrorismo', in Pasquino, op.cit., pp. 95–120.

L. Weinberg (1982) 'The Violent Life: an Analysis of Left and Right Wing Terrorism in Italy', report presented at the XII world congress of IPSA, Rio de Janeiro, August.

# 4
# The political ideology of the Red Brigades

## Luigi Manconi

## 4.1 Introduction

The aim of this chapter is not to make an analysis of the 'idea of the state' conceived by armed groups, but to trace the way in which the state, its apparatus and its institutions (that is, the sources of law, authority and administration) or, rather, their images, have been internalized by the very people who took up arms against them. In other words, the way in which the images of the state have taken the shape of the 'absolute enemy'.[1] This issue is important both from an ideological and a psychological point of view: ideologically, because it helps us to reconstruct the conceptual system of the clandestine militant; and psychologically because it allows us to decipher the system of motivations underlying the behaviour of the militant. The motivational and intellectual sequence I believe we can draw from the analysis – which is presented here in summary – is as follows: the perception of an 'absolute injustice'; the characterization of the enemy as the 'absolute enemy' (author of the 'absolute injustice'); the delegitimation of the enemy; and finally 'absolute legitimacy' of the 'war' against him.

On the basis of this sequence we may put forward the interpretative hypothesis that there is a close connection between the following: (i) the clandestine organizations' oversimplified definition of the state, its political system, the function of its apparatus and its 'faults'; (ii) the mirrored representation of a *counterstate*, its apparatus and functions; and (iii) the overturning of 'bourgeois' morality, with the consequent definition of an 'alternative' law and justice as the ethical foundations of the armed struggle. It is important to explore these links by means of theoretical and political statements, as well as through subjective perceptions processed by personal experience. That is, in the interviews with the clandestine militants, we need to trace the connection they have established between their idea of justice (the notion of '*what is right*'), and their motivation in the armed struggle. In this chapter the analysis will be restricted to the first period of the armed struggle in Italy, particularly from the early 1970s. For many Red Brigade militants, these were the years of their political apprenticeship and their entry into underground organizations, whereas for many *operaisti* militants it was exclusively the period of their political apprenticeship,[2] and only later in a second phase of their development would they choose the armed option. The years immediately following 1968 were the most influential ones for the political education of both those militants who were already active, and lived their militant experience intensively, and for those who were only partially or superficially involved, but who subsequently acquired a 'memory' of those years through what was related and written about them, or simply by their sheer impact.

On the basis of the observations we can formulate the following hypothesis: that both the Red Brigade militants who became clandestine in 1971 and the militants of the so-called *operaisti* groups who became active in 1976, were influenced by the same conceptual and symbolic model of power: the so-called *brigatista* model. Later on, this model, its foundations and implications were modified, expanded and in some cases, abandoned. But for a certain period of time – the period under analysis – it worked. Caselli and della Porta (see Chapter 3) define the kidnapping of the judge Mario Sossi as the final operation in the first period of the armed struggle; their suggestion seems feasible.[3] Until that episode 'the control of the organization remained in the hands of its founders'[4]; the cultural and ideological structure of the Red Brigades was compact and their political line unambiguous. This means that statements and publications issued by the BR during this period can be considered as a reliable representation of the organization. Later on, after the arrest of Renato Curcio and Alberto Franceschini in September 1974, the situation became more complex. Different opinions and interpretations started to emerge within the group and this marked the beginning of a process that ended in an open clash between the different political alignments of the mid-1970s. The emerging split also determined the different images of state power and, as a consequence, different strategies with which to combat it. After 1974, the ideological unity of the Red Brigades started to disintegrate: this rupture is clearly discernible in the contemporary literature. Thus, the interpretation of terrorism at the beginning of the 1970s cannot be applied to the terrorism of later years.

More generally, we should examine two variables: the gap between theory and praxis which occurs in terrorist organizations as in political organizations, and whose size is dependent on many different elements, not all necessarily pertaining to the internal life of the group; and secondly, the projection of an appealing and justifying image of themselves on the part of terrorists. This trend is clearly discernible in the contemporary literature and in particular in the *a posteriori* reconstructions of militants whose political opinion had sometimes undergone a drastic shift. In the interviews in particular, the search for consensus tends to produce a public image which is often far from reality.

## 4.2 The representation of power

Listening to many militants, including those interviewed for this chapter, at the beginning of the armed struggle in Italy there seems to have been a sort of 'original trauma'.

> about my personal story: it starts when the Italian left ... well, if one really wants to locate it historically, I can say that my own story starts when the Italian left decided to publicly defend Pietro Valpreda, and its shift from its earlier positions [taken] on the Piazza Fontana massacre ... [both] before and at the time an open 'mass' mobilization had begun – and I say mass in parenthesis – by the fascists.[5]

> then there was the strike in response to the Piazza Fontana bombing ... it was the first time we went to school and then instead of having lessons we went out on the streets. The rally gathered an incredible number of people ... there was a mass said, and I went too, or, at least, I tried to get into the cathedral with difficulty where the coffins were. ... some days later Pinelli died, and so there were angry meetings.[6]

> the first book I ever read, a political book I mean, was *La strage di Stato*.[7]

> it was clear to me that no popular struggle had ever got close to power – and this opinion was supported by the Piazza Fontana massacre.[8]

The bomb that exploded in Piazza Fontana, 'the state massacre', as the Left called it in order to identify the role played by part of the political ruling class and a part of the institutions, seems to have had a profound impact on young people's attitudes to power. There was a widespread – and to some extent documented – feeling that there was a close connection between right-wing terrorist groups and some state institutions. A belief that has proved to be well-founded by many enquiries.

> it was right to respond to such a reactionary state with street violence ... I remember, this was the time when we hunted down fascists, when the rallies started to organize their own self-defence against the fascists.[9]

As a consequence, in the 'common sense' of an entire generation of militants, the picture of the institutional system takes on a dramatic meaning. It is not surprising that in such circumstances a publication called *Il Collettivo* brought out by the *Collettivo Politico Metropolitano* (CPM) described:

the development of a very contradictory process which split the entire social body down the middle and which tends to create tensions — think about the Piazza Fontana affair — that could bring the country to the brink ... of civil war.[10]

In the same document the so-called 'latent' civil war was described thus:

There is no restraint. The old right mobilizes for the funeral of a policeman, [and] tends to create a 'lynch mob' atmosphere against 'extremists', basically directed against the [Italian] Communist Party. A bomb goes off and provokes a witchhunt, while there is talk of a *coup d'état*, there are rumours going around about the President of the Republic ... These are the faces of a latent, implicit civil war.[11]

A part of such 'civil war' was constituted by the sharpening up of the repression by the apparatus of the state:

Today two forms of repression coexist and are locked in grim competition with each other: (a) the old type of repression, punitive [and] based on open violence; (b) the active, legalistic, technologically skilled [type of] repression.[12]

and again:

the struggle against a generalized repression is already at a revolutionary stage.[13]

This document was the first theoretical work produced by the CPM where many of those who later became founder members of the Red Brigades first came into contact with each other. The quotations are a good illustration of the scenario (and it is important here that the word has a fictional implication) in which the strategy of the armed struggle took shape: they draw a picture and reveal a theory; they describe a system, thus making their concept transparent. Years previously this process had been initiated in the publication *Lavoro Politico*, partly edited by Mara Cagol, Renato Curcio and others who 'would all later be investigated for the BR'.[14] The culture that inspired the publication was pure Marxism-Leninism. Its theoretical structure was rigid, abstract and academic; its interpretation of the state and state institutions was a scholastic reading of basic Maoism in a national setting. But this Marxist bible — which interacted directly and brutally with reality — was conditioned by the environment and registered all its tensions. There is now little doubt that this perception of reality and its tensions was shaped by a marked subjectivism and was highly debatable and disputable. Nevertheless, it was a widely accepted approach at the time, that echoed a common-sense choice of political activity during those years.[15]

However imaginary this scenario that was slowly building up, of *coups d'état*, state idolatry, the unity of imperialistic control and many other abstract concepts, all probably different in reality, we had an enormous amount of confirmation.[16]

During this period, the mobilization was marked by a sense of social agitation throughout society and by strong mass movements. These movements accepted the simplistic concept of the state, which was then legitimated and absorbed into common parlance as an easy and effective idea. The 'Marxist-Leninist bible' version of the state became the 'vulgate' of the movement, a message easily understood and easily communicated, a jargon of an 'illusory community'.

I increasingly accepted what was then the Marxist-Leninist model: ... the class struggle, the proletarian dictatorship, and its political organization, the proletarian party ... There was some sort of coherent development. I didn't acknowledge the capitalistic society, I considered democracy a mere formality, a simple legalistic for the system, with the traditional political parties, starting with the PCI as the co-manager of power, being responsible for the capitalistic crisis and the attempts to resolve it by drastic social restructuring. At the time I thought there was no longer any room for unarmed opposition. It was normal for me to think that the clash with the State and the Christian Democrats was a consequence of this interpretation of our society and its possible transformation.[17]

This simplified and almost anthropomorphic vision of the state became even more distorted and unilateral when it encountered the physical expression of authoritarianism in the form of particularly aggressive police repression.

In the political arena of acute social conflict, the Piazza Fontana attack constituted an unexpected and unpredictable variable. It quickly upset the equilibrium between the two camps – or was at least perceived to do so – through the weight and the use of a weapon never before contemplated. Today there is little doubt that certain components of the state and of political and economic forces were at the time intent on a policy of revanchism and were considering exerting a 'strong' pressure on the legal institutions through an illegal intervention – which in some cases was even carried out. It is now generally accepted that the planting of the bomb in Piazza Fontana was made possible by the inertia – if not the active complicity – of sections of the state, or more prudently, to 'individual officers' of the state.[18]

It is still unclear today, unfortunately, after more than twenty years and a protracted trial, whether this inertia and complicity was part of the initial plan for the attempt, or whether it was only active in the subsequent cover-up. It is, however, unquestionable today that this episode planted in the collective imagination of the movement an idea, an image, a 'common sense' that labelled the attack a 'state massacre'.

The enduring strength of this image has been the result of a shock that sent waves through a large audience mainly made up of young people who had just started their political apprenticeship. They perceived it as, and it became, the symbol of the 'absolute injustice'. For a large section of the generation of militants in 1968–70, that massacre represented their 'loss of innocence'. This generated a tight theorem: that is, of the integration between the state apparatus, the Christian Democrats, economic power and the fascists. In communique No. 6 of 5 February 1971, the Red Brigades proposed a simplified version of their theorem (their signature at the time was still Brigata Rossa using the singular).

Piazza Fontana, Pinelli, shooting policemen, imprisoned comrades, Della Torre and many others killed, fascist hit squads protected by the police, judges, meddling politicians, the ruling class, the owners' lackeys.[19]

This is a simplification that can, nevertheless, sound credible and even acceptable if we consider the context of the time. This feeling of an 'absolute injustice' is summed to a frustration for a 'relative injustice'. In fact, none of the many public demands for social change expressed by a strong popular movement had been accepted within the political system.[20]

This unfairness and lack of receptivity provoked a move towards the 'substitution' of the institutions. The first expression of this trend was the practice of an 'alternative justice': the desire to correct the large imbalance of powers, which caused a clash – sometimes a violent one – between a material right and a formal but unfulfilled right. This is where a new collective action started. The practice of direct 'mass democracy' sometimes became the practice of 'justice' as counterpower. At this point, the direct clash with fascists and the power that protected them was one of the most common occasions for political involvement.

I remember when I woke up politically. There was Almirante who wanted to make a public speech. I was standing on the pavement and the police charged the crowd. They literally beat everyone up: Gallinari [and] Franceschini. So I became involved with them.[21]

during our mobilization we clashed with the fascists. They burned our things. They made attacks on us, and they attacked a nearby municipality.[22]

You must realize that there was this rather paranoid idea of the fascists, of an immanent *coup d'état* hovering in the air, and let's say the first step ... seems to me to be historically logical.[23]

On the other hand, a large section of non-extremist public opinion was for some time in agreement as to the impending likelihood of a *coup*.[24] It was this permanent feeling of threat that determined the twisting of the Marxist-Leninist analysis of the state, the core of the original theory of the Red Brigades, in a markedly anti-fascist direction.

The shift in emphasis had three important effects on the largest and most radical section of the movement. First, the focus of the struggle increasingly became the military confrontation with the fascists. Secondly, the focus of political tension increasingly became the Christian Democrat Party, as the instrumentalizer of the fascists. And thirdly, there was the development of a theory of 'authoritarian threat' and a consequent development of a strategy to resist and beat it. All three effects are clearly discernible in the 'publications' of that area of militants who later joined the Red Brigades and in the first documents of the BR. For example, from December 1970 to June 1971, a very active group – referred to as the 'Roman Red Brigade' by the publication *Nuova Resistenza* – existed in Rome. Its operations were exlusively anti-fascist: petrol bomb attacks on the studio of *principe* Valerio Borghese, the MSI headquarters in Quadraro, the offices of the Avanguardia Nazionale and the car of a right-wing union organizer. This sort of policy of action was defended thus:

> the fascists, all of them, are in some way an expression of the armed power of the owners. The struggle against all fascists is then a necessary step on the path towards the liberation from all types of oppression and exploitation ... This army of 'black' [fascist] soldiers who placed the Piazza Fontana bomb, takes orders from the generals who sit in parliament.[25]

The first issue of the publication *Nuova Resistenza*, subtitled as the 'communist newspaper of the new resistance', appeared in April 1971. The name was intended to 'indicate that there is a new horizon to continue the tradition of struggle that ... in the past has involved the best forces in our country'.[26] During the same period in the north of Italy another operation started up. This was the *Gruppi di Azione Partigiana* (GAP), which seems a revival of the partisan resistance because of the 'growing role of the state military forces and the fascist paramilitary forces'.[27] The GAP had a different political position to that of the Red Brigades, despite the fact that they later amalgamated with the BR. Curcio and Franceshini thought at the time that the main danger was 'fascist gaulisme':

> It is a given and indisputable fact that the goal of this repressive plan is not so much the institutional destruction of the democratic state as [in the case of] fascism, so much as the most ferocious attack on the revolutionary movement.[28]

This was the first conclusion reached in the analysis of the political system made by the Red Brigades. It was clear that in a certain way they had reduced the long-term strategy to a more immediate and material focus: the broader theoretical approach had been reduced to a provisional short-term programme. As a consequence, the focus became the

Christian Democrats, who were considered the brain behind and the real protagonists of this Italian version of 'gaulisme' and were an easily identifiable and reachable enemy in addition to the fascists. The concept of 'fascism' was expanded to include all the authoritarian trends within the DC together with the criminal activities of the right. Among other things, 'fascism' became factory-management policy: much attention was paid to 'Fiat fascism' and to the 'hard neo-fascist line that has been imposed within the factory'.[29] Two years later, in November 1973, at the Rivalta, Fiat, the BR distributed a leaflet that brought the issue up once more:

> What do the owners want? It's simple: a new dictatorship. But to obtain this goal they first have to strangle the mass struggle within the factory.[30]

This argument was to be constantly repeated in the analysis of the armed group. It was also a concept that encapsulated, yet again, the simplistic way in which the conflict was perceived at a grassroots level.

> As far as the factory struggle was concerned, nothing really, there was the fact that anti-fascism was always there in the struggle within the factory ... so there was a problem of self-defence, and during the occupation [of the factory] ... we had a tent [in front of the occupied factory and] some sons of the owners here – call them *padroni* if you like, but they're really just poor wretches – but they shared the opinions of the fascists – ... they threw molotovs at the tent and then ran off. The same evening ... within a couple of hours we knew exactly who they were and who did it; and we told the union, in the factory obviously, with names ... and during the night we waited for the *carabinieri* to come and arrest them, and instead nothing happened, we waited until morning ... and we organized ourselves just to teach them a lesson, so that something like that wouldn't happen again; seeing that the political forces didn't think about it, and the *carabinieri* didn't think about it, we would think about it![31]

This widespread perception evolved into a new strategic hypothesis called the 'line of resistance' which in March 1973 was explained thus:

> We do not look for exemplary actions, but we state together with the proletarian vanguard the following problems:
> – the *war against fascism* which is not only the fascism of Almirante's blackshirts but the fascism of Andreotti and the Christian Democrat white shirts;
> – the *resistance inside the factories* to strike the enemies, the saboteurs and the liquidators of the worker struggle who want to defeat the movement and reestablish further decades of exploitation and oppression.[32]

This 'line of resistance' with its 'partisan operations' developed in an atmosphere in which there was a new emphasis on the whole tradition of anti-fascism in Italy. At the time the idea of a 'new Resistance' had a central role in a political landscape dominated by the slogans, iconography, literature and mythology of the partisan experience: its memories, its messages, its aims and even its flags were brought back to life.

> I remember that we related to the partisan experience of the left, and to the salvaging of the values of anti-fascism and anti-imperialism. This was exactly the way I remember things, that's to say what we were reading, well, Pesce, I read all his books ... this rather mythological thing about people without many means yet capable of rebelling.[33]

> at the beginning, Che Guevara was the person who played the greatest role, there's no doubt about it ... then later it switched to the Italians: Pietro Secchia, Vittorio Vidali.[34]

> Yes, yes ... some partisan commanders ... But we met Moscatelli himself and from time to time we debated, we asked each other questions and it was very interesting. There was a strong closeness, physical, let's say ideological, moral ... And the songs, all the Resistance and working songs, we loved it.[35]

> [we read] the resistance literature ... oh, I don't know, *Senza Tregua* by Pesce, or the *History of the GAP*.[36]

> some studying, always about the Resistance, Giovanni Pesce, GAP.[37]

It is interesting to see how militants of different political areas, different clandestine organizations and different generations appeared to share the same cultural and mythical references, even the same 'formative book'. If we analyse the political plan generated by this culture, we can draw a first – albeit provisional – conclusion: in this scenario the *defensive* nature of the entire programme appears coherent and almost inevitable. Defensive even though armed, or rather armed *because* defensive.[38] If, in fact, the analysis of the political situation was 'catastrophic' – its 'militarization' – it is obvious that the answer is to adapt the type of struggle to the challenge and 'firepower' presented by the enemy.

> the silent majority in Milan, 'Giovane Italia' in other cities ... [there were] lots of problems for leftist militants to go out on the streets, and I'd say that it's here that the parabola of the defence squads starts.[39]

> This fundamental transition that is the assimilation ... of a concrete culture of violence is the real anti-fascism.[40]

> clashes because of the public speeches made by the fascists who killed a *Lotta Continua* militant in 1974, during a housing occupation ... for instance, the violence against the fascists was often sparked off ... by the fact that we often competed physically for the same spaces.[41]

Everything that has been said until now concerns only the beginning of terrorism, its 'dawn'. For dawn we mean: (a) the origins of the armed struggle in Italy between 1970 and 1974; and (b) the primary condition in which the individual shapes the motivational system that conditioned the choice of the terrorist option. Of course (a) and (b) do not always overlap, and (as in the case of many of those interviewed) these two sets of circumstances may be separated by a period of years. It is easy to see that in the later phases of the armed struggle (in historical-collective terms the mid-1970s and in terms of individual psychology the further formation of the choice for the armed struggle) the *defensive* element and the anti-fascist culture play a decidedly less-important role. But the defensive element returns in another much later phase, with the move towards the self-protection of the group and the preoccupation with the collective interests and survival instincts of the group. This opinion is also shared by Caselli and della Porta.

> The terrorist groups found themselves ever more isolated by the crisis of the youth protest and they increasingly concentrated their resources on the military defence of their members and the survival of the organization.[42]

and once again:

> this concentration of organizational resources on survival.[43]

> For all the fractions into which the BR is divided up then, criminal action – ever less rationalizable in terms of political and social conflicts – expressed the desperate search to testify to the survival of the group and, with it, to the group's existential identity.[44]

It was definitely a different era. At the 'dawn' of the armed struggle it is interesting to note that this *defensive* tendency was interpreted as a weakness, even by groups that had a serious dialogue with those first-armed commando groups. For instance, *Potere Operaio*, commenting on the kidnapping of an Alfa Romeo manager, on 28 June 1983 stated in its newspaper:

> It would have been right to strike Mincuzzi [the kidnap victim] even if he were a sincere democrat, instead of the fascist that he is. It is certainly useful to personalize the enemy, but it becomes damaging and confusing to define ideologically or – even worse – morally, positions of command that are *per se* abstract and interchangeable.[45]

More critical and inspired by different ideas, yet in substance similar to the criticisms of *Potere Operaio* were the comments that appeared a year later in *Bandiera Rossa*, a publication issued by the IV International:.

> In Italy there still is a regime of bourgeois and parliamentary bureaucracy in which the working class can impose respect for some of their basic rights ... the results of the 12 May Referendum ... show that the legal field for the working class is anything but closed.[46]

According to *Bandiera Rossa* to consider 'the legal struggle' totally closed would inevitably make the Red Brigades assume:

a gradualistic idea, as if it were possible for an armed alternative power to be built up slowly, starting off in some factory or neighbourhood ... The problem of the general armed struggle of the whole proletariat can only exist in an already revolutionary situation, in a dual power.[47]

Nevertheless, we cannot rule out the possibility that:

in a context of a general crisis of the system ... small groups of militants engaged in armed action could have some successes.[48]

According to *Bandiera Rossa* this was not sufficient because 'the revolution needs a global strategy.[49] The criticism was directed against a stance of 'defensiveness' that produced 'gradualism' and it pointed to how the grassroots armed-struggle would fall behind the real levels of social and political conflict, even when it was the target of 'white fascism'. During the same period, in April 1974, a document issued by the Red Brigades emphasized that the enemy was indeed 'neo-gaullisme',[50] which was defined as a 'reactionary block' based on 'the growing despotism of capital over the working class, the progressive militarization of the State and the class struggle, [and] the intensification of the strategy of repression'.[51]

The analysis and its programme continued until 1975. During this time the Red Brigades concentrated their fire on three types of target: clearly fascist targets, such as the cars and headquarters of CISNAL, the right-wing trade-union and the murder 'by mistake' of two MSI party activists; the rightist faction of the Christian Democrat Party, in the form of attacks on its study centres and on Massimo De Carolis; and factory targets, such as the attack on the SNIA storerooms, the headquarters of SIDA and attacks on and kidnappings of some managers.

According to the BR, the element that links all these attacks is the picture of the Italian ruling-class as a closely-knit 'bundle' of forces that includes the political right (basically the DC), economic forces (in particular Fiat and Pirelli), and 'black' terrorism. This analysis ultimately stops short of the state; it does not reach its 'heart', that is, the central apparatus and the real institutional system. In fact, it did not even reach the places where repressive decisions were made. Those sections of the state were in any case perceived as being utilized by 'this bundle of counter-revolutionary forces which are preparing a "white coup" according to the instructions given by their imperialist supermasters Ford and Kissinger'.[52] Only in April 1975 do we see a shift away from this sort of defensive strategy to one of attack. The BR then announced their plan to 'unify and turn all the expressions of proletarian antagonism upside down, converging in an attack on "the heart of the state"'.[53]

## 4.3 The representation of proletarian counterpower

Starting from their analysis of fascism and *gaulisme* the BR started to put their 'line-of-resistance' policy into practice. Their first interlocutors were the 'forces of Resistance':

> Forces that have been on the margins of the official institutions of the workers' movement since 1945, but which have always represented the continuity of the revolutionary tendency within the working class, and more recent forces whose experiences of 1968 and 1969 have made a rich contribution to autonomy.[54]

The reduction of the concept of the state to the phenomenology of the reactionary attacks by some of its sectors almost inevitably produced a focus on anything that could be used to oppose it. This is where the idea of 'counterpower' as the anticipation and progressive construction of an anti-state started to take shape. In the May 1971 edition of the Rome publication *Brigate Rosse* we could read that:

> [We must] organize our *proletarian power* in this attack, establishing armed political nuclei in the proletarian neighbourhoods of the city; because the attack and the destruction of bourgeois power, and the establishment of proletarian power are part of the same transition in the revolutionary process.[55]

A few years later, the language used had become even more explicit:

> We think that working to organize the masses means the establishment of sections of the proletarian state in the factories and working-class neighbourhoods: an armed state preparing for war.[56]

In these phrases there is an echo of an important, long-established tradition in the worker and Communist movement, an idea of the theory and practice that had influenced large sections of the class organizations. This idea emerged in some experiences of *Linkskommunismus*, councillorism and anarco-syndicalism.[57] It was a complex but respectable and appealing theory with its own 'ethical' references. This approach was already present at the beginning of this political experience. In a leaflet signed by the *Sinistra Proletaria* in the autumn of 1970 we read:

> The twenty families occupying this building have rejected the bourgeois system of law. And by a hard and rightly violent struggle they have imposed their own law. The legality of the proletarian masses. When the mass starts to rebel the owners get scared and don't know any better than to use their dull violence. This happened on Friday morning [when] 300 armed policeman sent by the owners attacked the squatters, men, women, children and comrades who were there to show their support for this cause, and at the end

they tried to 'do justice' using their weapons. But the masses are not afraid and for each attack their desire to fight is even greater. 'We won't leave this building until we all have a home even if that means that they'll kill us all', that's what they were shouting, and all the other proletarians came to support them. So the owners have withdrawn, and after this useless violence they switched to a new tactic, to the attempt to divide people by false promises. But if they cannot break the masses with violence how will they be able to do it with deceit? In fact, the answer of the squatting families has not changed. 'We have all fought, we have all resisted together, and we'll win together: we want houses, for everyone and now' ... the people's solidarity and unity was witnessed once again last night. This morning the families have won and their victory is shared by all the proletariat.[58]

At the time, this view was shared by many sectors of the left – not just the extra-institutional left – and *Sinistra Proletaria* and the Red Brigades took it to the extreme. The word 'justice' is central and repeated almost obsessively in all the written material. The emphasis is particularly on the concept of 'proletarian' justice as an assertion of an antagonistic 'bias' versus the bias of the establishment and as the application of a new 'norm' imposed by this bias. Theory though has often been the result of an emphatic and instrumental reading of the facts. Yet in BR Communique No. 3, where for the first time the BR claim responsibility for an attack, we read that: 'unless the spy Pellegrini resigns, in which case the Popular Court of Justice will grant him a pardon...'[59] The use of the phrase 'grant pardon' is significant and we shall return to it later on.

From the 'alternative court' there is an almost natural transition to the definition of an 'alternative law' and to the assessment of such as a central principle and as an ethical and existential turning-point. This alternative law had to be and was assessed in practice: this was in fact the 'rationale' of many actions, rallies and activities decided as 'proletarian' or 'popular justice'. Among other things, I am referring to the 'proletarian pillory' in Trent for fascists who had attacked striking workers at the Ignis works,[60] the 'masses trials' and to other instruments whose use for a while gave the left the impression that it was establishing and administering a system of grassroots justice; a justice whose legal foundation lay in different guarantees of the bourgeois law.

there was a progressive expansion ... of the legal limits to political violence ... that produce a *de facto* legitimization of violent actions ... The idea I had of the armed struggle was exactly one of a progressive expansion, but this idea of mine was rooted in the general dynamic that was investing the law system, the institutions and, perhaps even the constitution.[61]

In terms of the life of the individual this meant that:

this chap is responsible, it is him here and now, there is already a trial logic ... where you've already decided that he is guilty ... and what makes you different is the punishment, the punishment that you allot to that person who is guilty of those things. You go along and take on this sense of justice.[62]

There is a trend to transform this personal 'sense of justice' into an institution. Only much later did another armed organization – not the BR – reassess this point critically.

> Within *Prima Linea* a debate started based on some of the essays by Foucault. We discussed whether it was right to establish people's courts, if the model of society proposed by revolutionaries would not have some of the authoritarian elements already present, such as the right to administrate justice, for instance ... if this alternative society wasn't by any chance repeating the bourgeois model, with courts, police, carabinieri, the secret services.[63]

Such a discussion never took place within the BR. After Communique No. 3 the organization never dropped the language and praxis of 'counterpower' that they emphasize slowly in reference to alternative justice, a 'counterjustice'. In this way, the BR intended to launch an attack on the most important prerogative of the law: the prerogative of being unique and universally valid. For the BR, the power issue took the form of a challenge to the source of law. As a consequence it was important for the organization to establish its legality as an institution that produces justice. So in each action there was a growing emphasis on law and justice: trial and countertrial, state prison and people's prison, bourgeois army and proletarian army. The symbolism of the language and its pedagogical use became exaggerated. The same was true of the ritual – both macabre and grotesque – of 'captivity', 'interrogation, 'punishment': a system that mimicked the state in a perfect inverse mirror-image.[64]

> The arch-spy seems to have accepted the punishment of the People's Court in a disciplined way. If it's true [then] we will pardon him.[65]

> Now even in the bourgeois courts where the owners would like to punish proletarian illegality, the people will start to assert its own 'illegality'.[66]

> a Red Brigade group has taken [him], questioned [him] and put [him] on trial.[67]

> At the moment he is a prisoner in a people's gaol.[68]

> Today, Tuesday 18 December at dawn a Fiat manager has been freed ... He has 'collaborated' in a satisfactory way.[69]

> We have proofs and photocopies of documents about arms trafficking. Mario Sossi has given an extensive testimony on all this.[70]

The obsessive repetition became the structure of a didactic, ideological message. Once this conceptual and linguistic mechanism had been absorbed the next logical step was to absorb its forms: that is, those relating not only to the application of justice but also to its 'suspension', not only the rule but also the exception from the rule, hence the emphasis on the notions of 'pardon', 'recognition' and 'repentance'.

> We need ... a notion of proletarian justice that comrades cannot disregard. Sossi has been imprisoned as a persecutor of the revolutionary left. During the trial he criticized himself seriously and he has also collaborated in the reconstruction of facts, events and people [which are] very interesting for us, in a sincere and open way. He has to be given credit for this.[71]

The terms 'in a disciplined way', 'collaborate', 'testify', and 'pardon' used by the Red Brigades are interesting because they reveal not only the assumption of a definable authority in so far as this reproduces in an inverse sense the competences of the state, but also the search to establish an ethical base for such authority. This ethical base must be able to demonstrate not only power but also generosity. The moral foundation of proletarian power seems to require the maximum of strength and determination, but also a touch of humanity; it is a power that asserts its authority most when it is also capable of 'not punishing', capable of pardoning. This is, however, exactly the opposite of the interpretation given by the authors of the book entitled *Brigate Rosse*.

> imitating police language, news of the 'capture', 'trial' and 'provisional freedom' are given.[72]

If what we have said up to this point is true, this is neither an imitation of the police nor merely the language of propaganda. It is instead the expression of an ideological position and even of a philosophical stance. This is true to the point that even the most 'scandalous', 'illegal' or 'immoral' action – even by the standards of the left – is never justified on purely instrumental grounds, but is always defended as 'legitimate'.

> Expropriation shouldn't be thought of simply in terms of the need to finance the organization but should be considered as one of the basic instruments in the struggle to build up a proletarian counterpower.[73]

> In expropriation there is a conjunction of legality and revolutionary morality.[74]

## 4.4 The conception of the 'humanity' and ideology of the 'absolute enemy'

Eleven years after the 'pardon' granted to Mario Sossi, the concept of 'clemency' appears again in even more explicit and intentionally 'scandalous' terms in the BR communique that announced the 'liberation' of the magistrate D'Urso.

D'Urso has collaborated with proletarian justice .... Taking everything into consideration proletarian justice will allow an act of clememcy. The sentence will be suspended and the prisoner D'Urso will be freed.[75]

Immediately prior to this the *Comitato unitario di campo di Palmi* (an organization of imprisoned terrorists operating from inside the special prison in Palmi, Calabria) had made the following declaration:

The death sentence on D'Urso is just, but because the force of the revolutionary movement is such as to be able to allow acts of magnanimity, also taking into account that D'Urso has repented and has collaborated with proletarian justice, the Comitato unitario di Campo (CUC) of Palmi unanimously agrees to his release.[76]

In a previous text we can read the following still more significant words:

Without hesitation we declare that, due to his crimes and the politics of which he is an expression, the hangman D'Urso has been justly condemned. The decision taken by the BR is certainly a great act of humanity, the highest possible in this era and in this country where the Christian Democrat rabble run around, its multicoloured subjects and the stupid revisionist hyenas. For the proletariat, humanitarian acts are all those acts of revolutionary war that directly or indirectly hasten the ruin of the imperialist bourgeoisie and its state.[77]

Two and a half years earlier, Renato Curcio (who was presumably the author of the above cited text) had expressed similar concepts.

The action of revolutionary justice [carried out] on Aldo Moro is the highest act of humanity possible in this class-divided society ... For us there is no morality taken from outside society – morality is what serves to bring about the destruction of the old society.[78]

Consider carefully, *'the highest act of humanity possible in this society'*. This is the key phrase. And this is its origins in the words of one of those directly involved.

Renato and I simply repeated a phrase of Lenin's that we had happened to read quite by chance at that time, 'the death of a class enemy is the highest act of humanity possible in a class-divided society'. It would have been a simple but clear message ... The morning afterwards, in the courtroom we felt under observation more than ever, everyone was looking at our cages. Renato asked permission to speak, the president [of the court] gave him permission and he calmly, pronouncing the words well, spoke the phrase that we had agreed on. He was immediately dragged out of the courtroom. It was my turn and turning to the president, I repeated the words spoken by Renato. I was dragged out too. One at a time, in the security cells in the bunker, we saw our other comrades arrive. We smiled at one another, they couldn't resist it and they repeated too the phrase. The rite of the historical leaders was respected right to the end. We were tried three times and got fourteen years of prison for that phrase. It was the price that we knew we would have to pay.[79]

Alongside that phrase there is another which is, in my opinion, equally important.

well, this is all we can do, we are only doing it out of scrupulousness because, you know, a death sentence is not something to be taken lightly, not even by us. We are willing to take the responsibility that is ours, that is due to us and we just want ... among us there are some people who think that you haven't intervened directly because you've been badly advised.[80]

The basic concept expressed in both phrases is what we could term a 'state of necessity'.[81] For the author of the telephone call it was not a question of whether or not a death sentence could be carried out, but rather the way in which the decision was to be taken (lightly or otherwise). It was taken for granted that the death sentence could be carried out and that people had the power to do so. There are many reasons for such a belief but most of them (those of a political or 'juridical' nature) followed the primary and principle reason that was quite simply that the concepts of humanity, liberty and justice are 'forced' and 'limited' concepts, owing to the conditions. The extensive and universal interpretations of those concepts are either ideologically fraudulent or a giving-in to the bourgeois vision of the world. Only starting from the understanding of the condition of a generalized lack of liberty within relationships marked by class power can we speak of humanity, liberty and justice. Once this assumption is accepted, the path to be taken is obligatory, the choices rigid and the alternatives and options limited. Given the existence − albeit not *de jure* − of the death sentence that originates in and is applied by the state, it seems to be an automatic consequence that there can also be a death sentence that originates and is applied by another entity: in so far as this is 'imposed' by the existence of the enemy power. Consequently, the application of the 'revolutionary' death sentence is − given the conditions − a voluntary choice ('we are willing to take the responsibility that is ours'), but on the part of whoever is however subject to coercion: that is, of whoever finds himself in a situation that is 'limited' and for whom, therefore, an *absolute* criteria of justice does not apply. This generates yet other consequences: the only free act a constrained person can make use of is that which promotes the conquest of liberty. It is only here in the act of liberty itself that the principles and criteria meet and are legitimated. The act of liberty is, therefore, the litmus test for all behaviour and the only reliable and tangible measure of evaluation and judgement. The act of liberty takes in therefore – entirely – humanity and justice. Consequently, legality is determined by whoever breaks the dominant legality that dominates the oppressed. Justice is determined by whoever attacks the class justice that judges the exploited. Humanity is determined by whoever denies the pacific coexistence between the oppressed and the oppressors – and who thus asserts another possible humanity and coexistence.

Within capitalist society, which generates death and poverty on a daily basis, the fact that someone other than the state assumes the power to apply the death sentence appears an indisputable and incontestable right: it appears as a 'free' choice even if this is 'imposed' by a regime of non-liberty. The contesting of that choice would appear then to be a negation of the existence of a regime of non-liberty.

If we try to rerun the entire logic expounded up to this point – accepting both its assumptions and mechanisms – it follows that we accept the final device contained in the last affirmation, together with its extreme corollary.

> there is something else underneath that says: I'm forced to do this. ... Forced by the fact that it's the only possible reality and so, in fact, all this story, I mean to say: I'm not a killer, I'm not a terrorist, I'm someone with a series of values, who wants to be active in politics and today the only way ... to be politically active is this, because there is no other way because they have been taken away from us, they have taken away every other type of intervention.[82]

If it is true that the capitalist regime is the 'machine of repression' for the social individual, the breaking of this machine – by the mechanical application of a basic dialectic – is then the first act towards freeing these repressed energies. Perhaps only potentially, as the allusion and representation of a possibility. If the breaking of the machine (even if only, I repeat, by allusion or symbolic gesture) reaches the apex of the system of domination, the 'quality' of the act is heightened. In this way it is not difficult to arrive at the phrase used by Curcio: the killing of Moro as an affirmation – both concrete and symbolic – of the chance to negate the dominant meaning of the concept of humanity and to 'un-veil' another possible meaning. In the context of this unveiling, the 'perfect' and 'deadliest' action is also the 'supreme act'. That possible meaning of humanity is based on its 'limited' and 'finite' nature. The concept of humanity that interests the BR was located within a delimited and interrupted field: or rather, it was formulated with a guarantee that its meaning was strictly connected to a logical, behavioural and normative space (because it comes afterwards, is more formulated and less unlimited) with respect to that prescribed by common sense (false consciousness) and the dominant ideology. A concept of humanity, then, that starts from the assumption that there are *many* concepts of humanity and that it intends to take on immediately the limits imposed to its own conception as the very ground of the ideological and political clash.

Having said this, we are still apparently in an area of debate that was habitual for the revolutionary left in that period and for the entire Marxist tradition in general (but which also applies to the progressive left): it stressed the classist and biased nature of the ideologies and their conceptual categories and rejected the work of mystification carried out by the ruling class. On the other hand, it is this tradition that stresses the potentially non-biased and non-classist character – hence not limited and not finite – of a possible *other* ideology, in so far as it is the expression of values and categories endowed with a universal meaning: a meaning that the class struggle carries into the open, which is affirmed by the hegemony of the workers within a revolutionary social bloc, which the proletarian victory transforms into dominant concepts and which the abolition of classes translates into universal culture. We are back with purely scholastic Marxism that establishes the working class as the bearer of a general worldview, entrusted with the historical task of affirming it.[83]

Essentially, then, this is the reaffirmation of a vision of the world that, with its insistence on the existence of the class bias, tends to reinforce its potential and future universality. Where, then, does terrorism break – if it is a break – with the tradition of the Marxist left (old and new)? The answer lies in the desire to affirm and impose (here and now with the instruments available) a certain hegemony – that necessitates the use of pressure, power and violence – for a future society. Why is this desire presented as a break and why is it only a question of an apparent break? The fact that the affirmation of hegemony can resort to murder is not simply the last step in the traditional escalation in the *use of the instruments*; it is rather the explicit expression of the fact that the *alternative emerging right* (which also emerges through the act of political murder) is incomparable. That is, it does not recognize other values to which to submit itself, against which to measure itself and in relation to which to *exist*; it is, *as of now*, the supreme judicial principle.

Here we undoubtedly register a new element with respect to the past, but it is difficult to say whether the element of interruption prevails over that of continuity: at least as far as the tradition of the Italian left and the theory of counterpower – that in itself has had some diffusion – is concerned.

The phrases cited earlier on ('the highest act of humanity' and 'a death sentence is not something to be taken lightly') date back to years that fall after the period under consideration. I have dedicated so much space to them because, in one sense, they constitute the conclusion of the course of subversion and reflection undertaken by the 'historical group' of the BR; and in another sense, because they represent the synthesis of the 'negative anthropology' of terrorist thought. This terroristic thought was already active, however, as we have seen, from the initial phase: when there was a short circuit in the experience of 'injustice'. The first effect is the singling out – albeit in a questionable and 'confused' way – of the 'absolute enemy'.

> The discussion was sometimes exaggerated, sometimes by the demands of a particular action which in the long-run meant clearing up any confusion [also] from the political point of view and the human point of view. So you'd find yourself needing to – let's put it like this – needing to think about political murder as being necessary for the political line of the organization, for the activity of the organization itself ... It's obvious that this way of relating to things, in the long run, could produce the moments of rejection, in the sense that, in so far as every single aspect was examined in detail, there was still a black point, a black hole where you more or less hushed up the uncertainties that you nevertheless felt. That is, in any case, the weight of deciding on the life of another person, in so far as this was painted in black colours [was] something that I felt rather deeply. There wasn't any antiseptic complicity, even if you did everything you could to get it, just to reduce it to a mere exercise of a political activity of the organization. It's a bit like the comparison ... with a war for soldiers who have to deal with the problem of death in ... brutal terms.[84]

> I hinted at the depersonalization of the enemy ... this translates into an action of concrete annihilation ... a mechanism of hate ... of contempt ... for the man himself ... I believe that it is part of ... any form of political contraposition, at least up to a certain level of the polarization of real interests.[85]

In this uncertain and approximate synthesis of an *a posteriori* reconstruction, this is how the question of human life ('the problem of death') is dealt with by those young people who chose the armed struggle: the scheme outlined earlier in the chapter seems to fit perfectly with the conceptualization of political murder produced by the militaristic-terroristic culture. The transformation of the adversary into an enemy and into an 'absolute enemy', whose elimination will generate political advantages, seems to come from that 'physicality' of the direct relationship with the antagonist.

> I thought about it ... and organized to do things, I did [things] in this climate, which was a climate, among other things, that motivates strongly from a point of view of feelings that pushes you towards violence, that is ... by dint of hearing it said. But when it is no longer something referred [to you], it's something lived as a concrete experience, that 'that head of section is a bastard', that 'that chap deserves what's coming to him', ... 'I'm getting this illness in the paintshop because they don't give me enough breaks', and things like that, then it's clear that you are in a system of ... measuring the relationship with whoever belongs to, let's say, an enemy alignment, [measuring] that is really ... motivated by feelings ... I thought that ... there was a very strong component of ... then one said of proletarian hate ... in what happened, ... there was very little ideology, I mean, it wasn't a problem so that ... certainly, a mechanism of depersonalization acts ... [this is]

accentuated when the level of violence is accentuated ... a violence exercised against whoever is physically against you, who immediately and directly represents ... this polarization of interests, of alignments, of ... of ways of life, it was something that ... I thought motivated ... motivated logically, I mean there was ... really a school ... a school of war, a school of violence ... there it is, the problem is exactly that sort of friend–enemy polarization ... this process of depersonalization just gets worse as the gap widens.[86]

That 'process of depersonalization' is more efficacious the more one relies on the 'emotional' impact of a pain just suffered (once again, the theme of 'injustice'):

the day afterwards, when the news got to the demonstration that ... that this guy from the Digos was dead ... something which was accepted ... at least from the emotional point of view as a fact ... as a real fact, as an experienced fact ... just as the death of Lorusso was experienced as a real fact, that is, there was this ... this feeling of hatred, of enmity that, [which] in some cases [was] hardly ideological at all, it was just ... a polarization of institutions, of feelings and of things ... things like this.[87]

All this was brought about by the internalization – in 'absolute' terms and in terms of the inverted mirror-image – of the category of 'justice' as *ragion fattasi*.[88]

Street battles are different, they are ... something legal, something experienced with other people ... but [in the case of organized and premeditated violence] you start to do something different, you carry out an enquiry on someone so there is a sort of political enquiry beforehand, but psychologically it becomes something different, you single out someone who is responsible; it is not the State as before ... with policemen, and the Flying Squad [but] real physical people, this chap does this ... and has done that and you start a trial ... The trial begins when you single out someone on paper, that is to say, you make a person correspond to a political need ... that chap is responsible, it is him right here and now, that is already a trial logic ... where you've already decided that he is guilty ... and what makes you different is the penalty, the penalty that you allot to that person who is guilty of those things. You go along and take on this sense of justice ... so in actual fact he is not even a person any more, he has been emptied and you load him up with other crimes, other responsibilities ... At this point you can't afford to be totally involved ... you are someone who is meting out justice, who is stating values, and so there is no place for ... strong emotions even if you have them inside, even if the situation is charged with feelings ... but not in that role, not at that time.[89]

In the phrase 'in that role' it is important to note how the mechanism of reciprocity works automatically: the 'emptying' of the person chosen as the target precisely corresponds to the 'emptying' of the instigator of the action.

If we consider again the phrase 'We are willing to take the responsibility that is ours, that is due to us ...' we can see that these words take on the sense of a regulatory and bureaucratic formula: one that alludes to an organization that is located consciously – within the whole of its 'social justification' and in the perception that its individual members have of it – within the general division of labour, powers and competences. The 'role' carried out by the 'target' is part of that general division of labour. It is interesting (tragically interesting) to note how that conceptual schema is activated during the terrorist action and becomes the impulse and motivation for death:

> my first action of wounding was Girolamo Mechelli. I was part of the cover operation ... yes, I think he was a bastard that one ..., but he was an old man and [these things] always turn out for the worst. Why? Because then you're there and you say: I have done the inquiry, politically I know who he is, I know that he has done this, I know that he is responsible for this and that. You have done the operation of singling him out and of *emptying* him [ed's. italics], you give him all the other 'crimes' that you have to give him. In fact it's not him any more and then you find that person there, facing you, well ... I had to spot him because I had to give the go-ahead in the operation and so I had to go into the bar ... where this man was having breakfast, well ... what I mean is, we had a photograph of him and that's all, but Balzarani had seen him before and ... said to me 'look, he's that one there' and so I had to go in and so ... There was a moment in which hate took over, that is as a healthier feeling, I'd say, that is to say 'bloody hell, there he is that bloody demo-christian wretch, you are the worst'. Just, you know, it would have been much better if it had finished in a fight there ... well, I don't know ... if I'd have grabbed him by the scruff of the neck and I'd have said to him 'You bastard! You've done this and that.' ... Then instead, no, it's not that thing there, it becomes something else, it becomes the fact that he has other responsibilities and so he must be dealt with in another way. And so there the hate goes away and it becomes impersonal ... it becomes social. Social, that is, not relating to society as a whole, but to that group that you belong to. So it's not your job to sort out society's conflicts ... [that depends on] the rules determined by the ideology, by the way the organization [decides] to operate.[90]

In any case what prevailed was a 'culture of negation of the enemy'.[91]

## Conclusions

It seems to me that the analysis of interviews and documents about the rough path towards political murder confirms our hypothesis: that is, that the perception and the conceptualization of the 'absolute enemy' ('a culture that denies the enemy') is the element that welds together some of the key points relating to the sphere of experience of the armed militant, to the mechanisms of ideological legitimation formulated by him or her. At the beginning of this chapter we presented this intellectual and psychological sequence: perception of 'absolute injustice' (definition of the adversary as author of absolute injustice) or 'absolute enemy' (delegitimization of this enemy) and the absolute legitimization of the war against him. The different stages in this chain can also be regrouped in the way in which we have organized this chapter. The representation of power (see section 4.2) is the context in which the enemy operated and became responsible for the 'absolute injustice'. This responsibility delegitimizes the enemy to the point where he becomes a mere 'function' that can be eliminated. To do this, we need to create new spaces where traditional law has no legitimacy and where, instead, the law of the people operates (see section 4.3). On the other hand, when a counterpower starts to administer alternative justice, it needs a moral foundation because it destabilizes the way society is organized by the state. This moral foundation is found in concepts such as 'state of necessity' and 'class bias' as limits, both real and theoretical, to the use of universal categories and valid *erga omnes* (see section 4.4). But the 'absolute enemy' is the key figure in the sequence. This enemy is responsible for 'absolute injustice' (for which he deserves to encounter 'absolute hatred'),[92] and in doing so he makes the acceptance of universal categories such as 'humanity' impossible, thus imposing a 'bias' as a consequence. Provisionally at least, if we examine it more closely, morality also has to be, or become, universal even for the terrorist.

This is the first answer to the question about the relationship between ethics and policy when policy becomes war. As Nando dalla Chiesa (1984) put it, 'the discussion revolves around the dilemma as to whether terrorism cancels the ethical dimension or expands it to the point of fanatacism'.[93] If we re-reconstruct a life-course, the predominant tendency is to give a positive, gratifying version. Yet, even after this consideration, I think we can accept the second hypothesis presented by dalla Chiesa.

The 'expansion of the ethical dimension' seems to be the context and the foundation of the value systems of the clandestine militant. He is not a 'terrorist without a cause' but a man with too many 'causes'.[94] It is an excess of 'morality' that seems 'unavoidable'. It brings to mind that 'inevitability' of a 'moral duty' that, according to Schmitt, brings the 'partisan' to 'define the adversary as criminal and inhuman, an absolute non-value'. Thus we return to the words at the beginning of this analysis and we return to Schmitt who says that the terms 'friend' and 'enemy' have to be understood in their concrete existential sense. This premise allows Schmitt to define better than anybody else the cruel and uselessly tragic nature of the terrorist's human condition.

The enemy questions our role. If your role is well defined without uncertainty how can this duplicity come from the enemy? The enemy is something that cannot be brushed aside for any reason or who can simply be cancelled out because he is of no value. The enemy is on the same level as me. For this reason I must dispute with him while we fight, in order to get my own measure, my own limits, my role.[95]

In other words:

I define this person as the enemy and as such, since we are at war, to take his life is part of my argument.[96]

and this is precisely the argument of 'war'.

## Notes

1 The work of Carl Schmitt (1963 and 1975) offers interesting suggestions for an interpretation of terrorism. I have used his definition of 'absolute enemy' and 'absolute antagonism' throughout the chapter.

2 According to Franco Piperno in an interview with the Italian weekly *Panorama*, these organizations are the 'legitimate children of 1968' and were 'established by militants who developed politically during the red two years of 1969–71'. Piperno claimed that the ideological references of these militants were mainly *operaista* and very different from the 'the old orthodox PCI tendency'. The *operaista* line links the essays published in *Quaderni Rossi* (the short-lived organ of the *operaista* left-wing of the PSI) to a variety of political experiences in the factories (Classe Operaia, Gatto selvaggio), up until the organization of *Potere Operaio* was first established in the Veneto and Emilia regions of Italy and later became national. It is a transition with no continuity, full of contradictions and irreversible breaks. The use of the term *operaista*, then, is better understood as a reference to certain origins and to a broad cultural and linguistic attitude.

3 G.C. Caselli and D. della Porta (see Chapter 3) date the beginning of the second phase (1974–6) to the Sossi kidnapping, whereas I am inclined to interpret this episode as the end of the first phase. This indicates a difference of opinion as to the interpretation of the turning-point, but clear agreement as to its location.

4 Ibid., Chapter 3, section 3.1.

5 Interview with P.L., p. 6. Interview carried out by the author.

6 Interview with M.Fe., p. 10. Interview carried out by Donatella della Porta.

7 Interview with A.S., p. 15. Interview carried out by Giuseppe De Lutiis.

8 Interview with M.Fe., p. 16.

9 Interview with A.S., pp. 17–18.

10 *Collettivo Politico Metropolitano* (1970) p. 11.

11 Ibid., p. 12.

12 Ibid., p. 17.

13 Ibid., p. 21.

14 *Soccorso Rosso* (1976) p. 32.

15 In their preface note to the influential book, *La Strage di Stato* (1970), the authors wrote that, 'we are neither surprised nor indignant at the use of the

massacre of sixteen people to create a new government equilibrium. Neither are we surprised or indignant at the fact that this apparatus covers the responsibilities with the murders and imprisonment of innocents ... The meaning of this alternative inquiry into the bombings is to offer the comrades a modest instrument to expand the understanding of the bourgeois state to a popular level. Because as Lenin and Gramsci said, "the truth is revolutionary"'.

16 Interview with M.Fe., p. 43.

17 Interview with I.R., pp. 60–1. Interview carried out by Giuseppe De Lutiis.

18 Reference to the section entitled 'da Piazza Fontana a Ordine Nero' in the very well-researched work by De Lutiis (1984).

19 *Brigata Rossa*, Communique No. 6, 5 February 1971, in *Re Nudo*, 1971.

20 Melucci (1982) writes that, 'The expectations created during the struggle are not satisfied by the 'realistic' conclusion within the institutions. It is inevitable that disillusioned fringes of militants who long for the original purity of the movement and resist what is perceived by them as the betrayal of the first goals will be formed.' The dissatisfaction contributes to produce that 'excess of militancy' defined by Pizzorno (1978). The issue of the 'realistic ending' or 'lacking translation' of the struggles, with the consequent 'frustration' is a different issue from the 'system blockage', but there are nevertheless many links between the two. Bonanate (1979b and 1983) and Pasquino (1984) are references for the debate on relations between 'system blockage' and the 'quest for terrorism'.

21 Interview with A.C. Interview carried out by Donatella della Porta.

22 Interview with A.B., p. 17. Interview carried out by Luisa Passerini.

23 Interview with M.Fe., p. 17.

24 In Italy during the period under analysis, between 1969 and 1974, there were five massacres. 'It is now clear that the "protagonists" of the Piazza Fontana massacre were neo-fascists, both from within and outside the structures of the state. One cannot deny that Giannettini has been, and may still be, an intelligence agent with the SID. With him many others appear: officers, generals, ministers, prime ministers ... On 22 July 1970 while in the city of Reggio Calabria a popular rebellion was at its peak an attempt to the *treno del sole* near Gioia Tauro caused six dead and fifty injured. It was clearly a neo-fascist operation. On 17 May 1973, a neo-fascist threw a bomb into the courtyard of the police headquarters. ... On 28 May 1974, a bomb exploded in the Piazza della Loggia in Brescia during an anti-fascist rally, and left eight dead and ninety-four wounded. A few months later in August 1974 a bomb went off on the train *Italicus* leaving twelve dead and 105 wounded. *Ordine nero* claimed responsibility for the action. ... The massacre was indiscriminately against civilians. It was done not to hit particular victims but to intimidate the rest of the people. It is meant to provoke fear, the need for protection and security.' The quotation is from Tranfaglia's work in the collection of essays edited by Galleni (1981).

25 *Soccorso Rosso* (1976) p. 87.

26 Ibid., p. 91.

27 *Potere Operaio* (1971).

28 *Soccorso Rosso* (1976) p. 104.

29 Ibid., p. 175.

30 Ibid., p. 125.

31 Interview with A.B., p. 20. See chapter 6 for a full quotation relating to this episode.

32 *Potere Operaio del Lunedì* (1973a).

33 Interview with A.S., p. 17.

34 Interview with L.B., p. 2. Interview carried out by Giuseppe De Lutiis.

35 Interview with A.B., pp. 19 and 24.

36 Interview with M.Fe., p. 12.

37 Interview with L.B., p. 8.

38 According to Boato (1982), 'at the very beginning leftist terrorism is mainly a defensive hypothesis and strategy based on an "old-fashioned resistance" notion of the fascist offensive and the danger of a military *coup*'. Boato (1980) also states that 'One can say that during the period 1975–80, leftist terrorism would have been of smaller dimension and less political influence had the development of the strategy of tension, massacres and coup in which not only were right-wing military commandos involved but also a part of the state police and state intelligence, been prevented'.

39 Interview with L.B., p. 6.

40 Interview with M.S., p. 19. Interview carried out by Claudio Novaro.

41 Interview with M.S., pp. 19–21.

42 Caselli and della Porta, Chapter 3, section 4.

43 Ibid., section 4.2.

44 Ibid., section 4.2.

45 *Potere Operaio del lunedì* (1973b).

46 *Bandiera Rossa* (1974).

47 Ibid.

48 Ibid.

49 Ibid.

50 *Brigate Rosse* (1974).

51 *Brigate Rosse* (1971).

52 *Soccorso Rosso* (1976) p. 265.

53 *Brigate Rosse* (1975).

54 *Brigate Rosse* (1973).

55 *Soccorso Rosso* (1976) p. 87.

56 *Brigate Rosse* (1973).

57 We also find the notion of a 'dualism of powers' in the mainstream of the worker movement. See, for example, Lenin in his *Letters from Afar* (1971) and the writings of Mao. For references on the left opposition with its many nuances, see the work of Rosa Luxembourg, Karl Korsh and Anton Pannekoek.

58 *Sinistra Proletaria* (1970a).

59 *Soccorso Rosso* (1976) p. 87.

60 The publication *Foglio di lotta della Sinistra Proletaria* – which announced the news that the Red Brigades had established themselves as examples of the 'new legality' – , also refers to the 'kidnapping and pillory imposed by the Ignis workers on the fascist in Trent'.

61 Interview with N.S., p. 33. Interview carried out by Donatella della Porta.

62 Interview with A.S., p. 45.

63 Interview with M.Fe., p. 37. Michel Foucault (1972) refers to the 'popular justice' promoted in France by the 'cause du peuple' and goes on to state that 'the forms of the state apparatus that the bourgeois apparatus has transmitted

to us cannot in any way be used as a model for the new forms of organization ... For this reason I was against the people's court'.

64 According to Carlo Marletti in Villa (1979), the 'symbolic function of this trial is to represent the terrorist actions as a popular justice, to legitimate them as a revolutionary subject. Popular trials appear in all modern revolutions. But we must remember that at the beginning this phenomenon was part of a spontaneous and collective reaction, in the wake of already existing and widespread military or guerrilla operations. The modern terrorist uses this formula in a different way.' Marletti goes on to comment on the transformation of the popular trial during the kidnapping of Mario Sossi and Aldo Moro.

65 *Soccorso Rosso* (1976) p. 80.

66 Ibid., p. 97.

67 Ibid., p. 156.

68 Ibid., p. 167.

69 Ibid., p. 175.

70 Ibid., p. 231.

71 From an internal document quoted in *requisitoria Brigate Rosse*, by Bruno Caccia (1975).

72 *Soccorso Rosso* (1976) p. 110.

73 *Nuova Resistenza*, May 1976.

74 Renato Curcio (1975) in *L'Espresso*, No. 1.

75 *Il Manifesto*, 15 January 1981.

76 *Il Manifesto*, 11 January 1981.

77 Ibid.

78 *Il Manifesto*, 11 May 1978.

79 The account of Alberto Franceschini in Franceschini, Buffa and Giustolisi (1988).

80 From the text of a telephone call to Eleanora Moro on the afternoon of 30 April 1978 by a member of the BR, published in *Paese Sera*, 17 October 1978.

81 At this point we have used concepts and arguments already widely dealt with in Dini and Manconi (1981).

82 Interview with A.S., p. 46.

83 Karl Marx (1844).

84 Interview with Marco, pp. 56–7. Interview carried out by Giuseppe De Lutiis.

85 Interview with N.S., p. 53.

86 Ibid, p. 21.

87 Ibid, p. 41.

88 Ferrajoli (1986).

89 Interview with A.S., p. 45.

90 Ibid, pp. 46–7.

91 Interview with M.S., p. 64.

92 In Baum and Mahler (1980) we find this affirmation of the RAF: 'total hatred is at the basis of this class contradiction that the ruling imperialist class must maintain unchanged ... Only the solution of this irreconcilable contradiction

and the elimination of the exploitation by the ruling class with the class struggle are human [*sic.*] for the oppressed and create humanity'.

93 Nando dalla Chiesa in della Porta (1984).

94 Raymond Aron (1976).

95 C. Schmitt (1975).

96 Interview with Marco, p. 57.

## References

Various authors (1970) *La strage di Stato*, Rome, Samonà and Savelli.

R. Aron (1976) *Penser la guerre, Clausewitz, II, L'age planetaire*, Paris, Gallimard.

*Bandiera Rossa* (1974) Organo dei Gruppi Comunisti Rivoluzionari, Italian section of the IV International, No. 9.

G. Baum and H. Mahler (1980) *Der Minister und der Terrorist*, Hamburg, Rowholt Taschenbuch Verlag GmbH, Spiegel-Verlag Rudolf Augstein GmbH & Co., KG.

M. Boato (1980) 'Il terrorismo e il caso italiano', *Mondoperaio*, No. 10.

M. Boato (1982) 'Un 'terremoto' traumatizzante in una società in crisi', *Ottantagiorni. Racconti di notizie*, January–February.

L. Bonanate (ed.) (1979) *Dimensioni del terrorismo politico*, Milano, Franco Angeli.

L. Bonanate (1983), 'Terrorismo e governabilità', *Rivista italiana di Scienza politica*, XIII, April, pp. 37–64.

*Brigate Rosse* (1973) 'Autointervista', *Potere Operaio del lunedì*, January.

*Brigate Rosse* (1974) 'Contro il neogollismo portare l'attacco al cuore dello stato', *Il Tempo*, 13 May.

*Brigate Rosse* (1975) 'Risoluzione della Direzione strategica' (April), *Controinformazione*, 7–8 June.

*Brigate Rosse* (1976) 'Autointervista', *Soccorso Rosso*, September.

B. Caccia (1975) 'Requisitoria Brigate Rosse', in G. Guiso, A. Bonomi and F. Tommei (eds), *Criminalizzazione della lotta di classe*, Verona, Bertani.

*Collettivo Politico Metropolitano* (1970) 'Lotta sociale e organizzazione nella metropoli', *Il Collettivo*, single issue, Milan, January.

R. Curcio (1975) 'Intervista', *L'Espresso* No. 1.

N. dalla Chiesa (1984) 'Il terrorismo di sinistra', in D. della Porta (ed.) *Terrorismi in Italia*, Bologna, Il Mulino.

D. della Porta (ed.) (1984) *Terrorismi in Italia*, Bologna, Il Mulino.

G. De Lutiis (1984) *Storia dei servizi segreti in Italia*, Rome, Editori Riuniti.

V. Dini and L. Manconi (1981) *Il discorso delle armi*, Rome, Savelli.

L. Ferrajoli (1986) 'Il diritto penale minimo', *Dei delitti e delle pene. Rivista di studi sociali, storici e giuridici sulla questione criminale*, Vol. III, No. 3, pp. 493–524.

A. Franceschini, P.V. Buffa and F. Giustolisi (1988) *Mara, Renato e io. Storia dei fondatori delle BR*, Milan, Mondadori.

M. Foucault (1972) 'Nouveau fascisme, nouvelle democratie', *Les Temps Modernes*, N. 310 bis.

M. Galleni (ed.) (1981) *Rapporto sul terrorismo*, Milan, Rizzoli.

*Gruppi di Azione Partigiana* (GAP) (1971) 'Dichiarazione politica', *Potere Operaio*.

C. Marletti (1979) 'Il terrorismo moderno come strategia di comunicazione.

Alcune considerazioni a partire dal caso italiano', in R. Villa (ed.) *La violenza interpretata*, Bologna, Il Mulino.

K. Marx (1844) *Zur Kritik der Hegelschen Rechsphilosopie. Einleitung*, Deutsch-Französische Jahrbücher, Paris.

A. Melucci (1982) *L'invenzione del presente*, Bologna, Il Mulino.

*Nuova Resistenza*, periodical, May 1971, No. 1.

G. Pasquino (ed.) (1984) *La prova delle armi*, Bologna, Il Mulino.

A. Pizzorno (1978) 'Terrorismo e quadro politico', a debate between F. Cicchitto, L. Colletti, F. Mancini, A. Minucci and A. Pizzorno in *Mondoperaio*, Vol. XXXI, No. 4, pp. 5–18.

*Potere Operaio*, periodical, April 1971, No. 38 and May 1971, No. 39.

*Potere Operaio del lunedì*, periodical, 11 March 1973, No. 44 and 16 July 1973, No. 61.

*Re Nudo*, April 1971, No. 4.

C. Schmitt (1932 and 1963) *Begriff des Politischen*, Berlin, Duncker & Humblot Verlags-buchhandlung.

C. Schmitt (1963 and 1975) *Theorie des Partisanen*, Berlin, Duncker & Humblot Verlags-buchhandlung.

*Sinistra Proletaria*, September–October 1970, Nos. 1–2 and 20 Octtober 1970.

Soccorso Rosso (1976) *Brigate Rosse. Che cosa hanno fatto, che cosa hanno detto, che cosa se ne é detto*, Milan, Feltrinelli.

N. Tranfaglia (1981) 'La crisi italiana e il problema storico del terrorismo', in Galleni.

# 5
# Social networks and terrorism: the case of *Prima Linea*

## *Claudio Novaro*

## 5.1 Introduction

The theme of this chapter focuses on material drawn from the examination of the life histories of, and collected interviews with, members of *Prima Linea* (PL). This forms the basis for the hypothesis that entry into the sphere of terrorism presupposes the existence of previously existing social networks, and that such networks, and the maintenance of the ties of solidarity which they contain, play a potentially important role in orienting individual choices and decisions. It is a question then – already stressed by various enquiries into social movements[1] – of an approach that reveals how participation in forms of collective action is often preceded by a day-to-day individual involvement in a pre-existing social network (associational, family and friendship).

We intend to examine this hypothesis using a microanalytical and limited approach, and by examining the life histories and social interrelations of a limited group of militants who belonged to *Prima Linea* in the Val di Susa. Small-scale analysis seemed the most suitable instrument to concretely examine the individuals and groups concerned and to highlight the context within which the different life strategies chosen by single actors can be compared.

We shall attempt to reconstruct the individual life-courses with particular reference to the armed struggle mainly using the various personal accounts or 'autobiographies' of those interviewed, supplemented where possible with judicial sources, personal documents and, more generally, with various sorts of secondary sources.[2] In parallel, we shall consider the characteristics of the various social networks (their structure, degree of connectedness, and the content of contacts exchanged within them) in the belief that an analysis of the role they played will help us to make inferences about and give us an insight into both the modality of support for terrorism and the motivations underlying such a choice.

The decision to focus on the experience of *Prima Linea*[3] is primarily due to the particular permeability and flexibility of this organization which facilitated the simultaneous entry of entire networks of already-structured social aggregates. The Val di Susa is an important field of analysis in that it constitutes one of the places with the greatest presence and diffusion of PL membership in the history of the organization: a total of twenty-two people from this area were tried for belonging to *Prima Linea*, and pre-existing interpersonal ties prior to their political experience seem to have occupied, as we shall see, an important place among the reasons for such reproduction.

We shall start by reconstructing the links between Mauro, Fabio and Michele,[4] and the stages in their political activism up until their participation in the armed struggle, during the period when the plan to create *Prima Linea* was first taking shape within the *Senza Tregua* group. It is this 'basic' network which first became part of the organization and whose history had a significant impact on the development of terrorism in the Val di Susa. In the summer of 1977, Fabio and Michele moved away from Turin and the most important figure in maintaining links with the valley became Mauro. Following Mauro's life-course, we shall examine the activity of a series of people who joined *Prima Linea* on the basis of their previous ties with him: first Matteo, who joined individually at the end of 1977; and second, Gabriele and his friends, who joined collectively at the beginning of 1980.

## 5.2 Self-representations

The importance of the ties of solidarity certainly constitutes one of the central themes in the accounts of all the protagonists and is frequently highlighted as both an element of inspiration for personal decisions and in weighing up the importance of their individual experiences. This solidarity is part of a broader picture common to the different life histories in which the emphasis in the description of the individual life histories tends to be placed on the existential and individual elements of involvement. Even given the difference among the various life-courses and the variety of ways in which these are reconstructed, there is nevertheless a substantial homogeneity in the interpretation and evaluation of the biographical transitions. This is particularly visible in the accentuation of the emotional-type factors, rather than the rational-political-type factors, as a basis for the different personal choices. The often-claimed continuity with the experience of the mass movements is important not so much because of its political contents but because of the 'common feeling' that it induced – the feeling of breathing-in the same political climate and of an identity based on the same needs and the same impatience with the existing state of affairs.

In contrast, then, to the 'autobiographies' of left-wing militants of other generations,[5] these accounts do not overestimate the political aspects of choices made to the detriment of more strictly personal ones. This is partly due to the emergence of a new culture and sensibility with respect to the interdependency between the dimensions of private life and political activism. Moreover, we can hypothesize that the persistence of the elements indicated in all the accounts refers back to a common formula that took shape during the period of imprisonment: that is, to the consolidation of a sort of small-scale oral tradition that reconstructs different experiences by means of similar narratives.

We must emphasize that all the interviewees have openly dissociated themselves from terrorism and have subjected their own past to careful re-examination. Faced with the 'flattening-out' of the life-courses taken and of the reasons used to support them, such reflections certainly constitute an assertion of memory: that is, the formulation of a personal point of view that is then reflected in the different accounts through the convergence of common elements. In particular, the various autobiographical accounts seem to draw from a model of identity that makes personal coherence – that is, the capacity to 'take personal risks fully' on the basis of loyalty to one's own convictions or solidarity with one's comrades – as one of its foundations. This identity is emblematic; in the case of Mauro, for example, it is reaffirmed by his acknowledgement of other revolutionary figures:

> I identify myself intensely in those figures whose name appears ... once in the Kazan conspiracy, in the 'Young Russia' ... these revolutionary attempts that followed one another throughout the nineteenth century until the mythical revolution of the Russian proletariat ... I was moved to read the stories of these types of experiences where I recognized the unlucky, [those] unluckier than me ... dozens of generations which had taken risks [and] missed completely by decades and perhaps by even a century.[6]

All the figures of reference that appear in the various accounts are evaluated for the elements of existential challenge they contain, but in addition they are nearly always figures marked in some way by a former political or personal defeat. Mauro always related how, from when he was a child, he was struck by the *osterie* (pubs) in Val di Susa, the places where you found 'the ex-everything, ex-partisans ... ex-prisoners of war, well the ex, [those] defeated by life'.[7] Years later, during the period of militancy, he once again found himself faced with the atmosphere and sensations of those meetings; the fascination he had felt as a small boy was accompanied by a feeling of respect and human solidarity for people who had made sense of their own existence because they had 'experienced something'. It is precisely this anti-fascist tradition, filtered through accounts related by members of the family and by old partisans, which constitutes one of the key components of the personal and political education of many of those who subsequently became terrorists.

In the accounts given by those interviewed, however, anti-fascism is not only referred to as an historical or political experience, but primarily as an existential choice. What is highlighted in the individual accounts, over and above the events of the Resistance, and the references to a revolution that never took place – now blunted by time – is the notion of 'anti-fascists' as people who had chosen to take individual risks. It is this value of disinterested choice and individual propensity that is stressed and that, extrapolated from its historical context, becomes the vehicle for a comparison between different generations.

As is often the case in the reconstruction of history, these assertions are primarily effective at the symbolic level, as transmitters of the strong values in which we believe. They circulate in all the accounts that relate both to direct individual experience and those that are generated by a comparison with other events. In the accounts of Matteo and Gabriele, such factors emerge when we consider the elements marking the transition to terrorism.

> It wasn't so much the content of an armed action from an ideological point of view that I admired, so much as the talk about direct action ... the fact of risking something serious ... [something] determining like your own life, like the choice of a way of life.[8]

The interview with Fabio contains elements that are highlighted in his relationship with his grandfather. Fabio introduces the figure of his grandfather with a typical phrase of his, 'I have been in the PCI for fifty years, nothing has changed and I will certainly die before my dreams come true'. This is an often-repeated statement, a sort of narrative stereotype that, in addition to representing a real fragment of life, also has a symbolic importance in that it represents a particular orientation: the need – when faced with an old militant who fears that he will not live to see the revolution take place – to affirm a sense of urgency and to commit ourselves to bringing that revolution nearer. The account is almost a transition of testimony from one generation to another, represented by the attempt to redeem a different existential event by means of our own choices.

In fact, these examples of accounts and of self-representations are strictly linked to the interpretative level of the individual story. The autobiographical account necessarily implies an interpretative choice with respect to the protagonist's own past. The time when we are recounting plays a relevant role in the choice of identity. The source of the memory is in fact a point of intersection between different temporal levels, reconstructed through a continuous interaction between the past (of which we recount) and the present (from which we recount), and hence between memory and identity.

In this sense, then, all the autobiographical accounts appear to be inevitably marked by a suffered political defeat and the weight of this is clearly discernible both in the account of the events themselves and their actual outcome (prison). During imprisonment, the personal history of the prisoner constitutes one of his few available resources: to deny it would imply a loss of identity. We can then suppose that there is a direct relationship between the emphasis in the various accounts and the attempt made by the protagonist to master his own experiences, in which his personal circumstances are separated from his more directly political circumstances, which are linked to the experiences of the organization.

Hence, the accounts stress to varying degrees the aspects of solidarity and existential coherence; these aspects are reflected in the circumstances of the protagonist's own existence. The assertions made by Matteo at the end of his interview are a good example of this.

Personally, I believe that it was an important human experience, even given its negative aspects. But as far as the relational proofs of those years in prison are concerned ... I certainly have a ... positive judgement ... It is true that sometimes you felt you were scraping the bottom of the barrel and at other times you wanted to touch the sky with the tips of your fingers, but ... it is this strong contrast of emotions that certainly left its mark ... on our personalities, not only on our hair and our teeth which prison [life] is inexorably wearing away, but ... I believe that from the human point of view it was an experience worth living, also because, the way I felt it at the time ... I wouldn't have been able to *not* get to the bottom of this type of feeling.[9]

## 5.3 Mauro, Fabio and Michele

### The meeting

Fabio and Mauro, together with Michele, were the first young people from the Val di Susa to join *Prima Linea*. The link that united them accompanied the various stages of their political transition to the armed struggle. Fabio was involved in political activity from around the age of thirteen and in around 1972 he joined the *collettivo operai-studenti*, which included a large part of the extra-parliamentary left of the Val di Susa. Strictly speaking, Mauro's initiation into political activism began two years later when he left the Istituto Tecnico Pininfarina in Susa to go to the Istituto Tecnico in Moncalieri, but his life was already marked by a strong social commitment, in particular through the contact with the fundamentalist Christian milieu which made a strong impact on his future approach to militancy.

Their paths crossed during secondary school: the contact figure was mainly Michele, a close friend of Fabio and Mauro's schoolfriend. It was a relationship that was simultaneously located on two levels: that of friendship and that of militancy. It was strengthened through the sharing of an equal mix of individual feelings, personal restlessness and political aspirations, united in the need to travel to Turin every day and to reproduce these elements in a larger social and territorial environment. What emerged, however, were different approaches to political activism. Fabio and Michele completely immersed themselves in political activity, working immediately and directly in *Lotta Continua*,[10] whereas Mauro's position was less clear. Although he soon began to take part in the Turin meetings of the CPS of *Lotta Continua*,[11] the student coordination committees, and the meetings at Palazzo Nuovo and Corso San Maurizio (the old headquarters of the institution) through his two friends, he nevertheless did not share their hinterland of militancy: that is, that network of relationships and microsolidarity that constituted the basis of their political activism. For Fabio and Michele, political commitment, first of all the broadening of their own knowledge, acquaintances and personal contacts, marked by a feeling of communal belonging, did not relate solely to their political activity, but permeated all their daily experience.

> There was this sensation of never feeling alone because ... there was always somewhere to sleep, and there was always this thing about sharing everything we had.[12]

Mauro's situation was slightly different. He was a 'political agitator' but, when the march was over, he related that:

> I was practically 60 km away from home ... so my problem was to catch the train at midnight or even later and ... to get home.[13]

While Fabio and Michele decided to move to Turin, Mauro continued to commute, dividing his day between Turin and the Val di Susa. This was reflected in his position within the organization and in his relationship with politics.

> As a result I lived the political battle and the positions on the various questions through Michele and Fabio, in a relationship of total faith, because ... over and above [my] political commitment ... my public activity ... [in] my free time I caught the train [and] went back to the Valley, and there I had my friends.[14]

This sort of pluralization, or segmentation of life environments (Turin and the Val di Susa, politics and other activities, militant friendships and home friendships) made an important impact not only on social behaviour but also on identity. In Turin, Mauro was considered, as he says himself, 'as the friend of my Val di Susa friends', whereas when he returned home the situation was different.

> I was one who always talked, I held the floor, I was if you like, the figure of aggregation in my circle of friends.[15]

These different social roles which faced Mauro, and to which he was continually forced to readapt – even if, at least until the collapse in 1977 represented by the choice of the armed struggle, he was basically living his own private life – were not naturally separated. In particular, his political activism made an immediate impact on his relationships with his old friends, with consequences he could not evaluate at the time, but that strengthened his position as protagonist and front-line figure within his social environment in the Val di Susa.

> We had an 'extra gear' [Mauro, Fabio, Michele] because we had the fascination of the language of the metropolis.[16]

Later on we shall see how the tangle of the different social networks produced such a situation. It is interesting to cite what Mauro had to say on this subject.

> Within the group of friends there was no need for everyone to be active in politics in order to talk about it, it was enough to have someone who was the bearer of that type of experience, [and] in any case the solidarity of the group, the perpetual existential dimension in which the debates took place involved everyone emotionally in all the plans that had to do with the relationship 'with the outside world' and the realization of the strong values in which one believed.[17]

This is an interesting example of the links and interdependencies that exist between friendship and political choice – which we shall come back to later on – and which is partially confirmed by looking at the relationship between Mauro, Fabio and Michele.

The choice taken by Mauro to become an active member of *Lotta Continua* was also prompted by his friendship with Fabio and Michele. This friendship was, as we have said, nourished by common feelings and moods and reinforced by their political militancy. But in part, the more politically secure position of Mauro meant that the lines of communication with the movement was partly mediated by the relationships of friendship. For Mauro – who divided his time between Turin and the Val di Susa – the relationship with Fabio and Michele became an instrument of understanding of and access to a collective political identity and, above all, to a system of hidden relationships. It was to become a relationship that Mauro found himself having to face some years later, in a completely different political context where the roles were reversed.

## 5.4 Towards terrorism

The direct commitment of Mauro, Fabio and Michele to *Lotta Continua* had become worn out by the end of 1976. The subsequent stages of their journey towards terrorism, which were extremely close to one another, were constituted by the progressive approach to the sphere of the *Senza Tregua* group, and in the space of a few months, the joining of *Prima Linea* that had emerged within *Senza Tregua*. This was a complex and difficult-to-define transition, one that referred back in particular to the reconstruction of the experience of *Prima Linea* in Turin and of its relationship with the mass movements in which the elements of continuity and fracture were variously intertwined. Among these elements, the first was the relationship with violence. This has been one of the crucial points – albeit never completely explicit – that runs through much of a great part of the revolutionary left and of *Lotta Continua* in particular. It is a theme that – in addition to and perhaps more than from the discussion on a possible revolutionary break – originates in the conflictuality and from daily political practice.

Fabio, Mauro and Michele were active in the *servizio d'ordine* of *Lotta Continua*. This was an observation point that was closely linked – even more than other sectors – to a notion of politics as the ability to bring about immediate change in the relationships of power, translated, through the retrieval of the ever-present militaristic aspects in the culture of the movement, into the exploitation of street clashes. This was a question – at least initially – of a substantially contained level of violence, subsequently ritualized and broadened through the use of 'passwords' and slogans that were increasingly loaded with images of war. The first forms of the practice of violence took place primarily on the grounds of militant anti-fascism. At that time, anti-fascism constituted a sort of code of recognition and was the result of the intertwining between the so-called 'conspiratorial mentality',[18] linked to the political climate of the 1970s (the strategy of tension, the fear of an authoritarian coup, etc.), and the militant culture of the *servizi d'ordine* (the attacks on the offices of the MSI and the clashes during electoral meetings).

In fact, from a subjective point of view, this way of using force is internal to a collective dimension and relates to a common political culture. In this respect, Fabio's description of the clashes that took place after the death of Micciché is illustrative.[19]

A swollen stream of women and children ... led the march and went off ... to set fire to the MSI offices.[20]

In this case the use of violence was legitimated by the collective patrimony: that is, by the presence and intervention of 'the people' rather than just militants. But as Mauro reveals:

> The theme of anti–fascism ... already contains an *a priori* reasoning which legitimates the use of violence, even non-defensive violence; beating-up fascists was always OK for the Turin movement.[21]

Within the *servizi d'ordine* discussions soon started on a different way of organizing their force, in particular when faced with the radicalization of political conflict.

> It was clear that the use that you made [of violence] on marches was ... now unequal between you and the forces of law and order; on the other hand, in saying 'in fact the problem is to be armed [in order] to be on the same level' ... there was a real problem of [how to] unite these two things, so that automatically if you pose the problem of being armed, you began to talk about a level of violence that became subjective violence.[22]

Nevertheless, while the political plan and the organizational structure of *Lotta Continua* lasted, this debate remained on the level of intentions and only became concrete when people left the group.

From the interviews we find that during the period 1975–6 there was an air of imminent victory for the left, characterized by the charged atmosphere of political meanings and strong images (the great mass demonstrations, the marches, the factory-front picketings) that responded well to the left's need for intensity and radicality in spearheading political activism. Politics constituted a sort of common ground between the youth rebellion and ideology, between social struggle and revolutionary utopia: that is, it was the language with which to translate the questions of transformation or those of a personal existential search.

Towards the end of 1976, however, this link seemed to explode. The strategy of the *compromesso storico* (the strategic governing agreement between the PCI and the DC, which was followed by the irremediable break with the Communist Party, marked in Turin in particular by the clashes in front of the university in March 1977);[23] the electoral defeat suffered by *Democrazia Proletaria* (Proletarian Democracy, (DP)), and the disintegration of *Lotta Continua* is a stop signal that appears to refer back to the decomposition of a political model and the social groups that support it. In particular, the disintegration of *Lotta Continua*, which was preceded by bitter internal political clashes,[24] produced a situation of great uncertainty.

> Basically you feel abandoned in the middle of nowhere and everyone around you disappears.[25]

Faced with the high personal investment demanded by militant action and the sense of legitimacy that the forms of social conflict have produced in individual experiences, the interviewees relate that the only option open appeared to be the defence of the political and 'swerving' in order to legitimate their own life-course.

> There is in us the frustration to not have more than one instrument to transform the reality in which we believed and we made room for the state of mind and the conviction that we will have been able to compensate for this vacuum of references with a generic inclination to ... 'give more'; this, on the grounds of a social clash read through the eyes of ideology, [and] in the absence of a system of mediation with the reality, will automatically become an inclination to risk more.[26]

In this context, *Senza Tregua* seemed to be the suitable organization of transition, capable of giving form to the disappointment through a more radical qualitative leap; above all, able to retrieve the crucial political points, in particular that of the 'power', on which *Lotta Continua* had been divided. In fact, within a short space of time, Fabio, Michele and Mauro (but the first two in a more direct way) became involved in this group.

It was then a choice where the elements of political planning were strictly connected to those of friendship. The entry into *Senza Tregua* took place, albeit with a rather disconnected timing, through the transitions in which the social networks once again function as the place of socialization and exchange of experience. The network in question was, however, in turn part of a multiple, superimposed network of not-entirely coincident interdependencies of friendship and political activism; this extended system of solidarity was activated in the transition to *Senza Tregua*. In the autobiographical accounts, joining the organization is in fact described as the fruit of a collective discussion that permeated both personal relationships and those of militancy. Fabio, for example, stressed how the political confrontation with Michele preceded the decision to join *Senza Tregua* and that the latter was activated together with a breakaway group from the *servizio d'ordine* of *Barriera di Milano*, a peripheric area in the town of Turin. Michele's decision – taken a little before that of Fabio's – presumably functioned as the orientative setting that consolidated an already-existing individual propensity.

More specifically, we can hypothesize the existence of a double and reciprocal influence between individual decisions and friendships. The inclination to join appears to increase not only on the strength of the fact that the links of solidarity sustain such a choice, but also because this inclination tends to reinforce pre-existing collective solidarity.

In a period marked by a profound sense of political delusion and the disintegration of the elements of former identity, the action of joining *Senza Tregua* responded to the need for identification. In this search for identity the pre-existing associational networks were utilized. Political activism in *Lotta Continua* was based on a sense of common belonging, reinforced by ties of social solidarity. The failure of the organization's reading of the situation and hence the failure of political identification, nevertheless left the social ties that in turn constituted the basis that would facilitate the transition to another political experience intact. From the subjective point of view, that is, the existence of former relations provided the necessary identity resources on which to base the choice of militancy. From the organization's point of view, it allowed more rapid growth, precisely because it was supported by the mobilization of organizational resources and of already-active participation. The history of *Senza Tregua* in Turin is emblematic in this sense. By the end of 1976 it had broadened its membership through the inclusion of sectors of the ex-*servizio d'ordine* of *Lotta Continua* (especially Barriera di Milano, Borgo San Paolo and Pininfarina), which in turn increased its sphere of influence. *Senza Tregua* continued to operate on different grounds. Until March 1977 the group supported the need to defend and maintain the public spaces of political expression,[27] even if, when Mauro, Fabio and Michele were members, the plan to establish *Prima Linea* had already been formalized through a series of 'subjective pressures'.[28]

This attempt to marry public action with armed actions can perhaps explain the linearity with which the entire transition is described, in particular in the interview with Fabio. It was a question of progressive choices, recounted as an almost natural development due to the growth of the organization of violence and its legitimation. In the account given by Fabio, arms were first used on 2 March 1977, when various groups attacked the Circolo Monarchico at the Hotel Suisse and the headquarters of *Communione e Liberazione*.[29]

> It wasn't a big problem for me ... because once again the objectives which we had chosen were legitimated by the anti-fascist debate, and [were] understandable to everyone and then carried out with a procession of 10,000 people.[30]

Nevertheless, even in actions carried out by a limited nucleus, there remains the question of violence that is partly mediated by the procession, which then, perhaps in part unknowingly, contains the group that perpetrates such an action. In fact, not long afterwards, Fabio took part in genuine armed actions that raised the operational level of violence and for which the *squadre* (squadrons) or *Prima Linea* claimed direct responsibility. On 2 June, after the abortive attack on the Turin public-transport company, Fabio was forced to go into hiding. Shortly afterwards Michele also moved away from Turin.

Mauro's entry – he had for some time taken part in the internal debate of *Senza Tregua* – into *Prima Linea* was a little different.

> because of personal relations, because of friends in *Senza Tregua* you were willing to put up with talk about armed action. I was one of these, even if

there was no formal or practical occasion to act, [I had] a role that made me behave like a fighting militant.[31]

Mauro's full involvement came about at the end of the 1977 summer in a situation where – after the arrests of May and June – [32] the Turin group of *Prima Linea* was reduced to a few units. The other different parallel lives that he had until then managed to preserve (working on a radio station, an active interest in music and work) now appeared as poor alternatives; on a personal level it is clear he was affected by the choice made by Fabio and Michele and by the need to be loyal to the intense friendship that united them.

From September Mauro dedicated himself full-time to the reconstruction of the organization (for which he received a wage of 250,000 lire a month, approximately £115), relying on his acquaintances in the Turin movement and on the relationships with friends in the Val di Susa. Even before this, his militancy had constituted a sort of intermediation between the Turin movement and the social circles of the Val di Susa, in particular through an activity of mediation between different political cultures. Thus, at the end of 1977, when Mauro found himself having to reorganize the 'network of the proletarian struggle' of *Prima Linea* and having to activate direct resources of participation. He did so by utilizing those political elements already present in the context in which he carried out his recruitment activity. Of these elements, it was above all anti-fascism that constituted the patrimony common to all the militants.

We will develop a debate that will try to transform anti-fascist feeling, [which is] immanent, and always and everywhere present, [and] aggregating ... regardless of the type of aggregate, *piazza* [mass] or *non-piazza* ... and to make this anti-fascist feeling have an impact on the state, on the transformations of the state...relying on the most neutral and at the same time the strongest aspects of our political-personal identity ... generationally and territorially, this is the theme of anti-fascism.[33]

The activity of recruitment, however, was also mediated by an ideological influence: we notice a hint of this in the declarations made to the judicial authorities by another *Prima Linea* militant.

during demonstrations in which I had taken part Mauro told me that it was time to organize ourselves better because demonstrations were no longer of any use.[34]

In general, the progressive tightening-up of the spaces of political expression (the closure of some youth circles and the ban on demonstrations) increased the substitute role of armed organizations.

There were months – from the end of 1977 until the beginning of 1978 (in particular in Turin) – when the places for debate and contact between different sections of the youth proletariat tended to be markedly clandestine. This exaggerated extolling of our own importance thus produced a mechanism of self-legitimation.[35]

Armed action, which had the fascination of a conspiracy, became one of the possible responses to the vacuum of political initiatives characteristic of the Turin situation, especially after the tragic episode that took place in the bar Angelo Azzurro.[36]

The incredible speed ... with which we managed to structure the organization testifies to just how entrenched the tendency towards insurrectionary revolt [and] to violent revolt was in the circles of the movement (how widespread an anti-state identity was).[37]

The militancy of Mauro in Turin was interrupted in April 1978 with his arrest. When he was subsequently released some months later, after the period of protective custody had expired, the organization sent him to Bologna and he only returned to Turin at the beginning of 1980.

The entry of Matteo and Gabriele (whose life histories will be examined in the following pages) into the sphere of the armed struggle dates back to two different periods of Mauro's living in Turin. Matteo joined *Prima Linea* in the autumn of 1977; Gabriele, together with other friends, joined during 1980. Their courses lack that gradual transition found in the accounts of other *Prima Linea* militants, where becoming part of the armed struggle immediately followed political activism in other organizations of the extraparliamentary left and in the sphere of the *autonomia*.

This atypical feature allows us to estimate fully the impact of social ties on the life histories of the protagonists. The contact with, and socialization of, different experiences, and the friendships that these generated developed from a basis that was not strictly political. For many of them, for example, the opportunity was the shared love of music and belonging to small groups that met together to play. As one protagonist commented: 'Well, actually from the rock bands to armed bands, yes, the transition was quite linear!'

## 5.5 From rock bands to armed bands

### 5.5.1. Matteo

Matteo's brief period of political activism in *Prima Linea* only lasted from the autumn of 1977 to April 1978 when he was arrested. A few days following his arrest on 15 April, an article appeared in *La Stampa* entitled 'Investigation of the man found in possession of a *carabiniere* identity card'. The man in question was Matteo, who was described as an 'introverted' young man who 'had never been active in politics' and who 'worked as an electrician in a religious institute'.

In fact, one of the most striking elements in his story is constituted by the absence of a political past that could usher in such a radical choice. In around the mid-1970s, Matteo shared, with many others, the climate related to the participation in the struggles of the student movement. It was in this environment that, through the relationship with an Italian language-teacher, he began to be involved in the problems of the school and to develop a political commitment, even if the latter was restricted to school affairs. He became a representative for his school and often had to travel between the various branches (Bussoleno, Orbassano and Grugliasco) of the institute. This growing personal commitment led him to make more definitive political choices and to a generic sympathy for the historical left. In fact, in order to understand the transitions that in the space of a few months led to him becoming a member of *Prima Linea*, we need to examine the determining role – as Matteo himself defined it – played by his friendship with Mauro.

Matteo and Mauro first met at the end of 1976 as a result of being part of the same musical circles in the Val di Susa. Their subsequent contact was on the basis of their common love of jazz; and this in turn led to their forming a band together with Pino, another friend of Matteo's. During this period Matteo frequently met Mauro and his circle of friends (particularly Michele and Giulia, Mauro's girlfriend). In addition, Matteo had just come through a rather unsatisfactory period of personal relationships: important expectations about his personal life now focused on his friendship with Mauro. This was the beginning of an intense relationship, which started exclusively on the level of friendship and moved rapidly to a more strictly political level.

> He began to make me read the first issues of *Senza Tregua*, passed on clandestinely in coat pockets, but basically it was still a relationship free of organizational type ties ... [There was] a solid friendship between me and him, at that time he was going out with Giulia and so we were always together.[38]

Thus music became an important element of socialization, and contemporarily, of politicization.

> We began to discuss politics starting from talking about what music to play ... who to go and play for ... why not to do concerts for money and why discothèques in the Val di Susa were an attack on other more mature types ... of expression [and] aggregation for young people.[39]

The friendship with Mauro was one of intense contact and discussions and brought about a change in the political placing of Matteo within the group. As a result of meeting Mauro, Matteo readjusted and redefined the field of his own interests, shifting his personal investments into different spheres, in particular into that of political commitment.

> Among other things, I took up reading classical Marxism, ... increasingly developing my interest in politics [and] in this way I ... began to make my first contacts, [to have] my first limited discussions about what to do in the Turin area.[40]

Once again, social contact became the intermediary for an involvement in political choices, but by now politics for Mauro meant something much closer to the armed struggle, even if Matteo did not seem to be totally aware of this:

> Obviously, I knew that they had friends in these circles at the Turin level, but I wasn't officially aware that they were actually militants in *Prima Linea* ... because I read about the things that happened in Turin in the newspapers and ... it all seemed very distant from the people I knew.[41]

With the summer of 1977 the scenario changed substantially. There was, as we have seen, a progressive assumption of responsibility by Mauro within *Prima Linea* following the decimation of the Turin leadership. Mauro worked frenetically to reconstruct the networks and the bases of the group. In this type of activity it was natural that he should turn to his acquaintances and friends in the Val di Susa, first of all because this sort of contact was less risky if directed at people whose political pasts and potential commitment Mauro knew better. Matteo was obviously one of the various people contacted by Mauro: prior to a political commitment he had already shown a personal inclination.

> During that period [September–October 1977] Mauro made an official request to ... join the organization of *Prima Linea*. Obviously, at the time it was still linked to the experience of the *squadre* ... however, officially in so far as it concerned me it meant ... his official entry into the organization. He had clearly had quite a long time to check me out, living in contact direct with me, obviously feeding off the trust that I had for him.[42]

Matteo's entry into *Prima Linea* was immediate and was facilitated by the absence of any counterbalancing friendships. His entry was initially located on the level of mere personal commitment, but was rapidly reinforced, Matteo recounts in the interview, on the basis of two strong emotional incentives: on the one hand the events of Stammheim: 'There the talk about ... "yes, well, I'm on the right side" became concrete.'[43] On the other hand, and more importantly, the arrest of Michele which took place in Naples at the end of the year. 'I would never have been able to avoid getting to the bottom of things.'[44] Matteo admitted that his evaluation of his choice, more than in terms of practicability of a political plan, was posed as a commitment of trust in the existential value of friendship. It was then a question of a sort of spiralling involvement. The more he became involved in political activity, losing contact with the external world, the greater the intensity of his personal investment in that choice.

Within the organization, however, Matteo continued to have a special relationship with Mauro. In fact – because of the work that kept him busy for part of the day – he took part almost exclusively in operational meetings. As far as the more strictly political debate about orientation and general choices of the organization was concerned, so strong was the faith that Mauro placed in Matteo that he preferred to delegate almost entirely to the latter.

From November 1977 Matteo took part in various actions organized by *Prima Linea*, until April 1978 when – on the same day in which Mauro was also stopped – he was arrested. Some months later Mauro was released, whereas for Matteo it was the beginning of a long prison sentence. Among his comrades in the small community of the Val di Susa, his arrest induced solidarity and mobilization which pushed some, independent of their experience, in the direction of similar choices.

## 5.5.2 Gabriele and his friends

Gabriele was the person who, because of his friendship with Mauro that dated back to when they were students together at the Istituto Tecnico Pininfarina in Moncalieri, was in a certain sense the 'bridge' between the group and *Prima Linea*. They shared a passion for music (they played in two different bands that maintained close contact with one another) and had a common set of ideals, which, in the case of Mauro, were lived more actively through his political militancy. Gabriele recounts how, at the end of 1976, he progressively broke off his political activity. This was the result of a clear-cut judgement on the lack of concreteness and the excess of sectarianism of the extraparliamentary left. Nevertheless, the break in no way altered his ideological position ('I still felt I was a comrade'), or what appears in his autobiographical account as a diffident attitude towards institutions and a sympathy for non-stabilized models of life. During the first months of 1978, two episodes took place that marked a turning-point in the life history of Gabriele. On the one hand, the kidnapping of Aldo Moro, which was seen as the symbol of the operational efficiency of the armed struggle (and it was an image that counteracts the judgement as to the inconclusiveness of the extraparliamentary left). On the other hand, the arrest of Mauro and his girlfriend Giulia; the latter had been introduced to Mauro by Gabriele himself when Mauro was part of his circle of friends. This second episode in particular provoked an intense emotional reaction on Gabriele's part. This was immediately communicated to Sandro and Sara (respectively his best friend and girlfriend) and led him to express solidarity with his friends in prison.

Here, an almost *[sic.]* personal affair met up with something bigger, something that I had until then only followed from a distance as a spectator. In fact, I was no longer extraneous and only a spectator of what happened; ... I had been touched personally and my character, my personality prevented me from drawing back.[45]

After having attempted – in vain – to visit Mauro and Giulia in prison, Gabriele only managed to meet them when, after some months of imprisonment, they were released. Before they went into clandestinity they agreed to maintain contact.

There was just time to meet them a couple of times and the prevailing appearance of our meetings was not so much political, as a search for an exchange of existential impressions about their experiences ... the [sort of] relationship that I had with them led me to express spontaneous involvement, even if it wasn't easy for me to distinguish how much of this involvement was perhaps a question of solidarity with them, and how much was instead linked to the more complex phenomena to which they subscribed.[46]

They met again for the first time in Piacenza (in the autumn of 1979) and then in Milan at the beginning of 1980, where they agreed that Mauro would go back to Turin and live in Sandro's house. Mauro had been going through a rather difficult period. He had been temporarily expelled from *Prima Linea*, he found himself isolated (after a period of militancy lasting nearly three years and over a year of clandestinity); and he was keen to reconstruct a relationship with the organization. The attempt to patch up the difference produced between his claimed identity (that of the militant fighter) and being recognized, conditioned his relationship with Gabriele. It was the same as that recognized by Mauro in a declaration sent to the judicial authorities.

I was faced with two alternatives: to think of my relationship with Gabriele in extremely personal terms, accompanying it with a renunciation of any form of participation and involvement in the armed struggle; or given the high risk, however, that I posed for them, to construct a form of participation and involvement in the armed struggle. My psychological condition led me to the second hypothesis.[47]

In reality it was a transition facilitated by the attitude of Gabriele and, following him, Sandro. From the autobiographical accounts, it appears that for some, the chance of joining the armed struggle was a long-awaited opportunity. On the one hand, there was a desire to demonstrate concrete solidarity with Mauro and on the other a sort of fascination with the radical nature of the choice he represented.

those that knew ... would have put themselves, their lives, on the line ... [they had] a certain type of commitment to an objective.[48]

The arrival of Mauro in Turin reverberated within Gabriele's circle of friends, above all, among those he had known at the end of 1976. Among them, together with Gabriele, only four (Sandro, Sara, Carlo and Gianna) became involved in the armed struggle, or rather in the embryonic group that in 1980 was, as we shall see, initially formed around Mauro. In fact, this period was characterized by a crisis within the fighting organizations. The impact of the armed struggle on sectors of the youth world seemed to have largely subsided, so it is difficult to relate the choices made by the subjects to purely ideological motives, taking into account that it was primarily a question of people with little previous political experience.

In this case, the uncertainty (in terms of outcomes) of joining the armed struggle seemed to be balanced out by the fact that the involvement contained its own rewards. These rewards operated primarily on the level of solidarity, in the first place with Mauro (who, together with Gabriele and Sandro, felt himself involved because of personal experiences), and in second place within the group of friends. Indeed it is not accidental that among those who knew about Mauro's return to Turin (around ten people), those who chose to join or to become involved in the armed struggle were united by stronger affective ties with Mauro's life history or with Gabriele – who was a sort of internal leader of the group – and whose determination brought others with it.

As a matter of fact Sandro was fraternally bound to Gabriele by a relationship that operated simultaneously on various levels (work, friendship and interests). Sara, as well as being Sandro's sister was Gabriele's girlfriend and the two were engaged to be married. Gianna was Giulia's sister the girlfriend of Mauro who had been arrested at around that time in France. It was then a question of people that made up part of a more cohesive network, marked by almost daily contact and located within a more extended network of relationships.

In the light of these facts we can then hypothesize a direct link between the importance of the social milieu and the greater likelihood of accepting a political proposal. The only partial exception is represented by Carlo. He, too, was closely linked to Gabriele and Sandro but at a slightly later date. Carlo relates that after Mauro and Giulia had decided to go underground he thought 'they are mad, they have just got out and they are immediately at it again'.[49] Some months later, as Gabriele and Sandro gradually became closer to Mauro and to illegal activity, his attitude changed, also from the viewpoint of political judgement. For him (but the same was also true for the others with regard to Mauro) the image of the armed struggle was no longer an abstract model of fighting operations; it became something much more concrete represented by flesh-and-blood people with whom he shared a common friendship. The directly observable and assessable behaviour of his other friends became a possible choice that – reinforced by the group and by the desire to conform to the decisions taken by it – pushed him towards a progressive radicalization and into accepting Gabriele's request for collaboration.

From the point of view of political and organizational transitions, the group did not immediately join *Prima Linea*. From the outset there was a particular relationship with the Turin organization, which on the one hand was concerned with the political control of Mauro, but on the other was keen to exploit the opportunity to make new recruits.

> [Gabriele] himself ... became the focus of the organization's attention, since by offering to put me up at his house, he had expressed a high level of commitment which, in the logic of the armed struggle, was often the fruit of many months of organizational commitment with regard to the 'network relationships'. The organization therefore put into motion a sort of approach [with Gabriele] and the people connected with him, on the one hand making the relation with me 'informally stable', [and] on the other putting pressure on them – accelerated by the logistic crisis of the organization brought about by the crisis of the *ronde* (patrols) – that made the offer of a clandestine house very valuable.[50]

In any case, this initial phase of informal collaboration still allowed the group some operative autonomy; but this was destined, however, in a very short space of time, through an acceleration of the political choices caused by the first *pentimenti*, to be absorbed by *Prima Linea*. Some months later, the discovery of two flats rented by Gabriele and Carlo in their own names on behalf of the organization meant that everyone had to become clandestine. While Gianna was arrested immediately and Carlo went to Rome, Gabriele, Sara and Sandro stayed together and were sent first to Umbria and then to Puglia.

## 5.6 Social ties

We have so far tried to reconstruct – albeit imperfectly – the various 'entries' into the sphere of the armed struggle. As we have seen, each choice is located among the events that were simultaneously individual and collective and in which social networks played a different but equally important role. It is a question of aspects stressed by the interviewees themselves, as they re-evaluate the elements of social solidarity in interpreting their own life histories and who derive comfort from a reading of the various biographical life histories. This sounds like a confirmation of the fact that adherence and active involvement in the armed struggle – in the same way as other forms of collective action – did not generally take place on the part of single, isolated subjects but started from a network of relations of which the individuals were a part. That is to say, the process of mobilization implies the presence of pre-existing relational networks (associational or social) and is the result of complex interactions in which the single groups carry out an important mediating role.

As a matter of fact, the importance and the degree of influence of social relations in the process of joining the armed struggle vary markedly from one case to another. First of all, the social network functioned as a channel of communication for flows of information and knowledge that allowed the protagonists to orient their individual strategy. We have seen how the relationship with Fabio and Michele allowed Mauro to have a direct knowledge of the Turin movement and how, in turn, Mauro himself became the intermediary with the social circles of the Val di Susa, which allowed an enlargement and diffusion of the experience gathered in Turin.

On a more general level, then, there would appear to be a circulation of 'languages', experiences and behaviour between social movement and social network when a subject is part of both; this is even more easily realized when it is a case of a group of friends from a small town that cannot keep up direct contact with the movement.

The link of friendship allows access to a collective political identity and to an already-structured group through which the protagonist can decide whether or not to join the armed struggle: especially when the group is a clandestine organization about whose internal structure the protagonist possesses scarce information. However, the social link of friendship is also a channel for 'aimed' communication, made in view of a putative recruitment or request for collaboration; it is in this sense that the link has an important role in the life histories of the interviewees. From the point of view of the techniques of recruitment, an illegal organization can only use instruments of public and mass communication within certain limits. Even maintaining – as *Prima Linea* sought to do – at least initially, a clear and declared presence within the movement, the channels utilized largely took the form of face-to-face contacts.

The broadening of the so-called network of 'proletarian fighters' that took place at the end of 1977, through contact with and involvement of various more or less structured aggregates present in the territory, was realized in the form of direct contacts with individual militants or with whole groups, in an attempt to set in motion a debate in which to introduce their own 'passwords'.

Clearly, this recruiting activity was also directed at the persons to whom the protagonist was closest and whose possible involvement could be best anticipated. Indeed, after the summer of 1977, Mauro took up his contacts with his friends in the Val di Susa using the friendships and social ties of Fabio and Michele, not only because this entailed a lower degree of risk, but also because he could count on a higher level of loyalty, in so far as the relationship was founded not only on a political or ideological basis, but also on the solidarity of friendship.

Inversely – that is to say, from the point of view of whoever intends to *join* an armed group – the bond of friendship constitutes a condition that facilitates entry. In the case of Gabriele, for example, there would have been little likelihood of what he himself defined as a sort of generic sympathy for the armed struggle, to translate into some form of militancy and direct participation, without his relationship with Mauro. The social bond thus constituted the opportunity that joined the condition of potential commitment to its realization: that is, the direct transition through which to accede to the organization.

In fact, the simple knowledge of and the link with someone already active in the sphere of the armed struggle do not constitute *per se* a sufficient condition to determine a propensity to join. It is necessary that this be inserted into a personal feeling constituted by the sharing of the objectives and ideology of the group. But, as has already been seen, in orienting this individual propensity, the links of network have a role that is far from secondary. The ties of friendship in fact imply – through the exchange of information – contacts of reciprocal influence. We have seen how in the different life histories the meeting and the recognition of real-life experience or similar experiences generated mechanisms of identification in the subjects involved. The positive interchange of esteem and affection produced through these meetings and the subsequent assiduous contact generate a tendency to take on similar orientations and to share the same interpretative categories of reality. In particular, in cases where there was no previous politicization, the contents of information that passed via the social networks helped to redefine the hierarchy of the individual's aspirations and, consequently, to orient his life strategy.

Thus social ties have functioned time and again as a sort of precondition and as a facilitating element (from the point of view of the modality of access and ideological influences) in the decision to join the armed struggle. Their importance also operates, however, on the level of the motivations on which such choices are based. In particular, the solidarity generated by the interweaving of relations constituted a powerful element of orientation for the individual life-courses. From this point of view, however, it seems that there is a basic difference between the life histories of Mauro, Michele and Fabio and the others. In the case of the latter group, ideological incentives certainly carried less weight than solidarity. Look, for example, at Gabriele's social network in which the maintenance of the relationships of friendship functioned as an accelerator of his political involvement, in a situation where the reference group exercised a strong pressure of stimulus. It is conceivable that the group communicated its own norms indirectly: that is to say, information on the behaviour expected of each individual within the network, at a time when the energies on the part of the components were directed towards Mauro and his political proposal. This meant that those who did not participate in such activity would progressively lose contact with the others. Thus, the desire to preserve friendships, in a network of markedly cohesive structures, constituted one of the incentives for political adhesion. Conversely, in the case of Mauro, Fabio and Michele the tie of friendship operated essentially as a support for political mobilization, centred, however, on external objectives.

This diversity appears to correspond to two different models of aggregation already highlighted by existing research on political participation in the youth world and that deal with the relationship between solidarity and the action-objectives of a group.[51]

From an attitude that stresses the importance of aggregation as a means of operating in the social world, we pass to a vision of the group centred on itself, as the place of satisfaction of the needs of sociality and identity. Thus, if in the first model, solidarity and internal cohesion allow the group to act for its own ends, in the second case the objective of the action becomes the protection of the internal ties of solidarity.

It is clearly a question of two 'pure' models that do not correspond directly to the concrete reality of the groups examined, where diversified forms of both coexist. In the case of Mauro, Fabio and Michele, if the already-existing relations constituted a sort of support that facilitated the political transition, it is also true that at the base of the latter, as we have seen, there were elements connected to the processes of the construction and maintenance of the collective identity, in which the bonds of friendship carried substantial weight as the location of primary identification.

Similarly, in the life-courses of Matteo and Gabriele, the incentives and solidaristic motivations were intensely interwoven with more ideological and political factors. This in no way negates the fact that in these cases the ideology of the armed struggle represents the symbol of collective identity, whose actual cohesion was based on and guaranteed by – at least in the initial phase – the bonds of social relations.

The successive transitions could be read in terms of the activation of social ties. After becoming part of the organization, the protagonist is subject to a process of change and the extension of these ties (through mechanisms of ideological integration and building-up on the basis of the 'fighting' identity) from the social group to the political group. In the next phase, already marked by the first withdrawals and *pentimenti*, the incentives of solidarity become increasingly important. The autobiographical accounts mark this fact on several occasions: the bond with comrades in prison; the need to maintain commitments; persevering with the armed struggle in order not to abandon the persons with whom they have shared years of their lives. These are all decisive factors. The emphasis is progressively shifted on to the maintenance of the organization and on the identification around a plan for collective survival that foreshadows the extremes reached by the COLP,[52] where the sole objective was to free the political prisoners.

It remains to be seen whether the importance indicated by the ties of friendship constitute a more general key that covers the life-courses of single interviewees. Obviously, we cannot mechanically transpose the results drawn from the observation of these life histories to a broader level. Between the micro-situation analysed and the more general level there is no direct relationship but, rather, a subtle succession of affinity and resemblance whose links all deserve investigation. The particular and at the same time chance nature of the various life-courses makes each story unique. Nevertheless, even a summary examination indicates that the experiences of *Prima Linea* in the Val di Susa, and its degree of diffusion, appear to be based on a complex network of interlinked interpersonal relationships. To conclude, it would be worthwhile to consider these briefly, utilizing in particular those data drawable from the autobiographical accounts and from the judicial records.

## 5.7 Val di Susa

Among the elements that help to characterize the scenario of the history of *Prima Linea* in the Val di Susa, there are two in particular that emerge from the interviews. The first is anti-fascism, and has already been discussed with regard to the self-representations contained in the various life histories. We have seen how in many cases the culture and the history of the Resistance has played an important role, as the environment in which fragments of individual memory and collective memory are welded together, and as a base for the political education of some of those interviewed. Others have noted how traces of this tradition remained in the political-military representation of *Prima Linea*,[53] particularly in actions carried out with the participation of the Val di Susa militants. We have also seen how this influence operated not so much on the level of the political categories as on the more impalpable level linked to the imagination (that dreaming about 'experiencing a bit of risk ... that the partisans had felt') described by the young Fabio, and to an existential condition.

The second important element is the widespread presence of the extra-parliamentary left in the Val di Susa. In particular the *collettivo operai-studenti*, which emerged between the end of the 1960s and the beginning of the 1970s and which was an important point of reference until the mid-1970s. Its history is the result of the union between experience and different cultural matrices, but from 1974 in particular it reinforced the already-developing rapport with *Lotta Continua* produced by the withdrawal of some political components. The importance of this capillary presence of the revolutionary left evidently did not immediately translate into recruitment opportunities for *Prima Linea*. The autobiographical accounts themselves point out, as in *Lotta Continua*, for example, which was the stronger organization until its breakup, that there was a marked mistrust of the 'militant' culture of the Turin *servizi d'ordine*.

What is in any case significant is that this presence guaranteed an already-structured network of political contacts and participation resources on which it was easier to work in order to make converts, especially given the close interweaving between politics and personal relations, as is often the case in small towns, where loyalties and alignments are dictated, perhaps more than in other places, by friendship as well as by ideology.

> Despite the diversifications there will always and in any case be a capacity of interweaving and contact between the different political 'revolutionary' *anime* of the valley, where the tones of the political battle and the polemics arrived mixed up with and mediated by interpersonal relations.[54]

From this point of view it may be useful to define a sort of map of the relations among those involved in the trials of *Prima Linea* members, starting from a diachronical reconstruction highlighting the different times of entry into the armed struggle. In this respect, we should immediately make a qualification as regards the singling out of the people involved. This element has been drawn directly from the judicial records: that is, it has been verified by trial. Given that in judicial trials the parameter used to define behaviour is constituted by the penal norms, it must be specified that this fact could hypothetically be disproved on the level of historical reconstruction.

As seen in Figure 5.1, in September 1977 only three people from the Val di Susa were part of *Prima Linea*: Fabio, Michele and Mauro. Only Mauro still lived in Turin.

The second phase is characterized by Mauro's attempt to reconstruct the Turin network of *Prima Linea*. Mauro sought to convert a series of personal relationships and already-developed contacts into political relationships: in particular, that group of relationships that linked to Michele and Fabio. In addition to Matteo and Giulia, Mauro contacted Piero, Paolo, Gustavo, Giacomo and Nicola. In the same period, after the arrest of Michele, his girlfriend Delia also moved nearer to the sphere of the armed struggle.

In the third phase there was a further broadening of the sphere of the persons involved. The central figure in the contacts with the Val di Susa was Giacomo. It was primarily through him (he subsequently became one of the leaders of the Turin group and part of the National Executive in September 1979) that a group of people (Muzio, Vincenza, Cinzia, Roberto and Luigi) became involved in *Prima Linea*, some of whom went on to form the *ronde* of Val di Susa. Again at the beginning of 1980, the network essentially headed by Gabriele joined *Prima Linea*. Finally, in the successive phase, linked more to the experience of the COLP, Pino also joined the organization.

In fact, the judicial records reveal very little about the different modalities of joining and the importance of the relationships within the group of protagonists. In this respect, the autobiographical material and the reconstructions supplied by the protagonists themselves appear to be more useful.

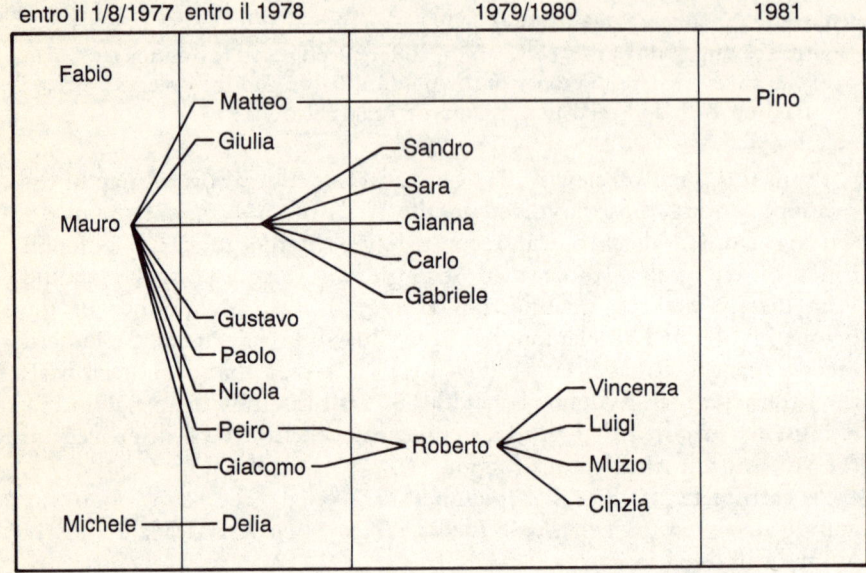

Figure 5.1: The times of entry into the spheres of armed struggle

From the point of view of social aggregates, there seems to be a complex mosaic of relations and relationships that cuts across this sort of map (see Figure 5.2) and the various networks constituted by it. Restricting ourselves to the networks of those persons whose life histories have been examined in this chapter, we find there is an intense intersecting and superimposition of networks and friendships. In particular, social group number 4, headed by Fabio and Michele, is made up of a group of friends from Bussoleno, who had been together since boyhood and shared a common past in the boy scouts, that subsequently maintained strong – albeit less frequent – links.

> a group that, thanks to the personality of its members, was exceptionally dynamic … a real place of generational intertwining, [a group that] was accepted in any environment.[55]

The other social groups (numbers 1, 2 and 3) have already been discussed in the course of the chapter.[56]

Finally, we must stress how within the sort of map outlined above, there are a series of individual relationships that revolve around the

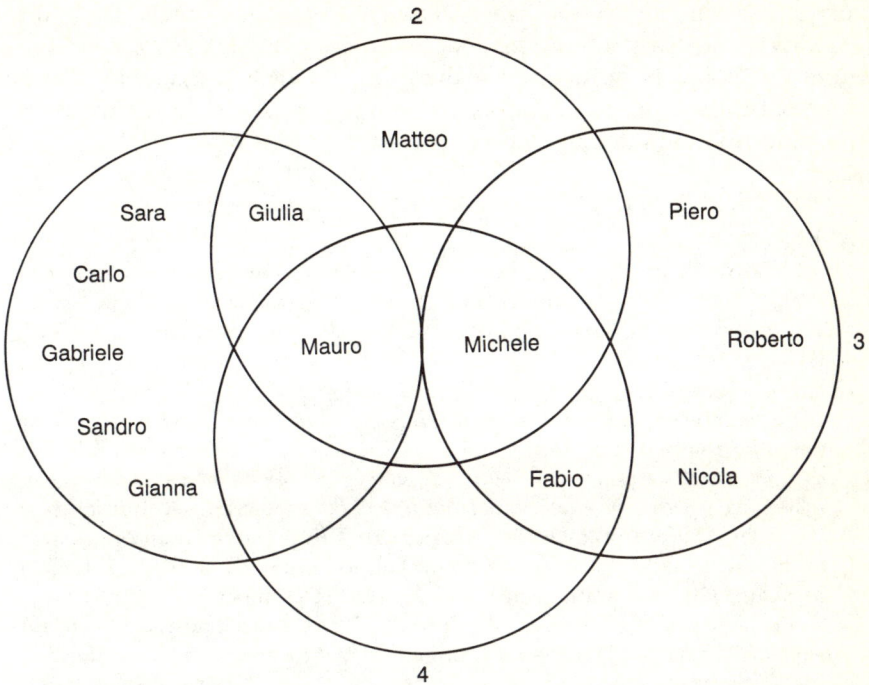

Figure 5.2: Social networks

figure of Mauro: Muzio, Gustavo and Piero had been his friends since childhood; Pino played with him and Matteo in a band. Within this picture are superimposed a series of emotional ties: in addition to the couple Mauro-Giulia, there are also Delia-Michele, Gabriele-Sara, Giacomo-Vincenza and Luigi-Cinzia.

In any case, without going beyond the examination of the different relationships, the existence of an interweaving between different social networks is sufficiently clear. Each has its own particular features and modality of relationships, but they nevertheless share a common characteristic: the link that unites them always predates the political 'formalization' of the network. This suggests that here too affective or social relationships have preconditioned and favoured individual mobilization and successive involvement in the armed struggle.

This is a hypothesis that remains for the time being a simple indication for further research and that undoubtedly merits further investigation. In particular, it would be interesting to carry out a parallel examination of the life-courses of those who had accepted the recruitment proposal and those who refused it, through a reconstruction of the social universe of the subjects active in *Prima Linea*, in an attempt to understand the mechanisms of differential participation in the armed struggle among subjects belonging to the same network. We could thus check the validity of the first indications emerging from the analysis carried out until this point, in particular for the group headed by Gabriele, which suggest the existence of a relationship between the degree of mobilization potential and the intensity and content of the social bond.

## Notes

1 See the work on the social network perspective. For example, Oberschall (1973), Snow, Zurcher and Ekland-Olson (1980), Gerlach and Hine (1979) and the works by Grazioli, Lodi and Donati, and Mormino in Melucci (1983).

2 Among these see some of the collective documents on the history of *Prima Linea*, compiled within the homogenous sphere of Turin, and in particular the collection entitled, *1983–1985 dallo scioglimento di Prima Linea alle aree omogenee*. See, *inter alia, Intervento sulla storia di Pl: contributo per una ricerca su riformismo, sovversione e lotta armata negli anni 70*, typescript. Declaration No. 1, sent by Mauro to the Ufficio istruzione di Torino. Declaration No. 2, sent by Mauro to the Ufficio istruzione di Torino. Tribunale di Torino, Ufficio Istruzione (G. I. Giordana) sentenza ordinanza 1 December 1977 in the trial of Grafta and others. Tribunale di Torino, Ufficio Istruzione (G. I. Carassi) sentenza ordinaria 7 January 1981 in the trial of Alberano and others. II Corte Assise Torino, sentence of 10 December 1983 in the trial of Alberano and others. II Corte Assise Torino, sentence of 16 July 1985 in the trial of Alfieri and others. *Seminario sulla ricostruzione storica della lotta armata negli anni 70*, typescript, compiled by Mauro.

3 Also referred to in the literature with the abbreviation PL.

4 For reasons of discretion, the names of all those cited in this chapter are pseudonyms.

5 Among others, see the works of Montaldi on the *militanti di base* (grassroots militants) in the 1960s.

6 Interview with Mauro, typescript, p. 9. Interview carried out by the author.

7 Ibid., p.3.

8 Interview with Gabriele, typescript, p. 35. Interview carried out by the author.

9 Interview with Matteo, typescript, p. 45. Interview carried out by the author.

10 Also referred to in the literature with the abbreviation LC.

11 *Collettivi politici studenteschi*: this refers to the *organismi di base* (grassroots organizations) among students of *Lotta Continua*, homologous to the CPU and the CUB, and respectively headed by the PDUP and *Avanguardia Operaia*.

12 Interview with Fabio, typescript, pp. 14–15. Interview carried out by the author.

13 Interview with Mauro, p. 30.

14 Ibid., p. 30.

15 Ibid., p. 31.

16 Ibid., p. 43.

17 *Seminario sulla ricostruzione storica della lotta armata negli anni '70*, typewritten document compiled by Mauro.

18 *Intervento sulla storia di Pl: contributo per una ricerca su riformismo, sovversione e lotta armata negli anni '70*, typewritten document, p. 9.

19 Tonino Micchiché, a member of *Lotta Continua* from Falchera, a strongly working-class neighbourhood in Turin with a recent history of immigration, was shot dead on 17 April 1975 by a *guardia giurata* (private policeman) of the *cittadini dell'ordine* (a private police corp) linked to the CISNAL, after an argument. His death made a profound emotional impact on the Turin movement and took place during the period when other left-wing militants were killed in Milan (Varalli and Zibecchi) and Florence (Boschi).

20 Interview with Fabio, p. 24.

21 Interview with Mauro, p. 46.

22 Interview with Fabio, p. 36.

23 This refers to an episode that took place at Palazzo Nuovo on 3 March 1977. The day before, during a meeting after a student march, a motion of condemnation had been passed against the FGCI for their separatist behaviour during the march. The FGCI was expelled and some of its militants were manhandled. The next day (3 March) the *servizi d'ordine* of the PCI was present in force at the entrance to the university. There were violent clashes following which the students of the movement took refuge in the Istituto Tecnico Avogadro, which was subsequently cleared by the police. The episode also had a journalistic after-effect, in that the PCI accused the daily newspaper *Stampa Sera* of having distorted the facts in the description of what happened and of having used the version of the extremists: that is, they accused the Communists of having provoked the clash. The newspaper responded by publishing photographs of PCI activists on their way to the university armed with clubs. The measure of the opposition and of the hostility towards the PCI by the movement is well-represented by some articles that appeared in *Lotta Continua* in particular on 4 March 1977 (*'300 funzionari del PCI attaccano gli studenti a Torino e vengono respinti'*) and the following day (*'Torino. Le fasi di una provocazione'*) in which it was claimed that 'in Turin too, the PCI has chosen to oppose the student movement head on ... the attack of the SDO *[servizi d'ordine]* of the PCI has demonstrated with a clarity that one has never before seen, the total absence, in the presence of an important movement, of margins of manoeuvre and mediation'.

24 In the provincial Turin congress, which took place shortly before the national congress, we saw, for example, lined up on opposing sides, the women and the workers allied with the *servizi d'ordine*. Fabio remembers how the opposition took place 'not only in political terms but in personal terms, in the sense that, within the space of a day one saw long-lasting friendships broken off ... in some houses where we went to eat there were comrades I was told to not go to any more'. Fabio, p. 35. On this point see also Bobbio (1979).

25 Interview with Mauro, p. 42.

26 Declaration No. 1, made by Mauro to the Ufficio Istruzione di Torino, p. 2.

27 See the national editions of *Senza Tregua*.

28 The first meeting of the organization took place at Salò in the autumn of 1976, followed a few months later, in the spring of 1977, by a sort of congress in which the Turin, Milan, Florence and Naples headquarters took part.

29 See *La Stampa*, of 3 March 1977, p. 4, in the article entitled '*Per protesta contro i fascisti assaltano hotel, monarchici, cattolici e comunisti*'.

30 Interview with Fabio, p. 39.

31 Declaration of Mauro, p. 3.

32 The most important leaders from Turin and various militants from the *squadre* were imprisoned. See also the ordinance of the Ufficio Istruzione di Torino (G.I. dott. Giordana) 1 December 1977 and the sentence of the Corte Assise Appello Torino of 19 April 1980.

33 Interview with Mauro, p. 46.

34 Cross-examination of Paolo, reproduced in the ordinance of the Ufficio Istruzione Torino (G.I. dott. Carassi) 7 January 1981.

35 *Intervento sulla storia di Pl*, op. cit., p. 9.

36 This deals with the episode that took place on 1 October 1977 during a march organized after the killing of Walter Rossi in Rome, in which Roberto Crescenzio died of his injuries after a fire in the bar.

37 Declaration of Mauro, op. cit., p. 4.

38 Interview with Matteo, p. 12.

39 Ibid., p. 22.

40 Ibid., p. 14.

41 Ibid., p. 13.

42 Ibid., p. 14.

43 Ibid., p. 15. This refers to the suicides of two members of the Red Army Faction in West Germany.

44 Ibid., p. 15.

45 Interview with Gabriele, p. 4.

46 Ibid., p. 5.

47 Declaration No. 2, made by Mauro to the Ufficio Istruzione di Torino, p. 4.

48 Interview with Gabriele, p. 7.

49 Interview with Carlo on 18 July 1987. Interview carried out by the author.

50 Declaration made by Mauro, op. cit., p. 5.

51 See in particular, Melucci (1982), and the essay by C. Caselli, 'Bisogno di socialità e innovazione culturale', in various authors, 1983.

52 Committees for proletarian liberation; one of their last 'flags of convenience' under which were gathered ex-militants of *Prima Linea*.

53 Bocca (1985), that indicates in relation to this the episodes relative to the wounding of Orecchia and the attack on the Val di Susa train on 26 June 1980.

54 *Seminario sulla ricostruzione*, op. cit., p. 41.

55 *Seminario sulla ricostruzione*, op. cit., p. 46.

56 See respectively sections 5.4, 5.3 and 5.2.

## References

Various authors (1983) *Tempo di vivere*, Milan, Franco Angeli.

L. Bobbio (1979) *Lotta Continua. Storia di una organizzazione rivoluzionaria*, Rome, Savelli.

G. Bocca (1985) *Noi terroristi*, Milan, Garzanti.

L.P. Gerlach and V.H. Hine (1979) *People, Power, Change*, Indianapolis, Bobbs Merril Co.

A. Melucci (1982) *L'invenzione del presente*, Bologna, Il Mulino.

A. Melucci (ed.) (1983) *Altri codici*, Bologna, Il Mulino.

A. Oberschall (1973) *Social conflict and Social Movements*, Englewood Cliffs, N. J., Prentice-Hall.

D.A. Snow, L. A. Zurcher and S. Ekland-Olson (1980) 'Social Networks and Social Movements: a Microstructural Approach to Differential Recruitment', *American Sociological Review*, No. 5, pp. 787–801.

# 6
# Subjective experience and objective reality: an account of violence in the words of its protagonists[1]

## *Raimondo Catanzaro*

## 6.1 Introduction

The idea of violence implies a high, if not infinite, number of references. Purely for the sake of argument, we can give an extensive list of the terms it evokes, either by analogy or contrast: conflict, social control, dictatorship, military force, justice, war, intolerance, liberty, the masses, power, revolution, the state, terror and torture. The list could be longer, but these terms are sufficient to indicate the complex range of thematic references implied by the term. Bearing this in mind, we have limited the field of analysis in two ways: by focusing on what the protagonists themselves relate; and by restricting the analysis to left-wing terrorism.

The first limitation regards the strongly subjective characterization of the account given by the protagonists. Here the notion of violence is mainly dealt with in reference to the interpretation of what the protagonists interviewed tell us: both about the experiences in which they were involved or in which they took part, the way in which they experienced them, and the sensations they felt and still feel in recalling them. In other words, this chapter aims to provide an image of the legitimation of violence and its use in the memory of terrorists.

It should be noted here that few of those interviewed talked at length or freely about the episodes of violence in which they were directly involved as protagonists, organizers or initiators. This process may be explained in terms of the need to maintain a degree of personality coherence and some respectable form of self-identification. Indeed, most of the protagonists interviewed belong to the *dissociati*. 'Dissociation' implies a repudiation of the use of violence as a means of resolving social conflict or as an instrument of political struggle. Nevertheless, these subjects do not deny having used violence during their terrorist experiences in so far as they believed in its utility and importance for the political struggle and for collective mobilization. The recognition of this reality is certainly a source of trauma and personal conflict in so far as it constitutes a marked break in their biographical history – and hence of the reconstruction of the subject's identity in his own memory. The first instrument used to reduce this trauma and to avoid having to deal with the contradictions implicit in the subject's life, thus enabling him to conserve a coherent rather than a despicable image of himself, is the glossing over of the particular episodes of violence in which the subject has been involved. The second instrument is the attempt to legitimize the use of violence: we shall focus on this in the course of the chapter.

The lack of detailed references to episodes of violence is an indication of the difficulty encountered by the protagonist in reconstructing a coherent identity of his or her own past. This has an important consequence from the viewpoint of the indications that emerge from these interviews: it confirms that the central problem – even in the sometimes unconscious eyes of the protagonists – is the legitimation of violence and the justification of its use. It is precisely on this subject that the reconstruction of the contradictions, ideologies and the terrorists' systems of thought is centred.

The singling out of this issue is a preliminary to the second delimitation of the field of analysis in that it only deals with exponents of 'red' or leftist terrorism. Part of the tradition of the left-wing is its problematic or traumatic relationship with violence. This is in strong contrast to the extreme right-wing, which conceives of society as being governed by violence; it does not propose to change this state of affairs but rather to take it to the extreme. Traditionally, the revolutionary left, in both its successes and failures, has often faced the problem of reconciling the use of violence with the blueprint of a self-regulating and violence-free society. We can in fact argue that the real problem of the historical experiences of the revolutionary left in the twentieth century has been its relationship to violence.

These elements – even if not explicit in the interviews with leftist terrorists – certainly constitute a deep substratum that conditions their justification of violence. On the other hand, there is little or no trace of such problems in the biographical reconstructions of personal histories made by right-wing terrorists. On the basis of our interviews, it appears that for the right-wing terrorist, violent action is primarily a value *per se* – its symbolic implications being secondary – as an exemplary expression of destructive behaviour. For right-wing terrorists, then, violence is primarily a starting point, rather than the finishing point in an ideological-political process of radicalization which in the 1970s marked the history of Italy and the lives of individuals within that country. This applies to the accounts of one of the critics of the destructive neo-fascist right who, after having lived that experience from the inside, confided that:

> The social vision that you have in neo-fascist circles is extremely simplified ... complexity is not even dreamt of; in spite of talking about the 'system', no consequences of the evaluation of this term are drawn; you imagine that society can be dominated by force.[2]

## 6.2 Collective movements and types of violence

Almost all the left-wing terrorists interviewed came either from or through organizations of the extreme left. Before opting to join the armed struggle and to 'go underground' or into clandestinity, all of them had had experiences of political struggle involving participation in mass demonstrations, marches and street battles with the police and groups representing their political opponents. Many of them had had experience in the organized branches of groups that practised more militaristic-style actions or forms of violent self-defence against, for example, the police. All of them had had some relationship with movements in the 1970s and there is more than an echo of this relationship in the accounts of those interviewed. These accounts are impregnated with the relationship between the use of violence during mass demonstrations and the choice of the armed struggle, and they are characterized by a series of contradictions.

The first of these contradictions is the justification of the transition from mass violence to terrorist violence, or to use terms more in line with the language of the protagonists, from the use of violence as self-defence to the strategy of offensive violence as an attack on the state. The difference between these two aspects of violence may be summed up with reference to their main characteristics: mass violence is a temporary and spontaneous explosion of destructive forces, whereas terrorist violence is premeditated and organized. This distinction is perhaps clearer if we consider the problem of violence directed against individuals, i.e. premeditated and cold-blooded attacks that interfere with the physical integrity of an individual and the marked difference between this and the action of, for example, striking someone in the heat of a street battle, at least as far as the justifications that a person must use to motivate either action are concerned. It is obvious that such justifications require a much greater degree of persuasiveness in the former case.

From a conceptual perspective, then, the move from spontaneous mass violence to terrorist violence is not a gradual transition but a clear leap or break. It is at this point that we confront the problem of the self-legitimation of terrorists and their need to justify the non-occasional use of premeditated political violence. Here the protagonist uses various sorts of justifying mechanisms, but these nevertheless point to an insoluble situation: that of a break or 'leap' between the two types of violence. Indeed, in the reconstruction of their biographical histories, most of those interviewed, albeit in different ways and using different tones, stressed the gradual nature of their 'ascent' to violence. From organizing marches to learning how to use molotov cocktails, from the preparation of 'provocative' strategies and inciting street battles to training in the use of arms, from 'proletarian expropriations' to the first armed robbery or act of arson, to kidnapping and attacks on individuals. These stages all tend to be relived as an almost natural and obligatory journey without problems of continuity.

> the problem of violence ... is not even discussed, it is passed over as something absolutely normal given the developing state of things.[3]

The mechanisms of justification and legitimation, however, provided by the interviewees, or that we catch a glimpse of, or which slip out during conversation, are different for the two types of violence (mass violence and terrorist violence). It is precisely this difference that points to the existence – albeit unconscious – of a leap. While in fact the legitimation of mass violence is given on purely ideological, social and political grounds, all three of these disappear when we go on to justify terrorist violence. Our analysis focuses on this second element in order to construct a profile of the relationship between the 'clandestine militants of the armed struggle of the left' and the use of violence.

The first type of legitimation of mass violence proposed by the interviewees is the reference to the political and moral climate of the early 1970s. The climate was one of an imminent *coup*, of rumours of attacks by the right and of *coup d'état*.[4] In some areas this climate was strongly interwoven with the reference to the strong anti-fascist tradition of the Resistance.

> In all the discussions one finds ... the partisan tradition ... this rather mythical vision ... and on the other hand the fascist tradition which regained strength through the strategy of tension ... mixed together with some considerable alarmism ... in reality at the time of the extra-parliamentary Left ... you saw paramilitary camps all over the place ... for a long time you could spend entire days ... looking for possible signs of paramilitary camps.[5]

There was, however, another element that was bound up with the anti-fascist tradition in the reconstruction of the protagonists: the workers' struggle. This is clearly summed up in an episode that took place in Piedmont recounted by a first-generation member of the BR.

> Anti-fascism was always present in the struggle within the factory ... so the

problem of organizing self-defence was always there, and during the
occupation ... we had a tent [in front of the occupied factory] ... there was a
very fascist, racist local newspaper, that organized ... the factory owners'
campaign against us, and we didn't bar them entry to the factory, we let them
in, we explained our reasons to them, which were obviously all distorted ...
and one evening we decided to demonstrate at the newspaper offices ... and ...
some of the old chaps, including my father and another chap, came up with
the idea of going there with a load of manure and of spreading it around the
newspaper offices. We did it ... and it was the straw that broke the camel's
back ... some sons of the owners here – call them *padroni* if you like, but
they're really just poor wretches – but they held the same opinions as this
other fascist – the next evening they threw molotovs at the tent and then ran
off. The same evening ... within a couple of hours we knew exactly who they
were and who did it; and we told the union, in the factory obviously, with
names ... and during the night we waited for the *carabinieri* to come and arrest
them, and instead nothing happened, we waited until morning ... and we
organized ourselves just to teach them a lesson, so that something like that
wouldn't happen again. Seeing that the political forces didn't do anything
about it, and the *carabinieri* didn't do anything about it, we would do
something about it! So we took one of them – we didn't want to beat him up
because he was still underage – we practically kidnapped him in his own
home saying, 'now you ... telephone what's-his-name and get him to come
here!' ... because it was the other one we wanted; something went wrong ...
so we went straight to his house to get him before he could get away, we
found his father there with a neighbour who was the headmaster of the *scuola
media* and a fascist too, and...we beat them up. Obviously ... we didn't run off;
we waited for the ambulance to come and get them, and for the *carabinieri* to
arrest us, quietly, in the sense that for us it was absolutely correct from a
political point of view. That evening in the factory ... everyone asked ... what
had happened to us ... and ... everyone ... came to the police station to
demonstrate and to call for us to be let out ... and for reasons ... of public
safety the magistrate and the captain of the *carabinieri* let us go ... The most
interesting thing ... was that absolutely everyone took part in it, not just the
group of the worker-students, the extremists, but absolutely everyone, from
the trade union officials down to the last worker in the factory.[6]

In this episode we should stress the combination of the various factors
that legitimate the violent action: the just nature of the workers' revenge,
the straightforward nature of the actions taken against the fascists, the
participation of the entire factory from trade-union officials to workers
and the mass demonstration for the release of those arrested. The range
of political, social and ideological factors that help legitimate violent
action are all present. The reconstruction of the protagonists (in this case,
by an armed militant from Milan) is again symptomatic of how a
relationship was established between the anti-fascist tradition and factory
problems in order to legitimate violence.

The violence issue [involved] something else, and that was anti-fascism ... In
the summer you'd often get back from holidays and they [the small factories]

had closed ... We'd organize a debate at the big factory, [because we had to] guarantee solidarity too, so that at the end the workers in the small factories [who were] sacked [would] be able to get into our firm for example ... [but] there was the problem that being from outside the factory ... the factory guards were against it; ... it's episodes like this that create ... conflict, there is very little ideology [involved] ... or general debate on violence, at least ... not in the factory.[7]

The idea of defensive violence – of a response to violence suffered – appears in another interview as a memory of the subject's first impact with the problem of violence. Here, too, the legitimation of the use of violence seems to be linked to problems of social justice and without doubt to mass situations.

Above all it appears ... [to be] a problem of violence suffered ...; the first images are linked ... to the attacks on various marches made by the police ...; the first clear signals of an impossible situation ... that had to be changed [occurred] at that time ... that is ... from these shocks of non–student demonstrations ... attacked and that bring ... as a cause a violent repression ... the death ... of [those] who went onto the street. These things ... are immediately part of the patrimony of reference, that is the violence is above all...a hostile system ... that needs a response by something that knows how to immobilize ... to change the plan of this situation ... The first demonstrations ... I don't remember them at all as being an imposition on the part of the march, on the part of the movement that wants to do certain things that are not possible, I remember ... simply as a reaction to someone who wants to stop you ... and you can't understand why ... and it seems to me natural to respond ... with stones ... with confrontation at a distance ... against people who are armed, who've got teargas, who've got truncheons ...; that is, this difference becomes ... in my view a motive of justification, that is a fact that legitimates for me the use of a different and antagonistic violence.[8]

To summarize, we can say that with regard to the relationship with mass violence found in the reconstructions of the protagonists of terrorism there are elements of legitimation that in the final analysis lead back to an underlying motivation for violent behaviour. What provokes violent action is the feeling of injustice suffered. This is because the defence by the organs of the state is lacking (as in the case of the missing police intervention in the molotov incident); or because of the disproportionate size of the the forces of law and order employed during street battles following a prohibition perceived as unmotivated. Finally violent action is seen as defence with respect to a form of violence that, as in the case of the unemployed workers coming back from summer holidays, consists in preventing people from realizing their own potential and in seeing yourself denied an essential right such as work. What must be emphasized is that the reaction to the perception of a suffered injustice is represented in the two aspects of the 'just' action, in so far as it is justified (for example, by the difference between the number of demonstrators and the size of the police force), and of the action that 'applies justice', substituting it for the inertia of the institutional forces that ought to deal with it ('the *carabinieri* didn't do anything about it, we would do something about it!'). This notion of legitimate violence was reinforced by the reference to a ready-made ideology that was treated as an immediately usable resource for its historical legitimation: the traditions of the Resistance and anti-fascism.

Up to this point we have looked at the justifications used by terrorist protagonists to support the use of violence during protest demonstrations. In the present analysis we are not interested in investigating whether – at the time when the facts narrated took place – such operations of legitimation were the same. What is important is to verify whether there is a coherence between the type of legitimation used at the time of the interview and those adopted to motivate the transition to the armed struggle and to a totally different type of violence.

## 6.3 Children of a futureless god

There are undoubtedly great differences between the generation of terrorists that went into clandestinity in the early 1970s and the post-1975 generation members of the armed struggle. One of the main differences is the attitude to violence and to the use of arms. In the words of one of the founding fathers of the BR:

all those of us who had been involved in politics before had tremendous problems [coping with the idea of] military action, the use of arms ... [it was] something frightening ... while those who were younger than us didn't have any prejudices, that is, those who were eighteen or nineteen years' old; ... let's say that to have been involved in politics at the legal level was a contradiction.[9]

Generational differences and differences in political experience are stressed as discriminating factors with regard to the use of arms. This is clearer if we examine another characteristic of the experience of post-1975 militants: the remarkable speed of the transition that was symptomatic of a sort of impatience or frenzy and of a desire to experience things immediately. One of the second-generation militants related that he left home at the age of fifteen, had become an active member of *Lotta Continua* (LC) in Turin before his sixteenth birthday and had become a *clandestino* (fugitive) before the age of seventeen.[10] It only needed an accident to tilt the balance in favour of the armed struggle: a choice that often became immediately operative without any time for a period of latency or reflection.

The most dramatic aspect ... was ... understanding that ... the day before ... I had been against violence, then something happened so that twenty-four hours later it became OK and I didn't even stop to think much about how I had changed my mind in such a short time.[11]

Certainly this attitude was the result of a malaise, and in the words of another interviewee:

[it was] a malaise where ... you didn't even know what you wanted, you wanted to go forward ... because there was this need ... this hurry to live and to get everything immediately.[12]

In the light of these considerations we can understand the sudden radicalization from the political struggle to the headlong leap taken by some militants, from leftist extremism to the armed struggle. The fact that it is a clear 'leap' is born out by the words of an interviewee:

There were people who were homeless, they needed a home ... and that in my view is where the leap took place ... [because] I began ... to say seriously ... that this thing [had to] be countered with an organization which dealt not only with needs, but with general armed clandestine politics ... An organization ... without an overall plan...can't always be fighting about housing problems because the [real] problem is the State and hence the holding of power.[13]

We should be mistaken if we believed that such attitudes are solely dependent on a greater degree of individual propensity to the use of violence. A more reasonable explanation is one that links this radicalization to the particular characteristics of the groups involved in the movements that started in the 1970s and to their organizational break-up. As another interviewee stressed, the link between movements and anti-fascism involved an implicit legitimation of the use of violence:

The theme of anti-fascism ... already contains an *a priori* reasoning which legitimates the use of violence, even non-defensive violence; beating-up fascists was always OK for the Turin movement; it wasn't only us who shouted death slogans against the fascists, there were marches where thousands of demonstrators shouted them.[14]

Nevertheless this potentiality remained such. The tradition of anti-fascism in the use of organized violence is due to two factors: first, the formation of the *servizi d'ordine*[15] of groups of the extreme left, and second, the loss of control over these groups by political organizations as the latter disintegrated, leaving only the military wing standing. This process is clearly illustrated in the accounts of the protagonists who stress that the basic problem within their groups during political demonstrations was to 'win over the masses'.

In this way the *servizi d'ordine* started to acquire their autonomy with respect to the political direction. Their logic became progressively inspired by their military function; this generated conflicts with the central political direction. The violence tended to become autonomous, no longer a mere instrument to achieve strategic or tactical objectives but a practice containing its own justifications. It is on the basis of this contradiction that one of the conditions for the formation of armed groups is determined; and in the account of one of the protagonists:

> if on the one hand there was discussion about violence ... and about the concept of 'military' action, and the use of force as an indispensable part of political activism, it was in this situation that the first contradictions began to emerge ... over the use of this force, over the use of the military, hence as a separate reality which is only reconstructable within the direction of the organization of the party as the armed struggle and as ... [a] situation that is constantly linked to the struggle and hence ... to the organization and hence united completely to political activity.[16]

Participation in the *servizi d'ordine* effectively socialized a large group of young militants in the use of violence partially or totally controlled by extremist political organizations. When organizations such as *Lotta Continua* or *Potere Operaio* (PO) started to disintegrate, these energies were 'liberated' and thus left without political outlets, but simply with 'military' outlets. Thus, the excess of militancy characteristic of these movements did not directly produce the propensity to the use of violence, or to terrorism; but indirectly this outlet was found via the growth of the *servizi d'ordine* following the disintegration of the extremist organizations of which they represented the military wing. The rapidity of the transition to the armed struggle that characterized the choices of entire groups of militants of the extra-parliamentary extreme left is consequently not surprising. Neither is it surprising to find that the protagonists have some difficulty in finding a form of self-legitimation for an experience that was the result of a hasty and often unmeditated choice. It is not incidental that the first legitimation mechanism is that of *myth*, that is of a sort of 'regeneration' seen in a romantic light that would have justified any kind of violence leading to its realization. This ingenuous and simplistic notion is accompanied by a perspective that does not go beyond the point of revolutionary regeneration.

> This question of the future yes, there was that, but it was very vague and misty ...; this society with the dictatorship of the proletariat in other words ... There was never any discussion as to what we wanted for Communist society, revolutionary society. All our discussions were negative [reflections] on current society; but we were unable to prefigure a [new] society through our ideology.[17]

If the future of society was not discussed, neither was the question of violence, or only in terms that were equally vague and well below the threshold of concrete debate.

> the question of political murder ... was a problem which was discussed too [by] *Prima Linea* (Front Line) ... but once again [it was] a bit over the heads of most people.[18]

In a picture of this sort, dynamic or aesthetic elements are reconstructed as the factors determining individual choice. The search for action became an expression of personal identity and the armed struggle acquired its fascination because of the novelty of the subjective experience it offered and because of the excitement derived from the use of arms.

## 6.4 The discrete charm of the armed struggle

In the memory-outline made by the terrorist protagonist in rethinking his life history, the acceptance of the armed struggle is reconstructed by scanning the stages where collective violence is diluted and by weakening the aspects of an actual qualitative leap, with all the problems related to the use of violence. This reconstruction tends to establish a coherent identity by which the protagonist, by re-running the account, can condemn the choice of the armed struggle today and simultaneously justify it when it occurred. This process requires a series of operations. The first of these emphasizes the justice, correctness and legitimacy of mass violence. Without this first reference point it would be impossible to establish a gradual transition to terrorist violence. Nevertheless, the gradual transition contradicts the speed – at times too swift – with which the option of the armed struggle is taken up. Moreover, if the gradual transition to terrorism were to be justified with arguments of a political and social nature, as is the case for mass violence, it would be difficult to prove ourselves to be *dissociato* on the basis of a choice that we held to be just at the time and that we consider seriously mistaken today. This kind of argument helps us to understand how the leap from mass violence to the armed struggle corresponds – in terms of terrorists' self-legitimation – to a leap from political arguments and notions of social justice to arguments where – even if these elements are still present – the emphasis has clearly shifted to aesthetic or 'naturalistic' factors characterized by elements of compelling inevitability. The first of these elements is the fascination exerted by the novelty of the armed struggle, which slowly but surely opened up the contrast between mass movements and their missing political outlets.

> [The armed struggle was] ... attractive because it was ... a break ... a break

with a castrated and obsolete world of politics, the old and unresponsive world.[19]

But the fascination and appeal of the armed struggle was not merely a factor of its political novelty. An important role was also played by the chance to handle firearms.

> arms have a fascination of their own, it is a fascination that makes you feel in some way more ... more virile ... this sensation of feeling stronger, more manly, ... I found myself ... showing them to women to try to impress them...; and then it seemed somehow more noble to use arms instead of, I don't know, fighting with one's fists let's say.[20]

The reference to the aesthetic element, in the twofold sense of the fascination exercised by arms and the sensations generated by their use, is emblematic. The relationship, however, with arms was not justified solely from the point of view of fascination, but also from the point of view of its being 'natural'. In this case the use of violence was legitimated as a fact that derived obviously and automatically from the education of the militant. Here it is worth noting part of the conversation about the use of molotov cocktails during demonstrations:

> this sort of thing was almost written into the physical makeup of those who took part in street demonstrations, [those] who lived the revolutionary experience.[21]

In response to the objection that molotovs had to be manufactured and that this implied learning how to make them, the emphasis of the reply, albeit affirmative, is on a technical factor: that is, on the fact that there was someone in the organization who dealt with the efficiency of the preparation and use of molotovs. In fact, the *brigatista* goes on to say that:

> you ... learnt how to make them, you also learnt how to use them, you learnt from the fact that some exploded and some didn't.[22]

Once again, it is clear that the use of violence was taken for granted; the discussion about it concentrates more on the technicalities of use than on the meaning or consequences of such violence *per se*, or on the limits that should have been placed on it. But where some stress the 'naturalness' of violence and for this reason take it for granted in a non-problematic way, others stress the influence exercised by the solidarity felt for those who had joined the armed struggle. It is in these terms that one of the protagonists stressed his decision to maintain his commitment to terrorism despite the outcome of an attempt to disarm a private guard that ended in tragedy with the guard's death.

I knew that it couldn't last ... but what pushed me on was the solidarity towards those *compagni* that I had known, people who were committing their lives to this venture, to this struggle, and with whom I had shared a part of myself.[23]

Here too, the element of solidarity matches up with the fascination of novelty, with the dynamic reaction against the alienating immobility of traditional politics. In this context, the protagonists also resorted to the weight of impelling external circumstances as an explanatory factor of their behaviour.

On the other hand, I thought that in any case the mark that the transition to the armed struggle would have left could only have an innovative effect on the alienating and unchanging scenario that I saw before me at the time.[24]

Once again, we come back to the extreme rapidity of the involvement, which left no room to meditate on decisions, so that in some cases protagonists speak of a sort of unavoidable destiny taking precedence over individual choice. The inevitability of such a choice is matched, however, by an emphasis on the casual nature of involvement in a combination of determinism and fatality that sets the premises for the elimination of any possible moral judgement as to the choices made.

## 6.5 The force of things, or the dominion of the case

Nothing demonstrates this mingling of the casual and yet inevitable nature of the choice better than the notion of solidarity as a reason for joining the armed struggle.

Ending up as a fugitive ... was a big shock for me, above all because of the strange way that I'd come to join the armed struggle, more or less because of a series of connected circumstances where a strong human involvement in a web of interpersonal relationships was more decisive than the ideological factor. So ... I found myself saddled with a warrant for arrest ... for ... belonging to an armed group, involved in and determined by something greater than me, that in part I felt was hostile, and which in part I accepted.[25]

This inevitability of finding themselves personally involved functions in an unmediated way to stop the protagonists from labelling themselves as terrorists.

I'm not a killer, I'm not a terrorist, I'm someone with a series of values, who wants to be active in politics and today the only way ... to be politically active is this, because there is no other way because they have been taken away from us, they have taken away every other type of intervention.[26]

In the eyes of those who rerun their experience of armed militancy, the loss of a degree of liberty in personal choice is the outcome of circumstances that left no other way open. The deterministic aspect of the choice is directly traceable to the characteristics of the historical climate in which the protagonists found themselves.

> in the particular historical [phase] that Italy was going through some experiences were in my opinion inevitable; ... it is useless to fool oneself that it was possible to do anything else given the state of things, the role of the parties ... the function of the parties and the function of society at that time, in that situation it was inevitable in my opinion that some people [chose the armed struggle].[27]

Personal choices then were just as impelling – in the sense of being necessary and inevitable – as collective and generational choices. The same applies to the contact with and use of arms.

> Some time afterwards, one of the times when these people [*Prima Linea* militants who the interviewee had until that time only known as acquaintances through a common friend] came to see us, they stayed to eat; ... they nearly always came at suppertime, and brought a bag with some arms which they said ... they had problems looking after for the time being, and asking us if we would keep them for a while. We agreed, also because it wasn't a very big parcel ... and only contained a sawn-off shotgun in bad condition, and ... some small handguns, things like that.[28]

Naturally, it is not important to ascertain if things really took place in this way. Indeed, the account could be interpreted as a need to justify involvement in the armed struggle. But it is precisely this circumstance that is indicative of the depth of the motivations underlying such an involvement. Indeed, in the development of the open-ended interview that forms the basis of these narratives, none of the questions refer to this argument; neither can the interviewer be compared – even in the eyes of the interviewee – to the investigating judge, to whom he must present a version of the facts that will allow the application of extenuating circumstances. If the interviewee presents that version of his acceptance of the armed struggle, it is the result of the contradiction created between a past and repudiated experience and the need to re-establish some form of coherence and continuity in his or her lifestory.

Here, too, in the 'parcel of arms' episode, the emphasis on the particular circumstances, as in the molotov cocktail episode, is on inevitability – matched by technical considerations that help justify the choices made. Indeed, as the interviewee said, they agreed to keep the parcel because it was 'not a very large parcel' and hence not very visible and which in any case could be easily hidden. On the basis of this account, we are faced with a leap to a further transition, not explicitly motivated with respect to the casual nature of the contact with arms. Even the motivation adopted to explain why they decided to keep the parcel contains an attitude of 'evaluative neutrality' with regard to the question of arms, or at least a stabilization between the problems that could arise as a result of looking after them and the need to express solidarity with friends that induced them to look after the parcel of arms. Unexpectedly, however, the 'looking after' was transformed into 'knowledge' of arms.

> This was the first time that we'd had any contact with arms ... and handling them, dismantling them, and in the end examining them ... the first time that – beyond the discussions, beyond the situations of an ideological character which we had been involved in – marked the first involvement of a different sort.[29]

In this way, the acceptance of the armed struggle is taken without any degree of liberty: the protagonist feels the need to explain and justify the use of arms by resorting to the explanatory combination of chance and solidarity or friendship. That is, the transition from looking after arms to actively knowing them, 'handling them, dismantling them, examining them', appears to be so obvious for the protagonists as to not require any further explanation. In this undisputed 'dominion of the case' recurs, combined with it, the inevitability of destiny.

It is this combination of chance and inevitability that constitute the logical premise so that the justification of the armed struggle given at the time, founded on political motivations, can be renounced without breaking the continuity of the biographical life-story in the eyes of the protagonist, who in his narration reconstructs his life-story. Indeed, in the same way in which the crushing predominance of the all-political motivations put forward to justify murder or cold-blooded and premeditated violence against individuals served at the time of personal involvement in terrorist activity to annul every possible reference to ethical questions, so today, in the reconstruction of the protagonist, the emphasis on the circumstances, on the particular case and on the inevitable nature of events help him to construct a system of justifications where morality simply ceases to be relevant.

## 6.6 The irrelevance of morality

The first way in which the need to settle up with morality with regard to terrorist violence and in particular with premeditated, organized and cold-blooded attacks against people, is presented in the interviews as the conviction of the impossibility of making a judgement; this conviction conceals the enormous difficulty experienced in commiting themselves to an opinion. In the words of one of the protagonists:

> this choice of the armed struggle ... was more a process of learning than of

changing myself ... This doesn't mean any judgement of a political or ethical nature as to what arms ... and political violence meant in our past.[30]

The need to avoid contradicting a probably fragile and difficult-to-reconstruct identity is demonstrated by the refusal to admit that the experience of the armed struggle has produced changes in their way of behaving. This is done by turning the admission into a feeble concept of learning, even though this learning did not stop them admitting their impotence and inability to pass judgement – either ethical or political – on the meaning of violence in the past of the individual and the collective. In addition to the recognition of this difficulty, there are cases where the admission of the irrelevance of an ethical judgement is quite open.

in terms of an ethical, moral, ideological judgement on the use of violence and hence a hypothesis of a break with the state of things, I never had any problems in the sense that I always shared ... a certain type of behaviour and way of presenting things ... with regard to the Red Brigades.[31]

Here some transitions appear to have been extraordinarily intense. In the first place the fact that the break with the existing state of affairs has to take place by revolution and that this implies violence, is seen as being absolutely non-problematic; it simply goes without saying. In the second place, we should note the reference to the Red Brigades, which is important because the interviewee was a member of *Prima Linea* and because his involvement in terrorist activity – and hence murder – is post-1977, which testifies, as we shall see later on, to the persistence of the strong pull exercised specifically by the BR with respect to other left-wing terrorist groups. Finally, we should note that this member of *Prima Linea* had previously spoken of the discussions on political murder being beyond the grasp of most people in his group. It is precisely this problem of political murder that shows just how irrelevant morality had become. One interviewee talks about the decision to kill in the following way:

It [political murder] was not totally antiseptic, even if we did everything to make it so, to reduce [it] to the mere exercise of a political practice of organization.[32]

There are, however, the *brigatista* who became involved in a series of contradictions that reveal an unresolved tension between past practice and a present critical attitude towards violence against individuals. An account is given of an action against the owner of a property company, held to be responsible for the evictions of people who had occupied housing and who had requested (and obtained) the intervention of the police in order to get rid of them. The group of armed militants decided to make raids on the offices of the property company; during the action the owner was wounded by gunshot. The action of wounding was not decided beforehand: the plan had only been to kidnap and 'expose' the person held responsible for the action against the evicted squatters. This is how the interviewee described his reactions after the episode:

> It's not a problem of the use of arms as such ... I wasn't shocked at all ... by the fact that someone could have been hurt; ... for ... my comrades the practise of murder worked as a barrier. That is, there was clearly no need to go beyond that point ... it was more of a direction linked to the identity of the movement rather than to, let's call them ethical, characteristics.[33]

In other terms, if political murder constitutes an unpassable limit, we could not, on the other hand, be scandalized if someone were to be hurt. The problem boils down to a technical matter – someone who does not know how to handle a gun in order to wound runs the risk of killing instead. The exclusion *a priori* of this as a possible circumstance does not depend on moral considerations but on the technical ability to use firearms. According to the interviewee in that case, he shot to wound and not to kill. This reduction of violence to its purely technical aspects – which excluded any reference to morality – combines with a political judgement; the limit for the non-profanation of human life arises from a political evaluation, from an identity of belonging to the movement and not from a value judgement. Indeed, the irrelevance of morality in favour of a combination of technical judgement and political judgement appears to be confirmed by the rest of the account.

> With regard to the action carried out ... what was laid down was that something like that must never happen again. That is, you could decide whether or not to injur someone, but it should be decided beforehand; you could use arms, but this sort of decision simply had to be clear.[34]

In other words, we can legitimize the decision – and hence remove any obstacle – to kill *a priori* by making a political decision. Another of these justificatory mechanisms was the reference to a higher degree of violence carried out by competing political groups. Faced with the question of what he feels after such an episode, the interviewee's response is again totally political; as a political action it is problematic, but he is indifferent about the ethical question.

> the most dramatic thing that happened inside me was, let's say, a process of political reflection ... there is an incredible disparity between the type of thing that we were doing, the type of logic that motivated us and what was happening around us, that is, in that same period the BR ... initiated a logic of destruction, killing magistrates, policemen. That is to say, exploding every possible level of reference.[35]

There is, however, a residual trace of uncertainty, in the account of a second-generation (post-1975) member of the Red Brigades who makes the explicit admission that political murder is a choice and not a problem. The decision to use violence depends exclusively on considerations of a tactical nature.

> The rules for sorting out conflicts are not your own ... they are rules determined by ideology, by the organization, by the way of carrying things out ... What we always said about the 'phase', that is, about murder, was not always valid, wounding someone was not always valid, it was valid at a certain time because of a combination of varied factors ... What point the relationship with the State had got to depended on one's own restructuring, what point the organization was at, the general relationship between guerrilla warfare and anti-guerrilla warfare and so things ... that ... really took this instrument away from you.[36]

At this point we have come full circle; we are back with the notion of inevitability, of necessary decisions, of judgements of technical rationality. If everything depends on the 'phase' then in individual decisions little or nothing depends on what you do; there is no possible degree of liberty. This latter level of self-legitimation coincides not only with the need to avoid breaks in the reconstruction of our biographical history, but also with some of the demands of the armed struggle – with regard to eliminating the importance of moral judgement in cases of political murder in order that such actions can be carried out – that is, the need to realize for a process of double depersonalization, of the victim *and* his murderer.

## 6.7 Double depersonalization and the reproduction of violence

The following description given by a 'second-generation' member of the Red Brigades is a perfect explanation of how the mechanism of coercion to use physical violence, up to the extreme of murder and which reduces the person to functions, works; that is, in depersonalizing the victim and the executioner. Let us leave the word to this protagonist of the armed struggle and to his way of defining the difference between street battles and premeditated, ends-oriented terrorist violence:

> Street battles are different, they are ... something legal, something experienced with other people ... but [in the case of organized and premeditated violence] you start to do something different, you carry out an enquiry on someone so there is a sort of political enquiry beforehand, but psychologically it becomes something different, you single out someone who is responsible; it is not the State as before ... with policemen, and the Flying Squad [but] real physical people, this chap does this ... and has done that and you start a trial ... The trial begins when you single out someone on paper, that is to say, you make a

person correspond to a political need ... that chap is responsible, it is him right here and now, there is already a trial logic ... where you've already decided that he is guilty...and what makes you different is the penalty, the penalty that you allot to that person who is guilty of those things. You go along and take on this sense of justice ... so in actual fact he is not even a person any more, he has been emptied and you load him up with other crimes, other responsibilities ... At this point you can't afford to be totally involved ... you are someone who is meting out justice, who is stating values, and so there is no place for ... strong emotions even if you have them inside, even if the situation is charged with feelings ... but not in that role, not at that time.[37]

The double depersonalization of the victim and the aggressor is a mechanism that induces the latter to carry out violent actions by deadening his ethical reactions to it. It is hence a necessary action in order to reproduce violence as an instrument of political action. It is, nevertheless, a mechanism that has limitations, as we can see – in contrast to the above testimony – in the account given below by a first-generation *brigatista*.

There was [the person] who insisted and perhaps managed to maintain a political point of view with respect to the adversary, to the person, so that ... there was this distance ...; then there were others who instead, became 'burnt out' let's say the moment when the handcuffs went on and they were taken away, and then they disintegrated ... I was one of them ... In fact, I remember this man here [the manager of a car plant]; five of us got him – all five were clandestines in order not to involve the local workers – and we took him away; three of us held him in the car, parked in a garage rented for the occasion, and then got rid of immediately afterwards; one took the recording, another kept a weapon in his hand ... and I ... was ready at the wheel to eventually rush off ... and the other two stayed outside with walkie-talkies to warn us if by chance there was a search going on in the area – and at a certain point I went to buy him some sweets and a drink because he [the victim] was thirsty, he felt ill, he was a bit ... [it was] the nervous tension, he couldn't salivate any more; and I remember this rule that we had practically broken – we shouldn't have left the place unless it was to take him away – and I felt so sorry for him, he was so pitiful ... yes ... pitiful.[38]

How then does the reproduction of the sort of violence that characterized the years of terrorism come about? We have seen how one of the mechanisms that pushes people into the use of arms and to the violation of the liberty and physical integrity of others up to the extreme of murder, is the interiorization, by the subject who carries out the violence, of a double depersonalization; of the person who is the physical target of the action and of the person who carried it out. Nevertheless, the process of depersonalization is neither simple nor unproblematic. Moreover, the greater part of terrorist activity in the period 1968–82 did not consist of attacks on individuals – even if these were the events that created the greatest uproar because they constituted the most serious offence that violence can commit against society – and the escalation of acts of violence cannot be analysed exclusively with reference to such attacks. The increase in the number of robberies, proletarian expropriations and other forms of violence against goods and property, was accompanied by an increase in the period 1977–8 of acts of violence against individuals.

We should be wary of thinking that the growth of violence is to be traced back exclusively or mainly to the socialization into violence of a generation of militants. If the mechanisms noted earlier actually work, then the growth and the feeding of violence are due to two elements that can be defined as factors of repression and factors of imitation. The first relates to the sudden falling off of the movements following the strong repressive response by the state. This caused a sudden rush into clandestinity by numerous groups of militants who had carried out semi-legal activity or activity on the verges of legality during their participation in the movement. It was not only those who committed serious crimes who went into hiding, but also militants who were not involved. In other words, there was a 'surplus of clandestinity'. That is, young people afraid of being given sentences over and above those considered 'adequate' for the crimes committed, or who were simply afraid of being involved in the general climate of repression, went into hiding out of fear, out of solidarity with friends, because the dramatic nature of events did not allow them to evaluate the advantages of alternative choices properly, or because they believed in ideological choices not in line with the state of social conflict at the time.

The high number of *clandestini* gave rise to serious problems of organizational management for the underground organization. It is well-known for example that *Prima Linea* found itself unexpectedly without adequate structures to support the weight of so many *clandestini*. The main problem was having to support and run an organizational network for militant *clandestini* without adequate support points or sufficient economic resources.

> Keeping up structures like those meant maintaining houses, paying wages, and slowly the number of *clandestini* increased [so that] where so much money used to last for a certain length of time, within two months the amount had to be tripled, so that ... for example ... I took part in robbery operations, bank robberies.[39]

Thus a mechanism of self-generating violence is applied – and as we shall see later – that took on aspects of economic instrumentalism for group survival, or tended to loose its immediate political meaning or perspective. The second mechanism, that of imitation, was based on the logic of competition triggered off between groups who had been involved in the movements or who had become clandestine for lesser crimes – who wished to establish themselves as members or potential members of the armed struggle.

> After the Moro kidnapping [there was] a proliferation of thousands of imitations ... each little neighbourhood group dreamed of its own small 'Via Fani' [the street where the president of the DC was kidnapped] ... all the collectives, the small armed groups that had been formed ... all over Italy, dreamt of an operation that would let them reach ... the level of an organization like the Red Brigades or *Prima Linea* or at least ... to be able to contact organizations like the Red Brigades, and in that period there were hundreds and hundreds of attacks taking place in every city.[40]

The growth of the use of violence – which was in turn built upon the ashes of the movements of the 1970s – was hindered by elements inherent in the organization of clandestine groups themselves; it was undermined by crises generated from within the clandestine milieu as well as by the impact of imitation and competition among terrorist groups.

## 6.8 The exterminating angel

For the *clandestini*, going underground meant a progressive reduction in their level of social contact. They were forced to reduce or eliminate certain contacts and relationships that might prove dangerous and lead to being discovered; they were forced to live a life where contact with others was limited and took place almost exclusively within the organization. This reduction of social horizons was particularly serious for those accustomed to an active life and created serious contradictions for them. One of the dilemmas facing the clandestine militant was his double identity: that is, the necessity to relate differently to the people he met.

> the houses where I stayed ... they were all houses where ... there was a regular comrade ... of the organization who knew who I was, but ... at other times I lived in houses where they had no idea about my real identity or what I'd done, so that there was this enormous problem of always having two lives ... you always had to have on the one hand an image ... so that even the things that you had to talk about – even the times that you needed to talk – were always bound up with your public image, and on the other hand, what you really were had to be constantly hidden, so that on the one hand you could talk to some people and on the other hand you had to keep up ... a public facade ... It wasn't easy ... to have ... two faces ... especially for someone who ... [was] used to living the immediacy of things, of relationships.[41]

The double identity of the clandestine militant became increasingly difficult to maintain when faced with the reasons for which the choice of armed militancy had originally been taken. Where such a choice had been a conscious and considered outcome related to a well-defined political objective – as was generally the case for first-generation members of the Red Brigades – to create the 'armed party', then the type of choice contained elements that allowed militants to withstand the privation of social contact. On the contrary, for those who had made a headlong decision to join the armed struggle, often with rather confused ideas as to the ends and objectives of such a choice, and who often felt they had literally been catapulted into clandestinity by events stronger than themselves, such privations proved far more difficult to bear.

Thus, two particular contradictions emerge: the first concerns the internal conflict between the need to respect determined norms of caution to avoid being recognized and arrested, and the need to have contacts – particularly emotional contacts – with a broader circle of people other than those with whom they mixed in order to respect the rules of clandestinity.

> In fact at the time ... I went on being a commuter for a bit because I would never 'fit in' in Milan if it wasn't in the *gruppo di fuoco* [armed nucleus] ... I saw the people in charge, I saw some 'safe' people ... It's not that I went to meetings, the problem was that at the time there in that house there was a rather marked traffic ... of people, of friends, because it wasn't a clandestine house ... there ... I got to know these ... girls ... from a feminist collective, they become friends. I mean to say that for a year and a half ... we lived practically together and went around together ... I began to construct an equilibrium in my emotional life linked ... to a situation that allowed me ... to have a space that was outside the organization ... In that period I had a very normal social life ... On the contrary I really didn't believe that I was clandestine because I ... regularly went to all the places where they met, I smoked joints too ... and this stuff was a continual bone of contention [between myself] and the organization ... relieved simply by the fact that a lot of the things I did weren't known and the fact that by living in a house like that I had a life which was obligatorily independent.[42]

This contradiction or unresolved tension between the demands made by a clandestine life and those of a normal life created continual uncertainty and doubts as to the bearableness of the armed struggle and its cost in terms of individual suffering. There is also a second contradiction that can be traced to the progressive predominance of forms of instrumental criminality with regard to the political struggle, in particular the need to carry out robberies for self-financing. It is interesting to read the accounts of armed militants to understand the complex nature of the problems involved in carrying out a robbery. This is not so much because of the organizational impact, which was often characterized by carelessness, improvisation and inexperienced behaviour even in relatively simple situations, as for the explosion of contradictions between this sort of illegal behaviour and the political and ideological values to which they are supposed to relate.

> Robberies are practically always carried out to guarantee ... the survival of militants and ... of comrades who don't work, to guarantee a relationship of solidarity and of comradeship with the prisoners ... to envisage different initiatives that in some way referred to the overcoming of the work relationship ... There were four of us in the robbery that I took part in ... and ... the thing that functioned then was a sort ... of redistribution of money ...; many comrades asked for and got money to go on holiday. To us it seemed to be a positive element ... that even in the so-called sacrificial life that induced that type of organization in actual fact there was room, let's say, for life, room for holidays, room for enjoyment.[43]

Besides the instrumental motivations for the survival of the organization, motivations and ideological justifications were also attributed to robberies: the 'overcoming of the work relationship', the need to have room for enjoyment and holidays for the militants. It it clear that this second motivation could have constituted a powerful incentive to overcome the obstacles that might, for some militants, interfere with the commitment to carry out illegal actions with no immediately political meaning. In this sense, though, it was clear that the problem of the 'technical' use of violence would have clashed with possible accidents: for example, the failure of a robbery.

> Immediately after this robbery there was a tragic accident ... because the robbery ... was carried out, and on the way back the car was stopped ... in a roadblock by the *carabinieri* and ... one of the group reacted ... pulled out a pistol and tried to open fire against the *carabinieri* who ... returned fire killing him, mortally wounding a second member of the group, wounding a third member who however managed to survive ... and by a pure miracle not hitting the fourth. Exactly the sort of thing [that would happen to] ... a band of common thieves.[44]

A band of common thieves; this then was the future that awaited them and that provoked a crisis in the subjective motivations for the armed struggle. In fact, the practice of robbery and the feeling of having themselves likened to common criminality threw the plan for the armed struggle of these clandestine groups into crisis. Paradoxically, given the moral irrelevance of the political assassinations, it was not their habit to have second thoughts, but the robberies – particularly those that caused deaths – to raise funds to live 'underground' do not have the teleological justification of, let us say, a political murder. The idea of being likened to a band of robbers, in the absence of a strong political plan, such as the construction of the armed party typical of the BR, constituted an element of potential crisis in the continuation of the armed struggle. But this crisis did not manifest itself immediately; notwithstanding the individual awareness, there was a sort of coercion to repeat, or better a sort of inertia in, the practice of violence that induced the terrorists to try again and again.

> it was always becoming more and more a story about a small group of robbers ... that didn't do any political work, that didn't have any contact with anybody any more, and for me this thing really didn't go down at all well.[45]

This disagreement, however, did not lead to a linear rejection of the armed struggle. The path was tortuous, full of contradictions, second thoughts and attempts to set up other organizations.

> I went along with all the territorial group which made up the greater part of the political force ... making myself autonomous ... I finally thought that I'd be able to get a job – even a military job – but linked to the masses; ... we got together with some other people who had taken a totally different political course, being Marxist-Leninists ... But as the months passed ... they gradually began to argue along increasingly militaristic lines ... and we split up again ... It was at that point ... that I became completely autonomous and built up a sort of mini-organization of my own with a territorial structure ... This group of people ... came up with the idea of a kidnapping; I was totally against it, saying that in my opinion it was sheer madness ... About a week after that I went back to them and said, 'OK, seeing that you've already decided to do it ... you can count me in' ... When ... they proposed something similar to me a few months later ... I said, 'No, that's enough'.[46]

Therefore, a relatively long and tormented period of latency characterizes the separation from the armed struggle. If in the case cited above, the rejection of the practice of robbery immediately led to the search for new political dimensions of armed struggle, in other cases this rejection did not come so quickly. But in all cases there is a sort of continuation of the commitment to clandestinity and the practice of violence that is almost a test for inertia. The emphasis again comes back to the inevitability of destiny and to technical motivations for doing certain things well.

> I experienced the dimension of the political debate – involvement in problems of an ideological and political nature – very little, and instead ... I had to face the demanding requests that came ... from other cities ... so that I was rather crushed by this situation ... Preparing robberies almost became a job ... so that the only form of creativity I could apply to the job was to do it well, to find an original way of doing it.[47]

Thus armed robbery became a job. The transposition of the means was complete, to the point that somebody actually considered the idea of doing it to earn a living in the future.

> In the organization the summer period was always linked to robberies. That

is, houses were taken in seaside places where you carried out robberies for self-financing and combined your holidays with this ... Sincerely, I must say that the only thing that at the time I wanted was ... one, to stay in Italy and to carry out some robberies in order to live, and the other [was] to go abroad.[48]

At this point the process of degeneration had reached its end. The accent on the inevitability brings the acceptance of a destiny that has little or nothing to do with the original plans. As in the case of the rich bourgeois protagonists of Bunuel's film they become prisoners of the party they organized; thus the force of the case that has brought them to the armed struggle is translated in the prospect of a destiny of common bandits. But this prospect cannot last long. The violence for inertia, of which the degeneration of the terrorist groups makes themselves prisoners of, is in contradiction to the original motivations of the armed struggle. The progressive breaking-away from political contacts as a result of the reduction of the horizon of sociality brings a growing inability to use the collective movements in an instrumental sense, as places of potential recruitment of armed militants.

The effects of such a process are those of the isolation of the group. If the use of violence involves a reduction of the social horizon, that in turn induces a growing fragility of the group and of the individuals that make up a part of it. The lack of sociality makes the use of violence – which had previously seemed to be the projection of a heroic ideal – appear empty and senseless. At this point the only element that still contributes to maintaining the terrorist perspective is myth; no longer the myth of a vague future society, but the myth of a fascinating, because mysterious, perfect terrorist organization – the Red Brigades.

## 6.9 The myth of the Red Brigades

It would be interesting to reconstruct the role played by the Red Brigades towards that broad quota of leftist-movement militants who found themselves, at a certain point of their experience, part of the armed struggle. The mysterious fascination of the oldest clandestine terrorist organization in Italy is confirmed in the words of a second-generation BR militant who was a member of the group from 1976 to 1982.

a part [of the terrorist group to which he belonged] went on, another part left completely ... and another part began instead to fall victim to the fascination of the Red Brigades ... Yes, I really mean 'fascination' of the Red Brigades because it really is just that, because no-one really knows what the Red Brigades are ... you think about an extremely compact and organized body and so on.[49]

But the fascination with the BR lasted beyond the period 1976–7 when the armed struggle was still on its upward phase. It extended into the phases of political and organizational crisis of the other experiences of armed struggle, for example in the period 1979–80, as a member of the *Prima Linea* testifies:

> At that time a lot of young comrades became *clandestini* ... and for some months they lived on the trains, that is they would catch a train in the evening, let's say from Rome arriving in Bari in the morning, so that meant that they slept on the train, stayed all day long in Bari, caught the night train back to Rome from Bari and so on for two or three months ... That evening there were around twenty of us *clandestini* in Naples without a place to stay the night. Finally, we managed to find a house ... there in Naples during those days there was a meeting mainly made up of five comrades more representative at the time because they had more experience inside the organization ... and at that meeting ... a comrade proposed to make contact with the Red Brigades.[50]

The attraction of the BR even extends to situations of utter confusion, so much so that even with the knowledge that with all hope for the armed struggle gone, we still attempt an extreme contact with it.

> A period of continual emergencies began when we tried to save what we could. We were in a tight corner; we carried out some armed robberies to meet the increasing costs of survival, but it was a thankless task. The chaotic climate in the organization and the closing of ranks meant that the difficult moments were lived as a reason to go on with what we were doing, even if everything by now seemed without any chance of success and ... destined to an unavoidable settling of accounts ... It was ... clear that the life of *Prima Linea* was over ... and along with some others I came to the decision to break away from those who still wanted to keep going within the ruins of that organized experience. So in April 1981 I moved to Naples with the other terrorist 'exiles', where I tried to set up contacts ... with other organized groups active in the armed struggle, in particular with the Red Brigades, but it didn't get off the ground. So then we carried out some operations for self-financing in order to keep going in hiding and some months later we were nearly all arrested.[51]

What is it that made the BR so compulsively attractive? There is no doubt that it was a question of its being the oldest of the armed groups, that it was the first to choose the armed struggle without being catapulted into it by circumstances and that it had always had careful, disciplined, selective recruitment strategies. The BR were also the first to formulate an ideology of armed struggle; they carried out the more spectacular actions such as kidnappings and the trials of kidnap victims, which in some cases kept the forces of law and order occupied for a considerable time. Given all this it is not difficult to understand the prestige and fame enjoyed by the BR among other terrorist groups.

Moreover, it is not by chance that even today this group still accounts for the organized presence of some factions that carry out armed robbery for self-financing and – until only a few years ago – the practice of political murder. These elements are enough to justify the appeal exercised by the BR on disintegrating terrorist groups. There was, as we have seen, a sort of inertia in the use of violence that was bound up with the reasons for the crisis that followed the inversion of moral values. In this way, it was the focus on the clandestine activity of armed robberies, and the instrumental demands imposed by the organization's mere subsistence that produced individual dilemmas and the splitting-up of groups rather than the use of violence against individuals and political murder. However, it is precisely this problem of the inertia of violence that needs to be understood. We need to focus our attention on it to bring together the threads of the analysis.

## 6.10 Conclusion

The thesis put forward in this chapter is that in the individual conscience and in the subjective reconstruction of the protagonists of leftist terrorism there is a tendency to hide the leap between mass violence and terrorist violence. The phenomenological manifestation of this leap is given by the ideological systems of legitimation used to justify the personal involvement in the two types of violence; political and rational in the case of mass violence and irrational (e.g. circumstances or necessity) in the case of terroristic violence. We have put forward the hypothesis that such a contradiction in self-legitimation is derived from the subject's needs to re-establish a coherent biographical identity in the face of the two fundamental breaks experienced in the course of his or her life: the choice of the armed struggle and that of *dissociazione*.

The repudiation of the armed struggle as an element of conscious choice implies indeed the admission of involvement in it, so that *dissociazione* represents a break with that choice and determines the need to re-establish a coherent biographical identity with reference to a life history that predates involvement in the armed struggle. But if this allows the subject to construct in his own eyes a coherent life history, he is still left with the impossibility of negating the existence of the other fracture: that is, the belonging to the armed struggle. This produces an internal contradiction that is resolved by attempting to eliminate, or at least to reduce to a minimum, all elements of rational consciousness in the choice of terrorism, in the first place by avoiding all use of the term 'terrorism', in the second by asserting that it was, however, a question of an experience of growth and learning, and in the third by finally resorting to elements such as the situation or inevitability as determining factors in the involvement in the armed struggle.

In the accounts of the protagonists we have seen how, together with and parallel to the systems of self-legitimation, there also emerge elements of reflection on the problems of the genesis of violence, of the individual's exposure to it, of its reproduction and of the internal reasons (both for individual subjects and groups) for the crisis in violence. It is therefore necessary to reconstruct the processes through which the subject passes from mass violence as a form of self-defence to the individual acceptance of terrorist violence and its organized practice. This process takes place in the form of a series of successive transitions that can be summed up in the following stages.

*The first step.* At the level of mass violence as a form of self-defence, violence is legitimized in the face of attacks from outside. The external forces are singled out as the fascists in the pay of the *padroni* (factory owners, industrialists, etc.) and the state that connives with them. The legitimation of mass violence is made by resorting to justifications and ideologies that are easily acceptable in so far as they are legitimated by the movements and by public opinion: that is:

— the needs for social justice bound to class inequality that impede the realization of individual capacity and that fail to guarantee essential rights;
— the unjust prohibition of spaces for freedom vindicated by the movement;
— the accusation of conniving between the State and the reactionary forces (*coup d'état* and *coup* strategies).

At this point a logic of competition between groups constituted inside the movement is triggered off. The aim of the competition is the conquest and government of the *'piazza'*. Organized competition is expressed in the formation and intervention of the *servizi d'ordine*, that is, in the setting up of 'military wings' of the groups.

*The exposure of the individual to the temptation of violence.* It is in this phase that the maximum potential of the exposure of the individual to the temptation of violence is realized. This happens for two types of reasons:

— for many militants adherence to the movement takes place while they are young and lack precedent experience in legal politics in precisely the phase when the military wings of the group are being built up in a frenetic and intense way;
— the exclusion (given equal commitment in the militancy) of a substantial quota of these young people as soon as they are recruited to functions of the politically 'pure' sort (formulation of lines and strategies of action, the chance to express speaking or debating ability); hence the impossibility of performing leadership functions, or in any event, to embark upon the career of leader.

These conditions produce the commitment of many groups of young militants in the *servizi d'ordine*.

*The formation of armed groups.* The precipitation of these elements and the organizational crystallization of armed groups takes places following two factors:

— the political and organizational disarticulation and the breaking-up of the groups of the extreme left that had developed inside the movements of the 1970s; only their organizational structures remained standing: that is, the military sections composed of individuals driven along the road to illegality by having already committed illegal or barely legal actions, or in order to bring an end to the political control exercised by the leadership over their military functions;

– the sudden collapse of the movements that caused an excessive dislocation of militants, until that time committed to group politics.

These factors, then, determine the taking-on of political functions by those who were the military wings of the groups, with the consequence that in the relationship between political action and military action the first is oriented towards and dependent on the second. This is the beginning of the process that quickly brings us to the political justification of murder and to its moral irrelevance. At the same time, following the sudden collapse of the movements and the disintegration of the political groups of the extreme left, there is an 'excess' of clandestinity. Excess in two senses: in the first place militants who had not committed sufficiently serious crimes became clandestine for fear of the excessive repression with respect to the crimes committed, or out of a sense of solidarity and support of friends who had committed serious crimes, or because they were driven along this road by the lack – in their eyes – of feasible political alternatives, given the disintegration of the groups to which they belonged. In the second place, the number of *clandestini* is 'excessive' with respect to the organizational and financial capacity of the armed groups to sustain so vast and territorially widespread a mass of clandestine militants.

*The generation of violence.* The conditions for the generation of violence are determined in the following two ways: internal competition within and between groups; and the need to obtain means of subsistence. In the first case, since there had been a substantial acceptance of the use of violence as an instrument of the political struggle against the outside (the state and political opponents), violence became an important resource for the future of the internal competition of single groups and between groups taking part in the armed struggle. Such violent competition was accentuated during the phases when political leadership was weak, lacking or in some way challenged. In the second case, there was an instrumental necessity to obtain means of subsistence by a high number of clandestine militants, who were often without, or lacking, contacts with a widely accepted, recognized leadership.

There was, therefore, an increase in three types of violent actions: direct political violence against external targets (kidnapping, shooting in the legs, wounding and murder); direct political violence aimed at internal targets (kidnappings, trials, the murder of those considered to be informers or traitors); and instrumental political violence aimed at obtaining the money to finance the armed struggle (robberies and other criminal money-raising acts).

*Limited reproducibility.* The sudden, massive explosion of violence registered after the second half of the 1970s contained elements of weakness that we have analysed in relation to the crisis of the groups due to the excess of clandestine militancy. These elements, combined with the repressive policies of the state, legislation favouring *pentitismo* and *dissociazione* and the more careful, efficient organization of anti-terrorist action by the state, produced a degeneration and a crisis in the use of violence by terrorist groups. In particular, the internal factors that constituted uncrossable limits for further violence were connected to the increase of the use of instrumental violence and the growing use of violence against members of the organization. These two elements, of 'settling accounts' and of copying the practices of petty criminals, produced a contradiction between the 'ideals' that constituted a motivational element in the individual choice of the armed struggle; they reduced the action of many groups to something not unlike that of a band of common thieves.

This situation led to the progressive crises that brought about the phenomena of *dissociazione* and *pentitismo* and to the disaggregation – the only relevant exception being the BR – of terrorist groups.

The protagonists related what they felt and learnt about the question of violence in discussions within terrorist groups; they have described how they lived the experience of the practice of violence. But what primarily emerges from their accounts is that somehow they did not feel themselves to be part of the violence they practised, first during and then after the extended season of political violence. For them more than for the others it was and remains true that:

> One carries out an act, and internally [it] has a completely different meaning than externally. With time, however, one has inside that which has happened outside. And one no longer has the force to change it. (From R. Musil (1982) *Die Schwärmer*, Cologne, Rowohlt TB.)

Perhaps nothing sums up better than these words the drama of a generation that believed in the myth of the armed struggle and that now has to face up to what remains within them of that experience.

## Notes

1 I should like to thank Arturo Parisi who read the first draft of this essay and who suggested useful ways of interpreting the problem of political violence.

2 Interview with S.C., pp. 62–3. Interview carried out by Maurizio Fiasco.

3 Interview with A.B., p. 27. Interview carried out by Luisa Passerini.

4 On the situation in the 1970s, see Chapter 4, section 2 of this volume.

5 Interview with M.Fa., p. 7. Interview carried out by Claudio Novaro.

6 Interview with A.B., pp. 20–3.

7 Interview with E.B., p. 40. Interview carried out by Luigi Manconi.

8 Interview with C.D'A., pp. 26–7. Interview carried out by Luigi Manconi.

9 Interview with A.B., p. 65.
10 Interview with M.Fa., pp. 6 *ff*.
11 Interview with G.A., p. 47. Interview carried out by Giuseppe De Lutiis.
12 Interview with M.Fa., p. 32.
13 Interview with A.S., pp. 27 and 35. Interview carried out by Giuseppe De Lutiis.
14 Interview with Gu.M., p. 46. Interview carried out by Claudio Novaro.
15 This term refers to the defence squads of extremist left-wing organizations (e.g. *Lotta Continua, Potere Operaio*, etc.), whose – initially defensive – role was to steward and protect demonstrations, speakers, etc.
16 Interview with A.S., p. 20.
17 Interview with P.L., pp. 72–3, first part, 15–16 (second part). Interview carried out by Luigi Manconi.
18 Interview with D.G., p. 16. Interview carried out by Claudio Novaro.
19 Interview with A.S., p. 41.
20 Interview with P.L., p. 79, first part.
21 Interview with C.D'A., p. 41.
22 Ibid., p. 41.
23 Interview with D.G., p. 17.
24 Ibid., ivi.
25 Ibid., p. 19.
26 Interview with A.S., p. 46.
27 Interview with A.S., p. 39.
28 Interview with D.G., pp. 9–10.
29 Ibid., p. 10.
30 Interview with P.L., p. 10, second part.
31 Interview with D.G., p. 34.
32 Interview with Marco, pp. 56–7. Interview carried out by Giuseppe De Lutiis.
33 Interview with C.D'A., p. 55.
34 Ibid., ivi.
35 Ibid., p. 56.
36 Interview with A.S., p. 47.
37 Ibid., p. 45.
38 Interview with A.B., pp. 58–9.
39 Interview with M.Fa., p. 46.
40 Ibid., pp. 50–1.
41 Ibid., p. 48.
42 Ibid., pp. 52–4.
43 Interview with C.D'A., pp. 56–8.
44 Ibid., pp. 58–9.
45 Interview with P.L., p. 89, first part.
46 Ibid., pp. 92–9, first part.
47 Interview with D.G., pp. 49–50.
48 Interview with M.Fa., p. 56.
49 Interview with A.S., p. 36.
50 Interview with M.Fa., pp. 68 and 74.
51 Interview with D.G., pp. 24–5.

# Appendix

Interview outline

## 1 Social and family background

### 1.1 Composition and socioeconomic characteristics of family of origin

- father's occupation/mother's occupation or activity;
- material and socioeconomic condition of family with particular reference to the position of the family in relation to the social stratification of the community (district, neighbourhood, etc.);
- standard of living of family.

### 1.2 Family environment

- family members: father/mother/brothers/sisters/other family and non-family household members;
- parents' attitudes on upbringing: perception of differences between mother and father, authoritarian-rigid/permissive-flexible;
- daily life of the family: description of a typical work day and a typical leisure day;
- type of emotional involvement;

*Emphasis on*: how well or how badly suited the subject is to his family environment and potential or actual areas of conflict.

### 1.3 Ideological-religious background of family

- religious beliefs or attitudes towards religion/the religious practice of family members;
- political and ideological orientation and forms of involvement.

*Emphasis on*: the degree of emotional involvement and agreement or conflict between family members.

## 1.4 Social background of family of origin

- type of neighbourhood or environment;
- relationship between the family and neighbourhood or area;
- associational or political involvement of family members (groups, societies, clubs, etc.)

*Emphasis on*: competition/cooperation/indifference towards the community; intensity/absence of social relations and their specialization.

## 2 Subjective experience during primary socialization

### 2.1 Informal social relations

- schoolfriends;
- friends, peer group, the group: its structure and composition, emotional and instrumental leadership;
- institutionalized forms of social life (church, clubs, bar, etc.)

*Emphasis on*: external relationships/informal or everyday relationships.

### 2.2 School experience

- schools attended;
- school successes and failures;
- like and dislike of teachers;
- relationships in the school environment.

*Emphasis on*: interests, hopes, frustrations; the meaning and importance of the school experience.

### 2.3 Leisure time

- when did the subject begin to have any;
- ways in which it was used.

*Emphasis on*: elements of conflict with the family; the sense of belonging to a youth culture.

## 3 Formation of adult personality

### 3.1 The emotional sphere

- friendships and affections;
- sexual relationships;
- the life of a couple, marriage, children.

*Emphasis on*: phases of transition and choice; conflicts between broad-based relations and emotional relationships involving two people.

### 3.2 Cultural and ideological formation

– cultural experiences; reading;
– the stages of ideological formation;
– the personal library: description.
*Emphasis on*: problematic and critical periods; phases of ideological and cultural change and development.

### 3.3 Cultural and ideological reference systems

– the image of power (from teacher to headmaster, priest, etc.);
– relationships with power groups or locally influential people;
– experience during military service.
*Emphasis on*: variations in the legitimation of power.

### 3.4 Work experience

– type of work;
– first work experiences;
– social relationships in the workplace;
– work relationships;
– dismissals and changes of work.
*Emphasis on*: reasons for choice of work; solidarity/instrumentalism; integration in work.

## 4 Political and association participation

### 4.1 Initiation into political militancy

– when did subject start to take part in political activity – age;
– when did subject begin to take part in political activity – subjective perception of the era and of the historico-political climate;
– places of political activity, factory, neighbourhood, school;
– places of political activity, groups;
– who (if anyone) introduced/inspired/convinced/persuaded the subject to take part in political activity (friends, relations, comrades);
– the circumstances of the beginning of political activity of subject;
– problems dealt with in the group;
– activity carried out by the subject.
*Emphasis on*: the meaning of this experience for the subject.

### 4.2 Evolution of political militancy before becoming clandestine

– transitions from one group to another;
– associational involvement and its development;

– the last group in which the subject was active before becoming
   clandestine, its main ideas, spheres of intervention, repertoire of action;
– militant comrades;
– level of involvement, duration and form of political activity.
*Emphasis on*: perception of own destiny as individual or generational.


## 5 Political commitment of terrorist

### 5.1 Entry into terrorism

– the image of the group before joining it;
– how did the subject get to know the group, modality and duration;
– age at which the subject joined the group;
– period of latency of decision to join;
– individual and collective experience of the decision;
– first action made by subject as a fighting militant;
– motivations for this choice (how and why the armed struggle became a
   possible and attractive choice).
*Emphasis on*: images of the terrorist future (what did the subject think
he/she would do, what actions would he/she carry out).


### 5.2 Armed militance: the characteristics of the group

– the sphere of action;
– type of activity;
– education and indoctrination of militants;
– activity of proselytism and recruitment.
*Emphasis on*: perception of surrounding political and social environment;
the 'climate' of the group.


### 5.3 The daily experience of a terrorist apart from the clandestine commitment

– division of time between: family, affections, work, other activities;
– social relationships;
– free time: what had to be given up, the advantages.
*Emphasis on*: perception of the difference between subject and others;
affectivity/instrumentalism.


### 5.4 The daily experience of a terrorist as a member of a clandestine organization

– duration in time;
– the development, quantitatively and qualitatively, of commitment
   within the clandestine organization;

– description of a typical day with reference to the following: political-ideological discussions; strategic decisions; distribution of responsibilities; exemplary actions.

*Emphasis on*: degree of meaningfulness/pervasiveness of the commitment in the armed militance and its development; the image of a future society.

## 6 The end of the terrorist experience

### 6.1 The process of abandoning terrorism (if this took place)

– the origins of the crisis: individual (when did the subject begin to think about leaving the organization);
– the origins of the crisis of the group;
– reasons;
– obstacles;
– duration of the breaking-away process;
– how did this breaking away finally take place.

*Emphasis on*: the processes of reflection, changing one's mind.

### 6.2 The judgement on terrorism and the armed struggle

– why did it emerge: what were the reasons (historical, socioeconomic, political) for individual choice;
– what was the meaning (political, historical, social and generational) of this experience;
– why did it fail.

*Emphasis on*: how the experience of the armed struggle has marked the life of the terrorist.

# Glossary

*Autonomia Operaia* – Worker Autonomy: extreme left-wing group which grew out of *Potere Operaio* and which declared the autonomy of the working class with respect to the party which historically represented them (the PCI); a substantial part of *Autonomia* subsequently transformed into a myriad of groups of the so-called *terrorismo diffuso*.

*Avanguardia Operia* – Worker Vanguard; extreme left-wing group operating in the worker tradition which emerged at the end of the 1960s.

BR. *Brigate Rosse* – Red Brigades: the main left-wing terrorist group in Italy which emerged at the beginning of the 1970s and which lasted despite the transformations in its strategy and leadership, and its splitting-up into various groups (cf. CCC. PCC.) and wings (fr *militarismo, movimentismo*) until the end of the 1980s.

CGIL. *Confederazione Generale Italiana Lavoratori* – General Confederation of Italian Workers; one of the three most important trade unions in Italy together with the CISL and the UIL; mainly communist, but with socialist and extreme left-wing components.

CISL. *Confederazione Italiana Sindacato Lavoratori* – Italian Confederation of Unionized Workers: Catholic trade union, once tightly linked to the DC, now more autonomous.

CISNAL. *Confederazione Italiana Sindacati Nazionali Lavoratori* – Italian Confederation of National Workers: a right-wing trade union linked to the MSI (Italian neo-fascist party)

CL. *Comunione e liberazione* – Communion and Liberation: political association founded in the 1980s with a strong Catholic integralist nature.

CPM. *Collettivo Politico Metropolitano* – Metropolitan Political Collective: a group formed in Milan in September 1969 by students from the Faculty of Sociology at Trent University together with Milan factory workers; it was this group that took the decision to initate the strategy of the armed struggle in 1969, and which gave birth to one of the historical nuclei of the BR.

COLP. *Comitati per la Liberazione Proletaria* – Committees for Proletarian Liberation; groups organized by ex-militants from *Prima Linea* with the objective of freeing imprisoned terrorists.

DC. *Democrazia Cristiana* – Christian Democratic Party: the political party, with a strong tradition of Catholic political commitment, which has been in power in Italy without interruption from the end of World War II to the present day, either alone or in coalition with other parties to its left and right.

DP. *Democrazia Proletaria* – Proletarian Democracy: political party of the far left of the political spectrum (dissolved Spring 1991).

FGCI. *Federazione Giovanile Comunista Italiana* – Federation of Young Italian Communists: the youth wing of the PCI.

GAP. *Gruppi armati proletari* – Armed Proletarian Groups: political groups founded in the 1970s, particularly in Milan, which championed the armed struggle; the name is reminiscent of the *Gruppi di Azione Partigiana* (Partisan Action Groups), active during the Resistance and the War of Liberation against the Nazis.

LC. *Lotta Continua* – Permanent Struggle: political organization of the extreme Left which published a newspaper of the same name; a part of the *servizi d'ordine* of LC subsequently formed themselves into armed groups which first became *Senza Tregua* and subsequently *Prima Linea*.

MPRO. *Movimento Proletario di Resistenza Offensiva* – Proletarian Movement of Offensive Resistance: term used by the BR to refer to all those who did not share the political strategy of the parties of the official Left and who constituted fertile ground for recruitment to the armed struggle.

MSI. *Movimento Sociale-Italiano* – Italian Social Movement: extreme right-wing neo-fascist party.

NAP. *Nuclei Armati Proletari* – Armed Proletarian Nuclei: terrorist group which was particularly active in the South of Italy, especially around Naples.

OCC. *Organizzazioni Comuniste Combattanti* – Organizations of Fighting Communists: one of the factions into which the BR split.

PCI. *Partito Comunista Italiano* – Italian Communist Party.

PCC. *Partito Comunista Combattente* – Fighting Communist Party: armed party created by the BR and subsequently one of its factions.

P-2. *Propaganda Due* – the secret Masonic Lodge, which counted almost 1,000 prominent national figures from the world of politics, defence, and law and order among its membership, and was implicated in a range of criminal activities including right-wing terrorism in the late 1960s and early 1970s.

PGPM. *Partito della Guerriglia del Proletariato Metropolitano* – Guerrilla Party of the Metropolitan Working Class: the prison-wing of the BR.

PL. *Prima Linea* – Front Line: the other main trend in Italian left-wing terrorism apart from the BR; PL had 'movimentist' tendencies and was an instigator of the so-called *terrorismo diffuso*.

PO. *Potere Operaio* – Worker Power: political organization in the 'works' tradition: a part of PO, in particular part of its *servizi d'ordine* gave birth to terroristic groups.

PSI. *Partito Socialista Italiano* – Italian Socialist Party.

P-38 – the name of the gun frequently used by terrorists at the time and which became a symbol unto itself: see the book by F. Calvi in the bibliography to Chapter 3, entitled *Camarade P-38*.

SIDA. – 'yellow' or 'the owner's' trade union.

SP. *Sinistra Proletaria.* – Proletarian Left: grassroots collective in Milan which generated one of the historical nuclei of the BR.

ST. *Senza Tregua* – No Truce: organization formed by militants from Lotta Continua's *servizi d'ordine* who then joined *Prima Linea*.

UIL. *Unione Italiana Lavoratori* – Union of Italian Workers: Republican-Socialist oriented trade union.

# Index